Virginia
Hunting
Guide

BOB GOOCH

Virginia
Hunting Guide

University Press of Virginia ———— Charlottesville

THE UNIVERSITY PRESS OF VIRGINIA
Copyright © 1985 by the Rector and Visitors
of the University of Virginia

First published 1985

Third printing 1992

Library of Congress Cataloging in Publication Data

Gooch, Bob, 1919–
    Virginia hunting guide.

    Includes index.
    1. Hunting—Virginia—Guide–books. I. Title.
SK137.G66   1985   799.29755   84-21004
ISBN 0-8139-1041-2

Printed in the United States of America

CONTENTS

Contents   vi

PREFACE TO SECOND PRINTING

Hunting is not a static sport. Managing and protecting game animals that support it often require changes in bag limits, seasons, and sometimes temporary bans on hunting various animals. Since *Virginia Hunting Guide* was published in 1985, such needs have brought forth changes as noted below.

Effective July 1, 1987, the Commission of Game and Inland Fisheries became the Department of Game and Inland Fisheries, a name change only. The authority and responsibilities of the agency remain the same.

The snowshoe hare, a legal game animal then, is now temporarily protected during a restocking program.

Those Southwest Virginia counties south of Interstate 81 and west and north of U.S. Highway 19 have been temporarily closed to bear hunting to support a stocking program.

The lifetime senior citizens hunting license has been replaced by an annual license available at a reduced cost at all license agencies.

Owens-Illinois Company no longer has hunting land available in Virginia. Most of it has been purchased by Westvaco, and permits are available from that company.

The charge for a book of maps of the wildlife management areas of the Department of Game and Inland Fisheries has been increased from $1 to $2.

The cost of George Washington and Jefferson National Forests ranger district maps has been increased to $2.

The costs of hunting permits on corporate timberland in Virginia have been increased approximately 100 percent.

Primitive camping is permitted in wildlife management areas unless otherwise posted.

Fees for hunting on the military reservations have been increased from 100 to 200 percent. There is now a fee to hunt Fort Pickett Military Reservation.

Continental Forest Industries no longer owns hunting land in Virginia, but most of these lands have been acquired by Bear Island Timberlands Company, P.O. Box 2119, Ashland, VA 23005. Permits are available from that company.

The Department of Game and Inland Fisheries has established a new boat launching at Kingsland on the James River in the Richmond area.

Special deer and hog hunts are now held on Back Bay National Wildlife Refuge and False Cape State Park, both in Virginia Beach. Information is available from the Department of Game and Inland Fisheries.

Waterfowl hunts on the Pocahontas Waterfowl Management Area are no longer outfitted and guided. The hunter must furnish his own equipment. The cost has been reduced to $15.

The timberlands of the Forestlands Division of Lester Properties are available for hunting lease agreements but not by daily permits.

The Appalachian Power Company land in Carroll, Giles, Grayson, Montgomery, Pulaski, and Russell counties is no longer available for public hunting.

Virginia
Hunting
Guide

INTRODUCTION

Hunting is traditional in Virginia. Deer and turkeys from its
vast forests and waterfowl from its rich marshes nourished
Captain John Smith and his hardy little band through their first
bitter winter on Jamestown Island, as they had the native
Americans from time immemorial. Over the years, game resources and hunting emphases have changed considerably. The
thriving deer and turkey populations faded before the ruthless
exploitation of the rich hardwoods and unregulated hunting.
Early Virginians lived off the land, and later market hunting
raped the marshes of their abundant waterfowl. By the turn of
the century deer had all but vanished from the Old Dominion,
and the turkey flocks had dipped to alarmingly low levels. During the early decades of this century waterfowl hunting hit an
all-time low. Fortunately, as Virginia and America moved into

the twentieth century, serious hunters became alarmed, and the first attempts to regulate hunting were made.

Writing in the February 1929 issue of *Game and Fish Conservationist,* the official publication of the old Virginia Department of Game and Inland Fisheries, M. B. Mount asked the question, "By what right have we of this generation been deprived of the privilege of knowing and enjoying these birds and beasts with which nature so bountifully endowed North America?"

The old Department of Game and Inland Fisheries had come into being in 1916 under the Commission of Fisheries. Ten years later, after much stormy debate in the General Assembly, it was divorced from the Commission of Fisheries, and what is now the Commission of Game and Inland Fisheries was set up. Since July 1, 1926, the agency has been run by a group of commission members appointed by the governor. It is an independent agency financed solely by receipts from hunting and fishing licenses plus excise taxes raised at the federal level under the Dingle-Johnson and Pittman-Robertson Acts and released to the states. The federal excise taxes are levied on the sales of hunting and fishing equipment.

In an enlightened political environment, professional wildlife management evolved, and today the Commission of Game and Inland Fisheries is staffed by some of the most professional wildlife managers in America. Its mission is the management of the state's wildlife resources. The comeback from the dark days of the early 1900s has not been easy. In fact, it has been a slow and tedious process, but today there are more deer and turkeys in Virginia than when Captain John Smith stepped gingerly ashore in 1607.

Changes in land uses have had both good and bad effects on Virginia's game resources. Logging operations that leveled the rich forests also opened millions of acres of fertile farming land, and farm game flourished through much of the nineteenth century. Hunting the bobwhite quail with classy pointing dogs became a gentleman's sport, and the bobwhite moved to the front as Virginia's most popular game bird, a position the hardy bird held for generations. Cottontail rabbits flourished in the edges, and squirrels romped in the farm woodlots. In the mountains the ruffed grouse waxed fat on the fruit of briers and weeds that replaced the devastated forests.

Land uses still play a major role in Virginia hunting. The bobwhite quail is now fading as family farms give way to commercial ones and the popularity of cattle and grass farming increases. New agricultural practices seem to favor the mourning dove, and it may well be replacing the quail as the most popular game bird in the Old Dominion. Rabbits too have suffered, but the frisky little squirrel continues to prosper.

Millions of Ducks Unlimited dollars are sent to Canada each year to purchase breeding grounds, and they have helped return waterfowl to Virginia's marshes. Modern federal and state law enforcement has given them the necessary protection. Market hunting is now little more than a colorful chapter in the history of waterfowling in America. Goose and swan populations have grown to the point where they create problems in some areas.

By law, wildlife is the property of the state of Virginia. It becomes the property of the hunter only after he has taken it during an open season and by a legal method, be it hunting or trapping.

To become a legal hunter the aspirant must first purchase a hunting license. License requirements vary depending upon what species of game the hunter wants to pursue. Any form of hunting, however, requires a basic hunting license. City or county licenses are available to those who limit their hunting to their home city or county, but otherwise a statewide license is required. The only other exception is the landowner who limits his hunting to his own property, his or her spouse, children, minor grandchildren, and tenants who rent the property and have the owner's permission to hunt; these hunters do not need licenses. The hunter in search of bears, deer, or turkeys needs a big game license with the appropriate tags in addition to a general hunting license, and the duck or goose hunter must buy a federal migratory bird stamp if he or she is sixteen years of age or older.

In addition to the various licenses, special stamps are needed to hunt certain federal or state-owned lands. A national forest stamp is required for hunting in the George Washington and Jefferson national forests, and a state forest permit is a prerequisite to hunting in the state forests. Bear and deer hunters are also required to purchase county damage stamps when hunting a number of western counties. These counties are listed in the *Summary of Game Laws* issued by the Commission of Game and Inland Fisheries.

With the exception of migratory bird stamps available only at first- and second-class U.S. Post Offices, all licenses and permits are sold either through the clerks of circuit courts in most counties or through license agencies such as sporting goods stores and gun shops. State forest permits and damage stamps are normally available only in the counties concerned, though state forest permits are also available from Virginia Division of Forestry offices in Chester, Cumberland, and Dillwyn (for the addresses, see appendix A).

Residents of Virginia who are sixty-five years of age or older do not need a license to hunt or trap on private property in their home counties. For hunting on public lands or in other parts of the state they can purchase a lifetime license by applying in person at the Commission of Game and Inland Fisheries headquarters office in Richmond. A Virginia automobile operator's license, Social Security card, or some other proof of age is needed.

The hunting license year runs from July 1 through June 30.

The current hunting licenses required are:

County or city resident to hunt county or city of residence only
State resident to hunt statewide
Nonresident to hunt statewide
State resident bear, deer, and turkey—in addition to basic hunting license
Nonresident bear, deer, and turkey—in addition to basic hunting license
Special damage stamp in certain western counties
Nonresident damage stamp in some, but not all, western counties
Resident 65 or older lifetime license
National forest permit
State forest permit
Federal migratory bird hunting stamp

Nonresident to hunt on shooting preserves only
County resident to trap in home county
State resident to trap statewide
State resident to erect stationary shore blind
Nonresident to erect stationary shore blind
State resident to erect stationary water blind
Nonresident to erect stationary water blind
State resident to use floating blind
Nonresident to use floating blind
Virginia Beach stationary shore blind
Virginia Beach stationary water blind
Virginia Beach floating blind
Note: Waterfowl blind licenses are available only from the clerks
of the circuit courts in the counties in which the blinds are located.

For costs, consult the current *Summary of Game Laws* available at license agencies.

Young hunters or adults interested in becoming hunters should enroll in the Hunter Safety Training Program inaugurated in 1961 by the Commission of Game and Inland Fisheries in cooperation with the National Rifle Association. This is a ten-hour course conducted in high schools and at hunting clubs all across Virginia. It is usually taught by a local game warden or an instructor certified by the commission. The course has launched thousands of new hunters on lifelong hunting careers free of accidents. Complete information on this valuable training program is available from the Commission of Game and Inland Fisheries in Richmond or from a local game warden.

While most game is taken in Virginia with conventional rifles and shotguns, there is a wide interest in hunting with more primitive weapons such as the bow and arrow and black powder or muzzle-loading firearms. Many hunters enjoy the additional challenge of taking their game with these hunting tools from the past. Both the bow and arrow and muzzle-loading shotguns are legal during the regular firearms season, but these hunters also enjoy separate seasons. Muzzle-loading rifles are legal only in counties where conventional rifles are legal. The monthlong archery season precedes the regular hunting seasons, with bears, deer, turkeys, and squirrels legal from mid-October into early November. Archers and primitive-weapons hunters also enjoy a late December and early January season west of the Blue Ridge Mountains during which only deer are legal. The regular firearms season gives them the same opportunity in the east.

A rich resource of furbearers has always generated a good deal of interest in trapping in Virginia. In fact, trapping is just as old as hunting, but the interest tends to lag when the prices of furs decline. Beavers, mink, muskrat, and raccoon are the major furbearers, though the demand for fox pelts also creates occasional interest in both gray and red foxes. Bobcats, nutrias, opossums, otters, skunks and weasels round out the furbearer populations. Trapping, like hunting, is regulated by the Commission of Game and Inland Fisheries. Unlike hunting, there is a profit motive in trapping, but most trappers are drawn to this traditional pursuit for aesthetic reasons also. They enjoy being outdoors. Furs are usually prime in December and January, the major trapping months.

Hunting is good in Virginia today, in many ways better than it has been for generations. The supply of game promises to remain good as long as modern game management continues to receive the support of hunters and the public generally. A more serious problem for the modern hunter is finding a place to hunt. Still, Virginians are more fortunate than hunters in many states, thanks to the more than two million acres of public land open to hunting. Public-spirited corporations make available another 700,000 acres. These many acres offer some of the finest hunting in America.

Not to be overlooked is an even greater amount of prime hunting land under private ownership, not generally open to public hunting. Approximately 80 percent of the 25.5 million acres of land in Virginia fall into this category. Still, someone hunts the great majority of those millions of acres—the landowner, his friends, hunters who lease hunting rights, and members of the public who approach the landowner politely and do not abuse the privilege. All private land in Virginia is considered posted. If signs are placed on the property boundaries prohibiting hunting, anyone who enters that land to hunt or trap must have the written permission of the owner. Even if no signs are placed, the hunter is required by law to have the owner's verbal permission.

The public hunting lands in Virginia include thirty wildlife management areas totaling in excess of 170,000 acres, two national forests totaling a million and a half acres, three military reservations with a combined acreage of over 170,000 acres, and 250,000 acres of land in state forests and parks and lands of the U.S. Corps of Engineers that are managed for hunting.

There are hunting clubs in every county that lease hunting land for their members. Many of them are looking for members, and the local game warden is a good source of information on such clubs. There are also a number of national and state hunting organizations with either affiliates or members scattered throughout the state. These organizations are listed in appendix B, and letters to the addresses given will bring information on local chapters or members. This can often lead to private land that is open to hunting through a membership in such organizations.

Hunting guides are not licensed in Virginia, and listing all who operate as guides is just about impossible. Many do it only occasionally, but appendix C lists those who are most active in this field. A good guide is often the least expensive and most effective route to good hunting, particularly for the hunter who does not know the region and has no local contacts. Many guides have access to private lands.

Many hunters, particularly bird hunters, enjoy hunting and working their dogs on licensed shooting preserves that charge modest fees for the privilege. These preserves are licensed by the Commission of Game and Inland Fisheries, and a special season allows them to remain open from October 1 through March. Game, of course, is assured, but most preserve operators do not guarantee the hunter his limit—only that he will have the opportunity to bag a limit. The bobwhite quail is the primary species, but some also stock pheasant, chukar partridge, and mallard ducks. A list of public shooting preserves is included in appendix D.

The restrictions on firearms do not handicap the Virginia hunter generally. Shotguns larger than 10 gauge are illegal, and automatic or repeating shotguns must be plugged so they cannot hold more than three shells. Rifles and pistols of .23 caliber or larger are legal for hunting bears and deer in most western counties and in many eastern ones. Some counties prohibit the use of rifles larger than .22 caliber. These counties are listed in the annual *Summary of Game Laws*. The .22-caliber rifle is illegal for deer statewide, and this leaves only the shotgun for hunting deer in those eastern counties that prohibit the larger rifle. The .22-caliber rifle and pistol are generally legal for small game.

Generally the regulations that govern the use of rifles also regulate hunting with pistols or revolvers. The handguns cannot be carried concealed without a permit. Muzzle-loading guns used during primitive-weapons season must be of at least .45 caliber, fire a single projectile propelled by a minimum of fifty grains of black powder, and cannot be fitted with telescopic sights. When used during the regular firearms season they must be .23 caliber or larger. The bowhunter's bow must be capable of propelling his arrows 125 yards, and his broadheads must be a minimum of ⅞ inch wide.

The *Summary of Game Laws* should be consulted before taking to the fields or woods. It covers spotlighting, shooting from public roads, and other illegal practices. The summaries are available from license agencies.

Trichinosis in bears and tularemia in rabbits are diseases that are discussed later. Periodically, there are also epidemics of rabies in Virginia and neighboring states. Primarily affected are foxes, raccoons, and skunks, but any sluggish animal should be regarded with suspicion. Avoid it and report it to the local warden. Do not handle it. Fortunately, deer and most other game animals rarely carry the disease.

Northwest Mountains and Valley

The Commission of Game and Inland Fisheries calls this region the northwest mountains, but it also includes the fertile Shenandoah Valley and the western slopes of the Blue Ridge Mountains. The rugged Allegheny Mountains and the picturesque Shenandoah Mountains dominate the best hunting country, but there is also Massanutten Mountain, which stretches south between the North and South Forks of the Shenandoah River. The region reaches from Roanoke, where the Shenandoah Valley begins, north to the West Virginia border. The Skyline Drive and the Blue Ridge Parkway form its eastern boundary, and the western reaches back up against the West Virginia border.

Except for Lake Moomaw, a controversial U.S. Army Corps of Engineers flood control lake on the Jackson River north of Covington, there are no big lakes, but some of the state's best-known rivers form here. The Shenandoah River system formed by cold mountain streams flows north to join the Potomac River at Harpers Ferry, and to the south the Cowpasture and Jackson rivers gather their waters in the rugged mountains to flow south where they join at Iron Gate to form the headwaters of the James River.

The sprawling George Washington National Forest, the larger of the two national forests in Virginia, claims much of the mountain country, though a small section of the Jefferson National Forest juts north into Botetourt County. The Shenandoah National Park spreads over much of the Blue Ridge Mountains range in the north, and between Roanoke and Waynesboro the Blue Ridge Parkway rides the ridges of the Blue Ridge Mountains. The park and parkway lands are closed to hunting. While it is off limits to the hunter, the Shenandoah National Park is home to one of the best bear populations in America, and it feeds bears and other game into adjacent lands, as does the long, narrow Blue Ridge Parkway to a lesser extent.

Though the peaks do not challenge high Mount Rogers and other peaks in Southwest Virginia, there is a good deal of high country in the Allegheny Mountains, with Elliott Knob in Augusta County stretching to 4,458 feet and Jack Mountain in Highland reaching 4,378 feet. The Allegheny Mountains are among the most rugged ranges in eastern America.

This interesting region, like Southwest Virginia, is best known for its mountain hunting. In fact, these two big western regions offer the bulk of Virginia's mountain hunting. The fertile Shenandoah Valley is noted for its small game hunting, but most of it is privately owned. There is very little public hunting land in the Valley.

An abundance of game, the largest amount of public hunting land of any region in Virginia, and the good mountain hunting make this region possibly the most popular in Virginia. It

A swinging bridge over the Bullpasture River leads to the Bullpasture Mountain tract of the Highland Wildlife Management Area.

attracts many out-of-state hunters as well as Virginia hunters who live in the big population centers and are accustomed to traveling considerable distances to hunt.

The best big game hunting in Virginia is found in this region, with over half of the western deer harvest, almost half of the black bears, and a fourth of the statewide turkey harvest being bagged here. Turkeys are, of course, game birds, but for licenses and checking purposes, they are treated as big game in Virginia.

Bath, Rockingham, and Shenandoah counties are among the top half dozen deer counties in the state despite the fact that the season is considerably shorter than the eastern one, lasting only two weeks. Each of these three counties gives up in excess of 2,000 animals annually. Hunters in Alleghany, Augusta, Botetourt, Frederick, Highland, and Rockbridge counties consistently top the 1,000-animals mark, and Clarke, Page, and Warren counties produce good kills.

Rockingham County often leads the state in the bear harvest, with hunters bagging as many as fifty animals there in good years. Alleghany, Augusta, Bath, Botetourt, and Rockbridge counties are also dependable for good bear hunting. Page County is usually good, and Highland, Shenandoah, and Warren counties usually give up a few bears.

The turkey harvest in Alleghany, Augusta, Bath, Botetourt, Rockbridge, and Shenandoah counties is consistently high, with several counties often topping 300 birds. The hunting here is some of the best in the state. All of the counties in this region offer good turkey hunting, though the kill in Clarke and Page counties trails that in other counties. It was from the flourishing turkey population on the Gathright Wildlife Management Area in Bath County that birds were trapped live for release all over Virginia. This effort has brought the wild turkey from a dangerously low population to modern abundance.

The small game hunter will find excellent squirrel hunting in these western mountains and valleys. The gray squirrel is more abundant, but the larger fox squirrel occurs throughout the region. All of the counties that border on West Virginia offer good fox squirrel hunting. These big squirrels usually prefer the forest edges in more open country; they are often found along the larger streams.

The rabbit hunter will find some of the best cottontail hunting in Virginia in the rich Shenandoah Valley, but most of it is on private farms where the permission of the landowner is required. Unique to Highland and Augusta counties is the snowshoe, or varying, hare, an animal which is abundant in the north but rare this far south.

The ruffed grouse is king of the game birds here. Game managers say the best hunting is often found along the slopes of the Blue Ridge Mountains in the southeastern part of the region, but the birds are found throughout all of the mountain regions. The river valleys and farmlands offer limited bobwhite quail hunting. The dove hunting can also be good, but it too is limited to farmlands where the permission of the landowner is needed. The stream valleys here offer some of the best wood-cock shooting in Virginia, but few hunt specifically for wood-cocks and the major migrations come too early for the grouse hunters who take most of these birds while in pursuit of their favorite game bird.

Night hunters willing to follow their hounds through the rugged mountains will find good raccoon populations, an abundance of opossums, and a few bobcats.

There are scattered Canada goose populations in the Shenandoah Valley, but they are mostly resident birds that do not offer many hunting opportunities. The best waterfowl hunting is for ducks along the major rivers and streams. The Shenandoah River provides some of the best jump shooting for ducks of any stream in Virginia, partly because it flows through rich agricultural country where mallard and black ducks find good feeding. The region enjoys excellent wood duck reproduction, and both the North Fork of the Shenandoah River and other wooded streams offer good shooting for this brightly colored little duck. Beaver ponds and wildlife watering areas provide good shooting at times, and there is limited waterfowl hunting on Lake Moomaw.

The Gathright, Goshen, Highland, and Little North Mountain wildlife management areas, the George Washington and

Jefferson national forests, and the timberlands of the Owens-Illinois Company make up the major public hunting lands in this big region. Collectively, they offer in excess of a million acres of prime hunting land in this interesting region of rugged mountains, fertile valleys, and sparkling rivers.

WILDLIFE MANAGEMENT AREAS

Wildlife management areas are owned by the Commission of Game and Inland Fisheries and managed for wildlife and public hunting. In fact, these are the only public lands in the state managed exclusively for hunting, fishing, and trapping. There is no charge for hunting in these areas, other than the usual license fees.

Maps of specific wildlife management areas and more detailed information are available from the Commission of Game and Inland Fisheries headquarters in Richmond or from its regional office at Route 6, Box 484–A, Staunton, VA 24401. There is a nominal charge of $1 for a booklet containing maps of all the wildlife management areas.

Gathright Wildlife Management Area

Named for the late T. M. Gathright, who for years maintained a private hunting lodge on this land, the area was purchased by the Commission of Game and Inland Fisheries in 1958. During the early years of the current wild turkey restoration program, birds trapped here were released all over Virginia. Obviously, this is a good turkey-hunting area.

LOCATION: Bath County, mostly along the Jackson River.

SIZE: The original tract was 18,500 acres, of which 16,000 were in southwest Bath County and 2,500 were in Alleghany County. It also included 14 miles of the Jackson River and its rich bottomland. The U.S. Army Corps of Engineers, however, claimed 5,000 acres for Lake Moomaw on the Jackson River, reducing the area to its current size of 13,428 acres.

TERRAIN: Three mountains, Alleghany, Bolar, and Coles, are the predominating terrain features. Elevations range from 1,400 to 3,600 feet, and the country is rough, steep, and well forested with hard-woods and conifers.

CAMPING: The U.S. Forest Service maintains a developed camp-ground on the shores of Lake Moomaw.

ACCESS: Virginia Secondary Route 600 off Primary Highway 39 be-tween Warm Springs and the West Virginia border follows Mill Creek between Alleghany and Bolar mountains deep into the area and to the western shore of Lake Moomaw. Secondary Route 603 leads from Highway 39 to the Coles Mountain area on the eastern side of Lake Moomaw, and Secondary Routes 605 and 607 off U.S. Highway 220 north of Covington also lead to the eastern regions of the area. Foot and jeep trails within the area provide access to vari-ous hunting areas, and if the lake is free of ice, much of the area can be reached by boat. There is a public launching ramp near the dam.

GAME: Noted for its bear, deer, and turkey hunting as well as grouse and squirrels. Lake Moomaw offers limited waterfowl hunting, and there are a few rabbits and quail near the forest edges and what is left of the Jackson River bottomlands. Night hunting is good for raccoon, opossums, and a few bobcats, but the mountain hunting is physically demanding.

Goshen and Little North Mountain Wildlife Management Area

This huge wildlife management area is actually made up of two areas, the Goshen Wildlife Management Area and the Little North Mountain Wildlife Management Area. Both offer rugged mountain hunting plus a limited amount of jump shooting for ducks along the Maury River. The two mountainous areas merge in Rockbridge County and are generally managed as one by the Commission of Game and Inland Fisheries.

Geographically, this is a big, long area that stretches from a point just west of Staunton all the way to a point approxi-mately 12 miles west of Lexington. Four major mountains, Bratton, Forge, Hogback, and Little North, are the predominant terrain features, with elevations ranging from 1,326 to 3,451 feet. The Goshen area is particularly steep and mountainous, but the Little North Mountain section is a bit easier to hunt.

The northern stretches are drained by the Middle River,

which eventually enters the Shenandoah River system. To the south and west the Little Calfpasture is the major stream. The Maury River flows eastward through a portion of the area where it follows Virginia Primary Route 39. Both the James and Shenandoah rivers begin to gather their waters here.

The history of this region is one of cattle, logging, and raging forest fires. Wildfire destroyed much of the rich forestland, which was eventually converted to cattle raising. While the current wildlife management plan allows limited logging, the steep, rugged Goshen section does not favor it.

This area attracts hunters from all over Virginia. The bear, deer, and turkey harvest is good, but biologists feel the area is capable of producing a much greater hunting harvest.

LOCATION: The Goshen section is wholly within Rockbridge County, but Little North Mountain land spreads over both Augusta and Rockbridge counties.

SIZE: The total acreage is 33,666, of which 16,128 are in the Goshen section and 17,538 in Little North Mountain.

TERRAIN: Goshen is steep and mountainous, but Little North Mountain tends to roll more. The area is well forested with conifers and hardwoods.

CAMPING: There are no developed campgrounds, but camping is permitted in self-contained units.

ACCESS: Virginia Primary Highway 39 passes through the area, and access roads off this highway provide hunter access. Numerous secondary roads off Virginia Primary Highway 42 to the west and 252 to the east lead to the area. Secondary Routes 603 and 682 pass through it. Within the area there are 51 miles of roads and a 150-foot swinging bridge over the Maury River. Many miles of trails provide even deeper access.

GAME: Bears, deer, and turkeys are the big game attractions, with grouse the major game bird and squirrels the most popular small game. Opossums, raccoon, and limited numbers of bobcats attract night hunters, and there is limited jump shooting for ducks on the Maury River.

Highland Wildlife Management Area

This is another big mountain area. It consists of a pair of large tracts and a small one, all in Highland County. The largest of the three tracts claims most of Jack Mountain. Directly across U.S. Highway 250 from the Jack Mountain area is the smallest, the Doe Hill section. The second largest section is located between the Bullpasture and Cowpasture rivers, and it claims most of the Bullpasture Mountain. A corner of this section juts into Bath County.

The Bullpasture River, cutting through a corner of the area, has carved out the Bullpasture Gorge just north of Williamsville.

Most of the accessible timber on this area was cut after 1931, and some just before the acquisition of the area by the Commission of Game and Inland Fisheries. The first tract of land was purchased by the commission in 1961, and additional land is being bought as land and funds become available. Over the years numerous wildfires ravaged the cutover timberland, but they are now better controlled.

Hunting in this region has always been good, and some of the southernmost snowshoe hare hunting in America is found here. The Bullpasture Mountain section is noted for its deer, grouse, and turkeys, and Jack Mountain holds one of the best wildlife populations in the state. The Sounding Knob area is particularly good.

LOCATION: Except for a tiny section of Bullpasture tract that juts into Bath County, the entire area is in Highland County, in the general vicinity of McDowell on U.S. Highway 250 and Williamsville on the Bullpasture River.

SIZE: The combined acreage of the three separate sections is 13,977.

TERRAIN: The entire area is mountain country with some bottomland along the Bullpasture River. The Bullpasture and Jack mountains, Little Doe Hill, and Sounding Knob are the dominating terrain features in rugged country that ranges in elevation from 1,800 to 4,390 feet. The area is heavily forested with mostly second-growth hardwoods and conifers, a major exception being a 125-acre bluegrass field that is used for summer pasture.

CAMPING: There are no developed campgrounds, but camping in self-contained units is permitted.

ACCESS: The Jack Mountain tract is accessible from Virginia Secondary Route 615 off U.S. 250 just west of McDowell and from Secondary Route 678 between McDowell and Williamsville. An old CCC road and numerous trails lead deep into the area. U.S. Highway 250 skirts the Little Doe Hill tract, and a secondary road off U.S. 250 skirts its western border. This is a small area less than a mile across and two miles long. Access by foot is easy. Secondary Road 678 also provides access to the Bullpasture Mountain tract, while Secondary Road 614 along the Cowpasture River offers access to the eastern reaches. A service road that follows Hupman Valley into the area from the north and numerous foot trails offer deep access.

GAME: Bears, deer, grouse, squirrels, and turkeys are the major game species, but there are some cottontail rabbits in the cleared areas and along the edges. The snowshoe hare are most numerous in the Laurel Fork area, and there is some duck hunting in the beaver meadows of this area. Beaver ponds and wildlife watering holes also offer some duck shooting, and there is limited jump shooting along the Cowpasture and Bullpasture rivers. A few woodcocks also migrate through this area. Night hunters enjoy good opossum and raccoon hunting, and their hounds tree an occasional bobcat.

Lake A. Willis Robertson Wildlife Management Area

Various federal, state, and county government agencies joined forces to create this outdoor recreation area in Rockbridge County. A 31-acre fishing lake and a swimming pool are the big attractions, but the area also contains several hundred acres of land, most of which is available to public hunting.

LOCATION: Rockbridge County along the eastern slopes of the Alleghany Mountains. It adjoins both the George Washington and Jefferson national forests.

SIZE: Approximately 500 of its 581 acres are open to hunting.

TERRAIN: Rugged mountain land, mostly forested with conifers and hardwoods.

CAMPING: A few sites in a well-developed campground are kept open during the hunting seasons. Electrical hookups are available and water also if the weather permits. Sites can be reserved by writing Supervisor, Lake A. Willis Robertson, RFD 2, Box 251, Lexington, VA 24450 or calling 703-463-4164.

ACCESS: Virginia Primary Route 251 off U.S. 11 south of Lexington to Collierstown and Secondary Route 770 lead to main entrance. Hunter access during most seasons is via the west gate.

GAME: Big game, namely deer and turkeys, are the big attraction, but there are also a few bears. Bird hunters enjoy grouse hunting, and the squirrel hunting is generally good. There are a few cottontail rabbits near the forest edges. Night hunters will find raccoon, opossums, and an occasional bobcat. Ducks may use the lake, but hunting on the lake is prohibited.

FEDERAL LANDS

The George Washington and Jefferson national forests and a small amount of U.S. Army Corps of Engineers land adjacent to the Lake Moomaw Dam are the federal lands in this region. Collectively they offer approximately one million acres of public hunting land, by far the largest block of hunting land in this area.

George Washington National Forest

Except for 104,800 acres of land in West Virginia, all of the 1,054,922-acre George Washington National Forest lies in Virginia, and except for some land along the eastern slopes of the Blue Ridge Mountains in Amherst and Nelson counties, all of it is in the northwest mountains region.

There is no national forest land in Clarke County, but otherwise there is not a county in this region that does not contribute some land to the George Washington National Forest. In several of them the forest holdings are small, but in top hunting counties such as Alleghany, Augusta, Bath, Highland, Rockingham, and Rockbridge, there are vast blocks of national forest lands. Much of it is remote wilderness country.

One interesting region is Massanutten Mountain, a narrow strip of national forest land southwest of Front Royal between the North and South Forks of the Shenandoah River. It claims bits of Page, Rockingham, Shenandoah, and Warren counties. Another small but picturesque section flanks the western slopes of the Blue Ridge Mountains in Augusta and Rockbridge counties. The great bulk of the George Washington National Forest, however, lies along the western border of Virginia.

Since 1938 wildlife in the George Washington National

Forest has been managed by the Commission of Game and Inland Fisheries under a cooperative agreement with the U.S. Forest Service. This highly satisfactory arrangement has seen the dramatic return of the white-tailed deer and the wild turkey and the stabilization of a good black bear population.

Headquarters for the national forest is located in Harrisonburg, where maps and general hunting information are available. Such information is also available at the six ranger district offices located throughout the forest. Much of the wildlife management work is concentrated at the district ranger level, often a better source of information if the hunter has settled on a particular district. The current ranger districts are Deerfield, Dry River, James River, Lee, Pedlar, and Warm Springs.

The ranger district maps are particularly valuable. Contour lines spell out the terrain, and a quick look at most maps will reveal a good deal of steep mountain country that will tax the best-conditioned hunter. Elevations in the George Washington National Forest range from 500 to 4,458 feet. The maps also show all travel routes from the major highways down to trails and footpaths. I- 64 and I–81 are the only interstate highways passing through the national forest, but there are several U.S. highways and numerous primary highways. The real access, however, is provided by secondary roads, dirt all-weather roads, forest service roads, and trails. These are shown in detail on the ranger district maps but not on the larger general maps of the forest. Gate symbols show which roads are closed to normal vehicular travel, but most of these are open during the fall, winter, and spring hunting seasons. The district maps also show the location of campgrounds. Some are in recreation areas, but others are in more remote sections of the forest and often are the better choice for the hunter. Other features of interest include lakes and ponds, mountain peaks, streams, and valleys. The current cost of ranger district maps is 50¢ each, but the less detailed maps of the entire forest are free.

There is not a county in the George Washington National Forest that does not offer good deer hunting. In some the hunting is excellent. Bath, Rockingham, and Shenandoah all have vast national forest lands. So do Alleghany, Augusta, Botetourt, Highland, and Rockbridge. National forest land is more limited in Frederick, also a top deer-hunting county.

The George Washington National Forest counties provide the very best turkey hunting in Virginia with plenty of land in such top counties as Bath and Botetourt, which often lead the state, and other top counties such as Alleghany, Augusta, Highland, Rockbridge, Rockingham, and Shenandoah. Much of this prime turkey-hunting country is high and rugged, and the old toms gobble from the highest ridges. Getting to them means climbing these ridges, a feat many hunters handle year after year. The wild turkey began its modern comeback here, though earlier in the history of Virginia the big birds were more abundant east of the Blue Ridge Mountains.

There is a big chunk of national forest land in Rockingham, possibly the best bear-hunting county in the state. There is also good bear hunting on national forest land in Page County along the eastern slopes of the Massanutten Mountain and on national forest lands in Alleghany, Augusta, Bath, Botetourt, and Rockbridge counties. National forest lands in Highland, Shenandoah, and Warren counties also produce a few bears.

Just about any patch of national forest land is likely to hold some gray squirrels, but the best fox squirrel hunting lies in the counties of Alleghany, Bath, and Highland on the West Virginia border.

Cottontail rabbit hunting is limited on the national forest lands, but a few bunnies live along the edges of the forest and in the clearings. The national forest lands in Highland County offer a unique chance to hunt snowshoe hare in Virginia.

The George Washington National Forest is ruffed grouse country. The popular forest grouse prefer the clear-cuts and abandoned farms. Old orchards are usually good. Many open areas have been planted in autumn olive, an excellent food-producing shrub for grouse and other game.

This big national forest offers possibly the best woodcock hunting in Virginia, particularly along the North Fork of the Shenandoah River. Other stream bottoms are also good. Nearby in West Virginia is the major migration route of the timber-doodles, which head south to Louisiana for the winter. Migrating birds spill over into Virginia.

Much of the North Fork of the Shenandoah River, some of the South Fork, and long stretches of the Cowpasture and Jackson rivers flow through the national forest, offering good jump shooting for black, mallard, wood, and other ducks. Otherwise, waterfowl hunting is extremely limited. A few ducks use wildlife watering holes and beaver ponds, and some are attracted to small trout ponds like Braley Pond and Elkhorn Lake in Augusta County and Trout Pond in Shanandoah County. These lakes are shown on ranger district maps. Lake Moomaw in Alleghany and Bath counties may eventually provide some good waterfowl hunting.

Night hunters roam the rich hardwood forests and mountain valleys for bobcats, opossums, and raccoon. The coon is the most sought after. Bobcats are scarce, but opossums are abundant. There are also good populations of gray and red foxes, with the gray the more abundant.

Dove and quail hunting is limited and unpredictable, with a few birds found near the forest fringes and in cutover areas.

Bears, deer, turkeys, grouse, and squirrels are the major hunting attractions in the George Washington National Forest, and for these species there is no better hunting in Virginia or most of the South.

Deerfield Ranger District

ADDRESS: 2304 West Beverley Street
Staunton, VA 24401,
Telephone 703-885-8028 or 703-886-4277

LOCATION: Portions of Augusta, Bath, Highland, and Rockbridge counties.

ACCESS: Virginia Primary Highway 42 skirts the eastern and southern fringes of the district, and Secondary Routes 614, 619, and 269 along the Cowpasture River skirt the western edge. U.S. Highway 250 passes through the northern section. Various secondary roads and forest service roads off these major highways provide access to the interior.

CAMPING: Rough camping permitted throughout district.

GOOD DEER AREAS: White Oak Draft, Shenandoah Mountain south of U.S. Highway 250, Great North Mountain south of Secondary Route 688, and the east face of Bald Mountain north of U.S. Highway 250.

Dry River Ranger District

ADDRESS: 112 North River Road
     Bridgewater, VA 22812
     Telephone 703-828-2591

LOCATION: Mostly in Rockingham County, but includes portions of Augusta and Highland counties.

ACCESS: U.S. Highway 250 passes just south of district, and Virginia Primary Highway 259 provides access to northeastern corner. U.S. Highway 33 divides district north and south. Western region is in West Virginia, and access to west is from that state. Secondary and forest service roads off these highways lead into hunting regions.

CAMPING: Developed campgrounds at Hearthstone Lake, Hone Quarry, and Todd Lake and beside North River. Rough camping allowed throughout district.

GOOD DEER AREAS: Upper reaches of the Germany River, Hone Quarry Run, Little Dry River, and the east side of Narrowback Mountain.

James River Ranger District

ADDRESS: 313 South Monroe Avenue
     Covington, VA 22426
     Telephone 703-962-2214

LOCATION: Mostly in Alleghany County, but also in parts of Bath, Botetourt, and Rockbridge counties.

ACCESS: Interstate 64 and U.S. Highway 60 split the district north and south, and U.S. Highway 220 divides it east and west. Virginia Primary Highway 42 leads into the northeastern corner, and Primary Routes 18, 159, and 311 lead into the district from the south. Secondary and forest service roads off these major highways provide access to the back country.

CAMPING: There are no developed forest service campgrounds in the district, but the Douthat State Park Campground near Clifton Forge is open to hunters. There is also a developed campground on nearby Lake Moomaw. Rough camping is permitted throughout the district.

GOOD DEER AREAS: Pounding Mill, Big Ridge, Peters Mountain, Jerrys Run, and Oliver Mountain.

Lee Ranger District

ADDRESS: Route 1, Box 31A
Edinburg, VA 22824
Telephone 703-984-4101 or 703-984-4102

LOCATIONS: Mostly in Shenandoah County but also in portions of Page, Rockingham, and Warren counties.

ACCESS: Interstate 81, U.S. Highways 340, 11, and 211, and Virginia Primary Routes 42, 55, and 259 provide access to various parts of the district, with numerous secondary and forest service roads leading into the interior.

CAMPING: Developed forest service campgrounds at Little Fort, Good Falls, Camp Roosevelt, Hawk, Trout Pond, and Wolf Gap. Rough camping permitted throughout the district.

GOOD DEER AREAS: Cedar Creek, Cub Run, Little Stony Creek, Laurel Run, and the east face of Massanutten Mountain.

Pedlar Ranger District

ADDRESS: 2424 Magnolia Avenue
Buena Vista, VA 24416
Telephone 703-261-6105 or 703-261-6106

LOCATION: Amherst, Augusta, Nelson, and Rockbridge counties (see next chapter for discussion of Amherst and Nelson counties).

ACCESS: The Blue Ridge Parkway and U.S. Highway 60 divide this district east and west and north and south. U.S. Highway 501 and Virginia Primary Route 130 provide access to the southern region along the James River. Secondary and forest service roads off these major highways lead into the interior.

CAMPING: There is a forest service campground at Sherando Lake. Rough camping is permitted throughout the district

GOOD DEER AREAS: Big Levels and regions south of U.S. Highway 60 and east of the Blue Ridge Parkway.

Warm Springs Ranger District

ADDRESS: Route 2, Box 30
Hot Srings, VA 24445
Telephone 703-839-2521 or 703-839-2442

LOCATION: Primarily in Bath County but includes portions of Alleghany, Augusta, Highland, and Rockbridge counties.

ACCESS: U.S. Highway 220 and Virginia Primary Highway 39 split this district east and west and north and south. Virginia Primary Route 42 leads into the southeastern corner, and Route 84 passes through the northwestern corner. Dozens of secondary and forest service roads lead from these highways into the backcountry.

CAMPING: There are developed forest service campgrounds at Blowing Springs, Bubbling Springs, Peaceful River, and on Lake Moomaw. There is also a developed campground in Douthat State Park near the southern edge of the district, as well as rough camping throughout the district.

GOOD DEER AREAS: Forest service road north of Douthat State Park, Pads Creek, Limekiln Hollow, Hidden Valley, and Poor Farm.

Jefferson National Forest

The Jefferson National Forest is covered fully in the chapter on Southwest Virginia, where most of its approximately 600,000 acres lie, but a bit of it protrudes north into game-rich Botetourt County. That portion of it is discussed here.

Headquarters for this big national forest is located in Roanoke, but a good source of local information is the New Castle Ranger District Office at New Castle.

Botetourt is an excellent bear, deer, and turkey county, and the national forest offers an abundance of public hunting land. This is also prime grouse and squirrel country, with limited woodcock hunting. Night hunters enjoy bobcats, opossums, and raccoon, and there is some jump shooting for ducks on the James River, which divides the George Washington and Jefferson national forests here. The lower reaches of Craig Creek also provide limited jump shooting. Other waterfowl-hunting possibilities include beaver ponds, wildlife watering holes, and Cave Mountain Lake.

New Castle Ranger District

ADDRESS: State Route 615, Box 246
New Castle, VA 24127
Telephone 703-864-5195

LOCATION: Botetourt, Craig, and Roanoke counties.

ACCESS: U.S. Highway 220 crosses the James River at Eagle Rock, and Secondary Routes 615, 686, 759, 681, 682, and 684 off this highway lead into the district. Jeep trails lead into the backcountry. Another possibility is to launch a canoe on Craig Creek for access to the interior.

CAMPING: No developed campgrounds in Botetourt section of district, but rough camping is permitted. In other parts of the district there are developed campgrounds at Camp Mitchell, the Pines, and the Steel Bridge.

U.S. Army Corps of Engineers Lands

The U.S. Army Corps of Engineers owns a small tract of land adjacent to the Lake Moomaw Dam in Alleghany County, but the recreational facilities are under the supervision of the Warm Springs Ranger District of the George Washington National Forest. It is available for public hunting.

Possibly of more value to the hunter than the limited amount of public land is an excellent public campground that can serve as a base for hunting the sprawling George Washington National Forest or the Gathright Wildlife Management Area. There is also a publicly owned boat-launching ramp near the dam, and the lake provides access to remote parts of the national forest and wildlife management area.

Virginia Secondary Route 687 north of Covington leads to the lake and the boat-launching ramp.

A map of the lake and the adjacent land is available from the U.S. Forest Service, Warm Springs Ranger District, Route 2, Box 30, Hot Springs, VA 24445.

PRIVATE LANDS

The rich farmlands of the Shenandoah Valley offer good small game hunting, particularly for cottontail rabbits. There is also good hunting for fox squirrels, a big tree squirrel that prefers the farm woodlots to the deep woods of the national forest. There are also scattered populations of geese, some good dove hunting, and limited quail populations. Ducks use farm ponds and other private waters.

Possibly because it is located near the heavily populated Washington, D.C., metropolitan area, or maybe because the fine national forest hunting draws so many nonresident hunters to the region, getting permission to hunt the farmlands is difficult. No-hunting signs are numerous. Some farmers will grant permission to hunt, but most reserve the hunting for their families and friends.

The hunter who gains access to some of these farms will enjoy a degree of privacy he will not experience in the national forests or on other public lands. Many deer and turkeys are killed on private lands.

Much of the South Fork of the Shenandoah River flows through private farming country, and these farms feed the ducks jump-shooting hunters enjoy. Fortunately, the Shenandoah is considered a public waterway, and the Commission of Game and Inland Fisheries has developed a good system of public access points that allow hunters to get canoes or light boats on the river.

Owens-Illinois Company

The Owens-Illinois Company owns 82,000 acres of land in Virginia, all of which is available for public hunting. Much of this land, approximately 35,000 acres, is in Botetourt and Rockbridge counties, mostly along the border between the two mountain counties. This is James River country, where the big river breaks out of the mountains and heads east into the vast Piedmont region of Virginia.

Both counties are top big game counties—bears, deer, and turkeys. There are also good populations of grouse and both fox and gray squirrels, opossums, raccoon, and a few bobcats.

Hunting permits are available from the company's offices at P.O. Box WV, Appomattox, VA 24522. Annual fees are $4 for Virginia hunters and $10 for nonresidents.

PUBLIC LAKES

Big public lakes or reservoirs are few in the northwest mountains and Shenandoah Valley, the 2,500-acre Lake Moomaw being a major exception. Even it is small when compared to lakes such as Anna, Buggs Island, and Claytor in other parts of Virginia. There are a few small lakes in the George Washington National Forest such as 55-acre Elkhorn and 15-acre Hearthstone in Augusta County, but generally this region is more one of mountains, valleys, and racing rivers.

While Lake Moomaw is generally deep, there is limited shallow water that may eventually hold fair duck populations. A wide variety of ducks including black ducks, gadwalls, goldeneyes, mallard, and ring-necked, scaup, and wood ducks use the lake. Some such as blacks, mallard, and woodies are primarily resident birds, but others use the lake as a resting spot on their migrations south in the fall. While the lake offers fair duck hunting, it is doubtful that it will stand much pressure. Access to Lake Moomaw is good with the U.S. Forest Service providing a boat-launching ramp near the dam.

There are several other small city and county lakes in the general region, but few provide duck hunting.

The region is not one for big-water hunting.

PUBLIC RIVERS

While there is limited waterfowl hunting on public lakes in this region, there is some excellent river hunting that ranks with the best in the state.

The major river systems are the North and South Forks of the Shenandoah River and the Cowpasture and Jackson rivers. The Middle, North, and South rivers are the major tributaries of the South Fork of the Shenandoah River, the Bullpasture is a major tributary of the Cowpasture, and Back Creek, once a major tributary of the Jackson River, now flows into Lake Moomaw. To the south the James River headwaters offer some duck hunting before the river breaks through the mountains into the eastern foothills, and its tributaries the Maury River and Craig Creek are productive at times.

The ownership of these rivers is often in controversy. The North and South Forks of the Shenandoah are public waterways, a status that has not been questioned. So is the James River, but its tributaries the Jackson and Cowpasture are generally considered private waters. Craig Creek flows through the George Washington and Jefferson national forests, making it a public waterway, and so does much of the Maury.

When the U.S. Army Corps of Engineers acquired what was once part of the Gathright Wildlife Management Area from the Commission of Game and Inland Fisheries, it was agreed that a tailwaters trout fishery would be created in the Jackson River below the Lake Moomaw Dam. This meant opening the stream to public fishing, thus changing its status to a public waterway. The Corps of Engineers has proceeded accordingly, but a group of local landowners has challenged this change in the status of the river. Anglers and hunters are now awaiting the decision of a federal court.

Currently, the Jackson River is considered a public waterway downstream from the U.S. Highway 60 bridge near Clifton Forge, and the U.S. Forest Service is in the process of acquiring land for a public launching ramp that will facilitate use of the river.

There are also short stretches of the Cowpasture River that flow through federal or state lands and are thus open for public use. Downstream from Williamsville the river flows through national forest land and land acquired by the Commission of Game and Inland Fisheries for the Coursey Spring Fish Hatchery.

The George Washington and Jefferson national forests sprawl over big chunks of this mountain country, and any stream flowing through such land is a public waterway regardless of its status elsewhere. The same is true of streams flowing through wildlife management areas.

For the waterfowl hunter, the Shenandoah River system is probably the best choice. It offers good hunting for various species, and the access is good, especially on the South Fork.

Reading downstream, there are access points and launching ramps at Elkton, Shenandoah, Grove Hill, Newport, White House, Massanutten, Foster's, Hazard Mill, Bentonville, Karo, Simpson's, and Front Royal. Float time between these access points varies from an hour to two to seven or eight hours.

There are only two access points on the North Fork of the Shenandoah. One is the Chapman Landing located near Willow Grove, and the other is at Riverton just above the confluence of the two forks.

On the main stem of the Shenandoah River there are four access points between Riverton and the West Virginia line. Reading downstream, they are located at Morgan's Ferry, Berry's Ferry, Locke's Landing, and Castleman's Ferry.

Access to other streams in this region is informal and limited. National forest roads, wildlife management areas, and secondary roads offer opportunities, but setting up a jump-shooting trip requires some prior scouting for places to put in and take out a boat or canoe.

Public hunting in the northwest mountains and Shenandoah Valley is rich, varied, and a mecca for the big game hunter and those who travel from distant points to enjoy it.

Upper Piedmont
and Coastal Plains

This big region includes that part of Virginia's Piedmont and Coastal Plains lying north of the James River. It is a land of sharp contrasts. Gurgling mountain brooks that race down the eastern slopes of the Blue Ridge Mountains send clean waters to tidal streams that form many miles from the sea. In the western foothills thoroughbred horses and registered cattle feed in lush green pastures, while to the east acres of soybean fields and stately pines form a patchwork in the flat country below the fall line.

The hills roll gently in most of this region. Hunting is

relatively easy in comparison to the rugged forest country of the mountains. Elevations range from flat marshlands just a few feet above sea level to 4,054-foot Mount Pleasant in Amherst County. The region lies north of the James River, east of the Blue Ridge Parkway and Skyline Drive, and west of the counties that border on the Atlantic Ocean and Chesapeake Bay.

All of the rivers flow east here to enter the big Chesapeake Bay, historic streams like the James, the Potomac, and the Rappahannock and lesser ones such as the North and South Anna, the Hardware, the Mattaponi, the Pamunkey, the Rivanna, the Rapidan, and to the north Pohick Creek. Legally, the Potomac belongs to the state of Maryland, but it is part of the personality of this varied region. Big lakes are rare in this general region, the only major one being 10,000-acre Lake Anna in Louisa, Orange, and Spotsylvania counties. It offers waterfowl hunting.

Several of the state's major metropolitan centers are located here, including Richmond, the state capital, and Northern Virginia, the Washington, D.C., suburbs that claim much of Fairfax and Loudoun counties and continue to inch south and west. Hunters from these population centers put a good deal of pressure on the region's game resources, but by the same token their license dollars contribute substantially to its support.

Federal lands are not extensive. The major hunting lands are the 54,000-acre U.S. Marine Corps base at Quantico in Fauquier, Prince William, and Stafford counties and the 77,000-acre Fort A. P. Hill Military Reservation in Caroline County. Both provide good public hunting. To the west a chunk of the George Washington National Forest claims the western fringes of Amherst and Nelson counties, and the Shenandoah National Park follows the ridges of the Blue Ridge Mountains north to Front Royal. Hunting in the park is prohibited, but it feeds game, particularly bears, into Albemarle, Greene, Madison, and Rappahannock counties.

The Commission of Game and Inland Fisheries owns a half dozen wildlife management areas in this region that vary in terrain from the mountainous Rapidan Wildlife Management

The entrance to the Hardware River Wildlife Management Area on the James River in Fluvanna County.

Area in Greene and Madison counties to flat and marshy Chickahominy Wildlife Management Area in Charles City County. Several are small in comparison to the big wildlife management areas found in the northwest mountains and in Southside and Southwest Virginia, but collectively they offer almost 25,000 acres of prime and varied hunting land and hunting for just about every species of game found in the state.

Although most of the lands of the big timber corporations are concentrated in Southside Virginia, a number of corporations also own land in this region. Among them are the Chesapeake Corporation of Virginia, Continental Forest Industries, Glatfelter Pulp Wood Company, Owens-Illinois Company, and Westvaco. All offer public hunting.

Because of its proximity to the major metropolitan areas, much of the privately owned land is posted against hunting. Even so, the farmlands support a good deal of hunting. Some land is leased to hunt clubs, but many landowners limit their hunting to family and friends. Some hunters get access to good farmland hunting by simply asking for permission and showing the proper respect and gratitude for the privilege.

Except for the showshoe hare, there is probably not a species of game found in Virginia that does not live here. Some of the best bear hunting in the state is found in the counties along the eastern edges of the Shenandoah National Park, especially Albemarle and Nelson counties, and also including Amherst, Greene, Madison, and Rappahannock counties. In the eastern counties there is hunting for ducks, geese, sora rail, and snipes.

Deer hunting in this big region is as varied as the terrain. Foothills counties such as Albemarle give up good bags every season, but so do the flatland counties such as Caroline. Counties that traditionally produce in excess of 1,000 deer every season include, in addition to Albemarle and Caroline, Charles City, Fauquier, Fluvanna, Louisa, and New Kent counties. Fort A. P. Hill supports much of the deer hunting in Caroline County, but most of the harvest in the other counties comes from private lands.

While the best turkey hunting is found in the northwest mountains and Southside Virginia, there is good hunting here also. Albemarle and Caroline counties are good for turkeys, as are Amherst, Fauquier, Fluvanna, King William, Louisa, and Orange counties.

Squirrels are abundant in the farm woodlots, often the very best habitat for the little game animals. Fox squirrels are not plentiful generally, but the frisky little gray takes up the slack. Fox squirrels are fully protected in much of this region, the only exception being in Fairfax and Loudoun counties where the seasons on squirrels include both the fox and the gray. The farmlands also furnish good cottontail rabbit hunting in certain areas, but rabbit populations are spotty here as they are all over Virginia.

Where there is adequate cover the quail hunting can be excellent, but the gradual shift from crop farming to grass and pastures has eliminated thousands of acres of once excellent quail cover. Dove hunting, on the other hand, is excellent throughout this region. Except for the Marine Corps base at Quantico, the better ruffed grouse hunting is limited to the western part of the region. There are good populations on the Marine Corps base and generally in the counties of Albemarle, Amherst, Greene, Madison, Nelson, and Rappahannock. Much of the hunting is on private lands. Bird and small game hunters kick up a few woodcocks, but concentrations of birds are hard to locate. So are snipes.

The waterfowl hunting can be good on the Potomac River, and Lake Anna holds good populations of both ducks and geese. The James, Mattaponi, and Pamunkey rivers offer good jump shooting, and the hunting is sometimes good on other streams such as the Hardware, Rappahannock, and Rivanna. Beaver and farm ponds often provide good shooting. Resident populations of geese are becoming more common, and they offer limited hunting, but most of it is on private lands or ponds.

Both the opossum and raccoon are abundant here, and this is one of the most popular parts of Virginia for fox hunting.

WILDLIFE MANAGEMENT AREAS

Wildlife management areas are owned by the Commission of Game and Inland Fisheries and managed exclusively for wild-life and hunting. No special fees are required to hunt them other than the usual license fees. Maps and general hunting information are available from the commission headquarters in Richmond or from its regional office at HCO2, Box 238, Buckingham, VA 23921, for the Hardware River, James River, and Pettigrew wildlife management areas; Route 6, Box 484–A, Staunton, VA 24401, for C. F. Phelps, G. Richard Thompson, and Rapidan wildlife management areas; and Box 1001, Tappahannock, VA 22560, for the Chickahominy Wildlife Management Area.

C. F. Phelps Wildlife Management Area

Named for Chester F. Phelps, for many years the executive director of the Commission of Game and Inland Fisheries, this 4,425-acre area is located along the Rappahannock River in gently rolling hill country.

LOCATION: Mostly in Fauquier County, but a small parcel just above the Kellys Ford stretch of the Rappahannock River is in Culpeper County.

SIZE: The 4,425 acres include seven miles of riverfront.

TERRAIN: River bottoms and gently rolling hills with numerous streams including, in addition to the Rappahannock River, Fishing, Marsh, Mine, and Persimmon runs. Second-growth hardwoods and a good mixture of scrub and shortleaf pine make up the forest cover. There is also much open land, much of which is leased to local farmers.

CAMPING. No developed campgrounds, but camping in self-contained units is allowed.

ACCESS: The Fauquier County section is reached by Secondary Routes 632, 651, and 637 off U.S. Highway 17. The Culpeper County section is reached off U.S. Highway 29 by Secondary Routes 620, 651, and 674. There is a good network of roads within the area, but they may be gated during wet weather. There is also a boat-launching ramp on Marsh Run just above its confluence with the Rappahannock River.

GAME: Deer, ducks, grouse, rabbits, raccoon, opossums, turkeys, squirrels, quail, and a few woodcocks are the major species. The farming activities might draw a few doves, but there are no managed dove fields. Floating the river for ducks and squirrels is popular. The deer hunting is good, and there are several gangs of turkeys.

Chickahominy Wildlife Management Area

Located on the Chickahominy River, which forms its eastern boundary, this area provides good public hunting in a region where public hunting land is at a premium. Plans include the purchase of additional land as adjacent land becomes available.

This land has been under some kind of civilized activity since the seventeenth century. Much of it has been logged many times, some of it just before the purchase by the commission. The variety of wildlife habitat is rich, making it one of the most interesting wildlife management areas in the state.

LOCATION: Entirely within Charles City County.

SIZE: Now 4,846 acres, but expansion is planned.

TERRAIN: Rolling hills drop off to stream bottoms and guts. Morris Creek, a winding tidal stream, divides and drains the area, and numerous smaller streams drain the area and enter either Morris Creek or the Chickahominy River. There are also numerous beaver ponds and marshes.

CAMPING: No developed campgrounds, but camping in self-contained units is permitted.

ACCESS: Virginia Primary Highway 5 skirts the southern boundary, and Secondary Route 623 off this major highway provides access, with Secondary Route 621 leading deep into the area. Spur roads lead to the shores of Chickahominy River and Morris Creek. There are also seven miles of graveled roads within the area, as well as trails. There is also a boat-launching ramp.

GAME: Waterfowl hunting is excellent with good wood duck hunting early in the season and later a wide variety of ducks and geese. Only floating blinds are permitted, and hunters must furnish their own. The deer hunting is also excellent, and there is a huntable population of turkeys. Fall turkey hunting is now limited to a two-week season. There are good quail and rabbit populations in the cutover areas and in the open pines, plus squirrels, snipes, and woodcocks. Doves, opossums, and raccoon round out the game populations. Dove hunting is limited to Wednesdays and Saturdays.

G. Richard Thompson Wildlife Management Area

The G. Richard Thompson Wildlife Management Area is mountain country that spreads in two separate tracts along the eastern slope of the Blue Ridge Mountains. The larger parcel lies to the south, but a smaller parcel is to the north where it abuts on the Sky Meadows State Park.

Lake Thompson, a 12-acre public fishing lake, is located near the eastern fringes of the area.

LOCATION: Spreads over parts of Clarke, Fauquier, and Warren counties, but mostly in Fauquier.

SIZE: The two parcels total 4,007 acres.

TERRAIN: Generally mountainous with much flat land near the foot of the mountains and some near the top. Most is heavily forested with hardwoods, but vast orchards once covered much of the land and remnant trees are still present.

CAMPING: No developed campgrounds, but camping in self-contained units is allowed.

ACCESS: Virginia Secondary Route 688 provides access to the eastern fringes, and Route 638 skirts the western border, dipping across it occasionally. Both lead off Interstate Highway 66.

GAME: The area receives a lot of hunting pressure, but it produces a good deer harvest and a fair turkey kill. Squirrels are reasonably abundant, and the grouse hunting is fair, particularly in the old orchards. There are also good populations of opossums and raccoon, and a few quail, rabbits, and woodcocks. Footpaths, trails, and several miles of gravel roads provide hunting access.

Hardware River Wildlife Management Area

The Hardware River Wildlife Management Area is one of the smallest, but it offers good hunting along the James River. The James River here is studded with islands, and there is a good deal of fast, shallow water. Duck hunters floating the river find good shooting among the islands. The river is a public waterway, but the islands are privately owned and not a part of the wildlife management area.

Before its purchase by the Commission of Game and Inland Fisheries, much of the land was used to grow crops.

LOCATION: Wholly within Fluvanna County.

SIZE: A small area of only 880 acres.

TERRAIN: The area fronts on the James River and includes several acres of floodplain, but generally it is gently rolling Piedmont country easy to hunt. One patch of the floodplain is separated from the main parcel. While there is some open country, most of the land is covered with hardwoods and stands of mature pine that have claimed fields abandoned during the Great Depression. Two streams, the Hardware River and Doby Creek, drain the area.

CAMPING: No developed campgrounds, but camping in self-contained units is allowed.

ACCESS: Virginia Secondary Route 646 off Primary Highway 6 provides access to the eastern part of the area, and Kidd's Mill Road also off Highway 6 leads into the western part. There are several miles of trails, and a boat-launching ramp offers access to the river.

GAME: Deer to ducks, and also doves, grouse, quail, rabbits, opossums, raccoon, squirrels, turkeys, and woodcocks. Dove hunting is limited to Wednesdays and Saturdays. The turkey hunting is good, but not as good as the deer hunting. Squirrels are the most abundant game, and a good way to hunt them is to float the Hardware River in a canoe or light boat.

James River Wildlife Management Area

Before its purchase by the Commission of Game and Inland Fisheries, the James River Wildlife Management Area was owned by the Dunn family and operated as a cattle farm. It is located along the northern bank of the James River with 3,000 feet of riverfront, and it contains a shallow-water impoundment that is planted in millet to attract ducks.

LOCATION: Entirely within Nelson County.

SIZE: A small area of only 671 acres.

TERRAIN: The area ranges from flatlands along the river to rolling hills with an average elevation of only 500 feet. Some of the low-lying areas drain poorly but offer good wildlife cover. In addition to the shallow-water impoundment, there are several small ponds, numerous springs, and a pair of small streams. Approximately 200 of the 671 acres are open fields, but some of the older fields are reverting to pine forests. The remainder, mostly uplands, is in mixed oak and pine forests.

CAMPING: No developed campgrounds, but camping in self-contained units is permitted.

ACCESS: Virginia Secondary Route 626, which follows the James River here, passes through the property, and Route 743 skirts its southwestern border. There is approximately a mile of roads within the area as well as a boat-launching ramp on the James River.

GAME: Deer, doves, opossums, quail, rabbits, raccoon, squirrels, turkeys, waterfowl, and an occasional bobcat are present. The deer hunting is good, and the turkey hunting should improve as the forests mature. Squirrels are the most abundant game, but the area is also managed as a dove-hunting area with hunting limited to Wednesdays and Saturdays as is customary on public dove-hunting lands. The James River offers excellent jump shooting for ducks, and there is also some hunting over the impoundment and the several small ponds. Crops planted for doves attract a few quail and rabbits, and the hunter might sight an occasional bear.

Pettigrew Wildlife Management Area

The Pettigrew Wildlife Management Area is a relatively new one located in a part of the state where public hunting land is limited. It was once a part of Fort A. P. Hill and was acquired by the Commission of Game and Inland Fisheries when the federal government declared it surplus land.

LOCATION: Entirely within Caroline County.

SIZE: 934 acres.

TERRAIN: Gently rolling to flat and mostly wooded with mixed oaks and pines. A marsh is on one end, and there are numerous beaver ponds and small streams. A few open fields are leased to local farmers but are open to hunting.

CAMPING: No developed campgrounds, but camping in self-contained units is permitted.

ACCESS: The area is wedged between the old and new U.S. Highway 17, both of which offer good access, and a secondary highway leads into it.

GAME: The area has good deer and turkey hunting, ducks on the beaver ponds, and squirrels in the hardwood forests. There is also fair dove, quail, and rabbit hunting in the open fields and edges. Hunters kick up a few woodcocks, and night hunters will find fair numbers of opossums and raccoon.

Rapidan Wildlife Management Area

The Rapidan Wildlife Management Area is a big one in comparison to most wildlife management areas in this region of Virginia. It sprawls in almost a dozen separate patches across the eastern slope of the Blue Ridge Mountains. The biggest block is wedged deep into the Shenandoah National Park, but the park lands where hunting is prohibited are well marked.

Much of the rich mountain culture of a bygone era is still evident—old log cabins, rock piles and fences, and rusting barrel hoops from Prohibition days. Bootlegging was a part of the region's colorful past.

LOCATION: Greene and Madison counties.

SIZE: 8,882 acres in almost a dozen different parcels.

TERRAIN: The terrain is steep and rugged with elevations ranging from 900 to 3,000 feet. It is well forested, but most of it is accessible. With the exception of an occasional beaver pond or wildlife watering hole, still water is very limited. There is plenty of water, however, in the form of racing mountain streams, many of which hold native brook trout. The major rivers, all of which are well known, include the South River in Greene County; the Conway River, which forms the Greene-Madison County border; the Rapidan River, for which the area was named; and the Rose River, which drains a small patch of the wildlife management area.

CAMPING: No developed campgrounds, but camping in self-contained units is permitted.

ACCESS: Numerous secondary roads such as Routes 662, 615, and 642 provide access to various parts of the wildlife management area, but they are winding and steep in places. A four-wheel drive vehicle, while not an absolute necessity, is definitely an asset. The Commission of Game and Inland Fisheries has built six miles of roads within the area, including a pair of bridges over the Rapidan River. Miles of footpaths and trails lead deep into the area.

GAME: Bears, deer, grouse, squirrels, and turkeys draw hunters to the area, but it is the black bear that makes the hunting noteworthy. Hunters take approximately twenty bears per season here, making it one of the best bear-hunting spots in the state. Both deer and turkeys are on the increase. This is also good grouse-hunting country, but it is physically demanding of the hunter. Squirrels are abundant, and there are a few rabbits and woodcocks. Night hunters enjoy bobcats, opossums, and raccoon.

FEDERAL LANDS

A portion of the Pedlar Ranger District of the George Washington National Forest, the U.S. Marine Corps base at Quantico, and the Fort A. P. Hill Military Reservation comprise the federal lands in this big region. Collectively, they offer approximately 200,000 acres of public hunting land, considerably more than do the wildlife management areas. These federal acres offer a rich variety of hunting ranging from bears in the rugged Pedlar Ranger District to ducks on the Fort A. P. Hill beaver ponds.

George Washington National Forest

A small part of the George Washington National Forest, discussed fully in the preceding chapter, is located in this area—approximately half of the 141,621-acre Pedlar Ranger District, which stretches across the Blue Ridge Mountain ridges into this region. The forest headquarters is located in Harrisonburg.

This is an interesting section of the national forest. The James River skirts its southern border, separating it from the Jefferson National Forest to the south, and the Blue Ridge Parkway divides the east and west slopes of the Blue Ridge Mountains. Nearby is the spectacular Crabtree Falls.

The national forest here is ribboned with streams, including Buffalo and Otter creeks, the North and South Forks of the Buffalo Rivers, the South Fork of the Piney River, and the North Fork of the Tye River.

Pedlar Ranger District

ADDRESS: 2424 Magnolia Avenue
Buena Vista, VA 24416
Telephone 703-261-6105 or 703-261-6106

LOCATION: Portion of Amherst and Nelson counties.

ACCESS: The Blue Ridge Parkway and U.S. Highway 60 are the major access routes to this section of the forest. Numerous secondary roads and forest service roads leading off these two major highways provide access to most of the national forest. Some are all-weather dirt roads.

CAMPING: There is a developed campground in the Sherando Lake Recreation Area across the Blue Ridge Parkway in Augusta County, and rough camping is permitted throughout the forest.

GOOD DEER AREAS: Regions south of U.S. Highway 60 and east of the Blue Ridge Parkway.

Quantico Marine Corps Base

The Quantico Marine Corps base located on the Potomac River approximately 35 miles south of Washington, D.C., was established in 1917 and expanded considerably during World War II. Public hunting is permitted when it does not conflict with military commitments.

Wildlife and hunting are managed under a cooperative agreement between the military authorities and the Commission of Game and Inland Fisheries. A wildlife manager heads the reservation conservation staff.

A minimum of 15 percent of the land is reserved each day for civilians, and generally much more is available—particularly during the week. There are over three dozen hunting areas, and they are assigned on a first-come, first-served plan. Opening days, weekends, and holidays can be crowded, but usually there is room for all.

In addition to the basic state hunting licenses, Quantico hunters must hold an annual base hunting permit, available for $4 from the warden headquarters. A daily permit, available from the same office, is also required, but there is no charge for it.

As is generally true of military reservations, rifles are prohibited, but both shotguns and archery tackle are permitted. The wearing of blaze orange is mandatory. Deer hunters must use shotgun slugs or archery tackle, and deer hounds and deer drives are prohibited.

Hunters are required to complete game reports at the conclusion of their hunt, a requirement that enables the wildlife managers to keep accurate records of the game harvested.

LOCATION: Fauquier, Prince William, and Stafford counties.

SIZE: Originally only 5,000 acres, it was increased to 54,000 during World War II.

TERRAIN: Much of the base was farmland before its purchase by the military authorities, and many open fields remain. Many are planted with wildlife cover and feeding plots. The terrain is generally rolling, but marines who have trained there will recall some rugged hikes over hilly terrain. Generally, however, it is easy to hunt. A variety of beaver ponds, small lakes, and streams dot or ribbon the base, including Barrett, Dalton, and Upshur ponds, Aquia, Breckenridge, and Lunga reservoirs, Aquia and Chopawamsic creeks, and Beaver Dam Run.

CAMPING: Camping is not permitted on the Marine Corps base, but there are several developed campgrounds in the Prince William Forest Park, which borders the base lands. They are operated by the National Park Service and are open all year.

ACCESS: While Interstate Highway 95 and U.S. Highway 11 pass north and south through the Marine Cops base, all of the hunting land is to the west of Interstate 95. The game warden headquarters is located approximately 1.2 miles west of the I-95 exit to the Marine Corps base and on the left side of the road. A good network of secondary roads provides access to the various parts of the base. There are boat-launching ramps on Dalton Pond and Lunga Reservoir.

GAME: The squirrel is the most popular game animal, with hunters bagging in excess of 4,000 animals during the better seasons. The old farmlands, edges, and open fields are ideal for cottontail rabbits, and in good years the kill has topped 2,000 animals. The abandoned farmlands also favor quail, and in recent years the harvest has run approximately 400 birds. Deer hunters take in the neighborhood of 500 animals annually, and turkey hunters enjoy both fall and spring seasons, bagging approximately 50 birds per year. Quantico is noted for its grouse hunting, with a yearly bag of 100 to 200 birds, and occasionally there is fair woodcock hunting. The dove hunting is spotty as the migrants do not seem to linger long even though there is good food and cover. Hunters also take a few opossums, raccoon, and foxes. Located on the shores of the Potomac River, Quantico offers some good duck hunting. There are half a dozen duck management areas where ponds are drained, planted with millet, and then allowed to refill. The lakes, ponds, and streams also hold ducks.

Fort A. P. Hill Reservation

The third tract of federal hunting land in this region is Fort A. P. Hill Military Reservation, a U.S. Army installation. It is the largest of the three military reservations in Virginia where hunting is allowed. Hunting and wildlife on the reservation are managed under a cooperative agreement between the military authorities and the Commission of Game and Inland Fisheries that has been in effect since 1959.

Located close to Richmond, the state capital, and within a

couple of hours of Washington, D.C., this area gets a good deal of hunting pressure, but it provides good hunting year after year.

As is true at Quantico, the hunter needs an annual hunting permit costing $5 plus a daily permit for which there is no charge. Both are available from the hunt administrator's office on the reservation. Hunting permits are issued on a first-come, first-served basis, and lines sometimes form in front of the office, particularly on the opening day of deer season. During weekdays, however, this is rarely a problem. There are almost three dozen hunting areas, and usually there is room for all. At the conclusion of their hunt, hunters are asked to complete harvest reports, which are used for game management purposes.

Except for .22-caliber rifles, which are permitted during the squirrel seasons, no rifles are allowed. Archery tackle and shotguns are allowed, but slugs may not be used in shotguns. A minimum of 500 square inches of blaze orange is required except during the spring turkey season and during the special bowhunting season. The use of dogs for hunting deer is prohibited, but they may be used for ducks, quail, rabbits, squirrels, and turkeys during the fall season. The use of a retrieving dog or a boat is mandatory when hunting ducks on beaver ponds, lakes, or other waters.

LOCATION: Entirely within Caroline County.

SIZE: 77,000 acres.

TERRAIN: This is a region of Virginia where the Piedmont merges into the coastal plains. The land rolls gently, and there is much flat land. All of it is easy to hunt. Much of the area that makes up what is now the military reservation was in farmlands, and many large, open fields still exist. There are also numerous streams, beaver ponds, and other small impoundments including Buzzard Roost, Lonesome Gulch, and Meadow Creek. Hunting in the vicinity of Travis Lake, a wildlife refuge, is prohibited.

CAMPING: No developed campgrounds, but camping in self-contained units is permitted.

ACCESS: U.S. Highway 301 passes through the reservation, and U.S. Highway 17 skirts its northern border. Virginia Primary Highway 2 passes along its western border, but the major access is from U.S. 301 at Bowling Green. There is a good network of access roads to various parts of the reservation, and these are shown on a map issued to the hunter when he is assigned an area.

GAME: A deer herd estimated at 3,500 animals makes deer hunting extremely popular. A recent estimate places the turkey population at 1,200 birds, making the reservation one of the best turkey-hunting areas in eastern Virginia. Both fall and spring seasons are held. Squirrels also get plenty of attention, with a population estimated to be 15,000 animals. Most are gray squirrels. Fox squirrels released on the reservation are fully protected, but hunters are asked to report sightings of these big squirrels. The squirrel season is a long one running from mid-October through January. Cottontail rabbits are present but not nearly as abundant as squirrels. The big open fields make quail hunting a real pleasure, and a population of approximately 2,500 birds provides good shooting. Dove hunting is limited to Wednesdays and Saturdays, and the hunting varies but is occasionally good. A few snipes and woodcocks round out the bird hunting. The various beaver ponds and other small bodies of water offer fair waterfowl hunting, but Canada geese are currently fully protected. Foxes, opossums, and raccoon round out the game populations.

PRIVATE LANDS

Private farmlands support a good deal of hunting in this area, but most is reserved for family and friends. Some farmers permit hunting when asked, and others lease the hunting rights to hunt clubs. A number of corporate timber companies own large tracts of land that are generally open to public hunting. Some charge a modest fee; others do not.

Chesapeake Corporation of Virginia

The Chesapeake Corporation of Virginia, West Point, VA 23181, owns 2,300 acres of land in Nelson County that are managed for public hunting under a cooperative agreement with the Commission of Game and Inland Fisheries. This land is well marked, and there is no charge for hunting it.

Nelson County is one of the best bear-hunting counties in Virginia, and it also offers good deer and turkey hunting. The small game hunter will find rabbits and squirrels, and the night hunter will find opossums, raccoon, and possibly a bobcat or two. The grouse hunting is good, and there are a few quail and woodcocks.

The Chesapeake Corporation of Virginia also owns public hunting land in the counties of Amherst, Essex, Fauquier, Fluvanna, James City, King and Queen, King William, Nelson, New Kent, and Spotsylvania, much of which is open to permit holders.

Like Nelson to its north, Amherst is also a good bear county. Most of these counties offer deer hunting, with Fauquier, Fluvanna, King William, Nelson, and New Kent being the better ones. Turkey hunting is good in many also, but Fauquier, Fluvanna, King and Queen, King William, and Nelson counties are the better ones. Fresh cutover areas offer good quail hunting, and cottontail rabbits like the young pine forests. There are squirrels in the mature hardwoods, and usually good populations of opossums and raccoon. Ducks use the beaver ponds and marshes and a few of the streams.

Permits are available from the company offices in West Point for $5. The company will also furnish maps for specific counties but will not honor a blanket request for all counties in which it owns land.

Continental Forest Industries

Continental Forest Industries, P.O. Box 1041, Hopewell, VA 23860, owns approximately 300,000 acres of land in Virginia, most of which are open to public hunting. Many acres are located in the counties of Albemarle, Caroline, Charles City, Fluvanna, Hanover, Louisa, Nelson, New Kent, Orange, and Spotsylvania.

Both Albemarle and Nelson counties are near the top as bear-hunting counties. They also offer good deer hunting, but Caroline, Charles City, Fluvanna, Louisia, and New Kent counties are just as good.

Albemarle, Caroline, Fluvanna, Louisa, Nelson, Orange, and Spotsylvania counties all provide good turkey hunting.

The quail hunting can be good in the new clear-cut areas

and young pine forests. Such areas also offer fair rabbit hunting. Hardwoods left along streams or inaccessible cliffs provide fair squirrel hunting. They are also good for opossums and raccoon, and the beaver ponds and marshes offer limited duck hunting.

Permits are available for $8, and application should be made at the company offices in Hopewell in early October. A statewide map showing the location of all of the company's lands is also available when a hunter applies for a permit.

Glatfelter Pulp Wood Company

The Glatfelter Pulp Wood Company, P.O. Box 868, Fredericksburg, VA 22404, owns land in the counties of Culpeper, Fluvanna, Hanover, Louisa, Orange, and Spotsylvania.

Big game in these counties is limited to deer and turkeys with good deer populations in all counties, though Fluvanna and Louisa are the top ones. All except Hanover offer fair to good turkey hunting.

The clear-cut areas and young pine plantations provide some quail hunting in most counties, and there is limited rabbit hunting. Where there are stands of hardwoods the squirrel hunting is good, and night hunters will find a few opossums and raccoon.

Beaver ponds, old farm ponds, and the larger streams hold a few ducks.

Some of the company's land has been leased to hunt clubs, but the remainder is open to hunters who purchase $7 permits from the above address. Maps are available for specific counties, but blanket requests will not be honored.

Owens-Illinois Company

The Owens-Illinois Company, P.O. Box 28, Big Island, VA 24526, owns 82,000 acres of land in Virginia, much of which is in this big region. The company lands here are in Albemarle, Amherst, and Nelson counties, all good bear-hunting counties, and good for deer as well. Albemarle is one of the top deer counties in the state. All three also offer good turkey hunting.

There are also good populations of grouse and squirrels, a few bobcats, opossums, and raccoon, and scattered quail, rabbits, and woodcocks.

Hunting permits are available from the above address. Annual fees are $4 for Virginia hunters and $10 for nonresidents.

Westvaco Virginia Woodlands

Westvaco Virginia Woodlands, P.O. Box WV, Appomattox, VA 24522, offers some excellent hunting lands in the counties of Albemarle, Amherst, Fluvanna, Greene, Louisa, Nelson, and Orange, but most of its holdings are south of the James River.

Approximately 1,800 acres of the company's lands in Amherst and Nelson counties are under a cooperative agreement with the Commission of Game and Inland Fisheries, and there is no charge for hunting this land. It is clearly marked.

Albemarle and Nelson are two of the best bear-hunting counties in Virginia, and Amherst and Greene are also good. Albemarle, Amherst, and Nelson are also good deer counties, but Fluvanna and Louisa are probably better. The Orange hunting is also good, and Greene is on the upswing. Albemarle, Amherst, Fluvanna, Louisa, Nelson, and Orange are all good turkey counties, and Greene produces a few birds every season.

All of these Westvaco counties offer good grouse hunting. It can be quite good in Albemarle, Amherst, Greene, and Nelson, but rather limited in the remainder. Squirrel hunting is generally good, and cutover hardwoods and young pine plantations offer good quail hunting and some rabbit hunting.

Westvaco leaves approximately 20 percent of its land in hardwoods, and this provides good habitat for opossums, raccoon, and squirrels. A few bobcats range the western counties.

Ducks use the larger streams, old farm ponds, and beaver ponds.

Annual hunting permits costing $5 are available from the company's offices at the above address. Maps are available for specific counties, but blanket requests will not be honored.

PUBLIC LAKES

Except for the small ponds and lakes in the George Washington National Forest, the ponds and lakes at Fort A. P. Hill, and the Quantico Marine Corps base, 10,000-acre Lake Anna is the only sizable body of water where hunting is permitted. This popular Virginia Electric and Power Company lake in Louisa, Orange, and Spotsylvania counties offers good, though sometimes spotty, waterfowl hunting. During the course of the season both Canada geese and a variety of ducks use the big impoundment, and there are usually several big flocks of coots.

Access to Lake Anna is good. There are a number of public launching ramps around the lake available for use at a modest fee. There is also a public launching ramp on the Pamunkey Creek arm of the lake. It is owned and maintained by the Commission of Game and Inland Fisheries and is reached off U.S. Highway 522, which crosses the lake.

Some hunters build permanent blinds, but most of the land around the lake is privately owned and the permission of the landowner is required.

Just about any species of waterfowl using the Atlantic Flyway is likely to be found on Lake Anna at one time or another, but black ducks, mallard, teal, widgeon, and wood ducks are the most common.

The waterfowler willing to spend some time scouting the big lake is likely to enjoy some good shooting on Lake Anna.

PUBLIC RIVERS

Big rivers, the largest in Virginia, ribbon this region. There is the mighty Potomac, available to Virginia hunters willing to purchase a Maryland license. Licensed Virginia hunters can hunt the Virginia shoreline, of course, and generally within the coves so long as they stay shoreward of a line drawn between the two points of land that form the cove, usually indicated by markers. In its upper reaches west of Washington, D.C., the Potomac offers good jump shooting for ducks, but downstream the broad tidal river is more likely to be hunted from blinds. To the south is the historic James. Above Richmond, the river is good for the jump shooter, while below the capital blinds are more popular.

In between these two major rivers are the Chickahominy, Rapidan, Rappahannock, and the Mattaponi and Pamunkey, which join to form the York. In the foothills there are the smaller rivers such as the Hardware, the North and South Forks of the Anna, the Rivanna, Rockfish, and Tye. Most of these rivers are public waterways, at least in their tidal stretches, and in many cases all the way to their headwaters. That is the case with the James and Rappahannock, for example. If there is doubt, it is a good idea to check.

These rivers generally have good access. On the Potomac the Commission of Game and Inland Fisheries maintains a public launching ramp at McKimmey in Loudoun County. There are a number of access points and launching ramps on the James. Moving downstream from its headwaters there are landings at Monocan Park in Amherst County, Bent Creek in Appomattox, Wingina and Midway Mills in Nelson, Howardsville and Scottsville in Albemarle, Columbia and Cartersville in Cumberland, West View and Beaumont Ramp in Goochland, and Beaumont and Watkins in Powhatan County. In the tidal stretch of the river there are access points at Dutch Gap in Chesterfield County and Deep Bottom in Henrico.

The Rivanna has launching ramps at Milton in Albemarle County and at Crofton Bridge and Palmyra in Fluvanna County. On the upper Rappahannock there are access points at the C. F. Phelps Wildlife Management Area in Fauquier County and at Motts Landing and Fredericksburg in Spotsylvania County. In the tidal section of the Rappahanncok there are access points and launching ramps at Tappahannock and Hoskins Creek in Essex County and at Mill Stone, Saluda, and Mill Creek in Middlesex County.

There are Commission of Game and Inland Fisheries access points at Aylett in King William County and at Melrose and Waterfence in King and Queen County. The Pamunkey River has public access points at Lester Manor and West Point in King William County.

In addition to the public access points and launching ramps, there are numerous marinas on the tidal stretches of the Chickahominy, James, Potomac, Rappahannock, and York rivers that offer launching facilities at modest fees. Of course, there are all kinds of informal access to most of these rivers—farm roads, bridges, fords, and others which often require securing the permission of the landowner to launch a boat.

That is hunting in Virginia's Piedmont and Coastal Plains north of the James River, possibly the heaviest hunted region in the state.

The Northern Neck

The Northern Neck is a land to itself in Virginia, a mixture of tidal rivers, the upper Chesapeake Bay, a few gently rolling hills, marshes, and many acres of flatlands. It is bounded by the Potomac River on the north, the Rappahannock on the south, the Chesapeake Bay to the east, and the city of Fredericksburg on the west. Loosely, it claims the counties of King George, Lancaster, Northumberland, Richmond, and Westmoreland. Commercial fishing, oystering, farming, and forestry are the economic base, with a little tourism thrown in. The region is historically rich.

The deer is the major big game animal in the Northern Neck, and each of the five counties offers good whitetail hunting. It does not rank with the best in Virginia, but it is consistently good. Hounds and shotguns are the most popular hunting combination. Rifles are prohibited, but some still hunting is done with shotguns.

The wild turkey is doing well in King George, Richmond, and Westmoreland counties, and it is being reestablished in Lancaster and Northumberland counties. Doves and quail provide excellent bird hunting, and there are cottontail rabbits and squirrels for the small game hunter. Both bird and small game hunters kick up an occasional snipe or woodcock. Foxes, opossums, and raccoon are reasonably abundant.

Waterfowl hunting can be good in the Northern Neck, with the broad Potomac River, the tidal Rappahannock River, and the Chesapeake Bay offering almost unlimited opportunities. Small bays, sounds, and creeks probe deeply into their broken shorelines, offering migrating waterfowl good protection.

The Potomac and Rappahannock rivers and the Chesapeake Bay are all public waters, but Maryland owns the Potomac River to the mean low-water mark on the Virginia side. Licensed Vir-

The Simonson Landing of the Commission of Game and Inland Fisheries provides access to the Rappahannock River from the Northern Neck region. The river offers good duck hunting.

ginia hunters are limited to the coves on the Virginia shore, and generally they are required to restrict their hunting activities to the water shoreward of a line drawn between the points of land that form the cove. There are also delineation markers, but the safest approach is to purchase a Maryland hunting license.

Public hunting land is extremely limited on the Northern Neck, but public waterways are almost unlimited. There is no federal or state land in the Northern Neck region that is open to public hunting. The approximately 2,000 acres of land at the Dahlgren Naval Station in King George County has huntable populations of upland game and waterfowl, but the hunting is limited to base personnel. The Commission of Game and Inland Fisheries owns the 462-acre Lands End Waterfowl Management Area, also in King George County, but it is managed as a waterfowl refuge. Hunting is not allowed.

PRIVATE LANDS

Except for waterfowl hunting, the private lands of the Northern Neck region support its hunting. Most of this land is posted against hunting, with permits generally limited to friends and neighbors, though some landowners grant hunting permission. Fortunately, one Virginia timber corporation has opened its lands to public hunting. The rich farmlands support good game populations, including ducks and geese that use the rivers and the bay.

Chesapeake Corporation of Virginia

The Chesapeake Corporation of Virginia, West Point, VA 23181, owns approximately 200,000 acres of land in Virginia, much of which is located in four of the five Northern Neck counties— Lancaster, Northumberland, Richmond, and Westmoreland.

All four of these counties offer good deer hunting, with annual kills running 300 to 600 animals in most counties. Turkey hunters will find some birds on the company's lands in Richmond and Westmoreland counties and possibly in the counties of Lancaster and Northumberland. Only spring hunting is now permitted in the Northern Neck region.

The Chesapeake Corporation lands also offer reasonably good dove, quail, rabbit, and squirrel hunting. The dove, quail, and rabbit hunting is usually best on cutover areas that have been replanted in pine seedlings. It is good for the first three to five years after the timber has been harvested, and the rabbits will normally remain good for much longer. Squirrel hunting is good where the logging crews spare the hardwoods, normally on cliffs and near streams.

Night hunters find fair populations of opossums and raccoon, and ducks, mostly mallard and woodies, use the beaver ponds and old farm ponds.

Annual hunting permits costing $5 are available from the company's West Point office. Maps of company lands in specific counties are available upon request, but blanket requests will not be honored.

PUBLIC RIVERS

The Potomac and Rappahannock rivers, the big waterways that bound the Northern Neck region, could well offer its best public hunting. The Potomac River is owned by Maryland, however, and the reader is directed to the opening paragraphs of this chapter regarding the ramifications of hunting on it.

The Potomac River spreads to its widest point here, but there is good duck hunting—mostly close to the shore and in the many small bays, inlets, and sounds that probe the mainland. Access is no problem with dozens of boat docks and marinas along the shore. The Commission of Game and Inland Fisheries maintains launching ramps at Colonial Beach and Bonum's Creek in Westmoreland County. There is also a public boat ramp in Westmoreland State Park.

The Commission of Game and Inland Fisheries owns numerous access points and launching ramps on the Rappahannock, equally as good for waterfowling. Beginning upstream, they are at Fredericksburg in Spotsylvania County, Carters Wharf in Richmond County, Tappahannock and Hoskins Creek in Essex County, Totusky and Simonson in Richmond County, and at Mill Stone, Saluda, and Mill Creek in Middlesex County.

There is some jump shooting for ducks on the narrow upper reaches of the Rappahannock just east of Fredericksburg, but this is generally tidewater hunting. Floating and stationary blinds provide most of the shooting.

PUBLIC LAKES

There are no public lakes in the Northern Neck region that are open for public hunting, but the broad Chesapeake Bay offers duck-hunting opportunities. The counties of Lancaster and Northumberland front on the bay, and the coast here is deeply indented with bays, coves, and creeks. They offer good duck hunting.

The Commission of Game and Inland Fisheries maintains a boat-launching ramp at Shell in Northumberland County, and there are also numerous docks and marinas that provide access to the big Chesapeake Bay.

Public hunting opportunities are limited in the Northern Neck region, but the hunting available can be interesting for those who take the time to work it out.

Lower Tidewater Virginia

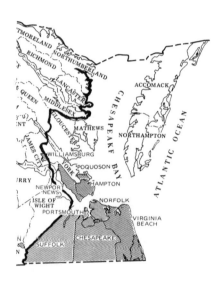

Far from the mountains and the big national forests, the big military areas where public hunting is allowed, and most of the wildlife management areas, hunters in the lower Tidewater look to the coastal marshes for much of their hunting. This land of marshes, pounding surf, tidal creeks, wide beaches, bays, sounds, and the mighty Atlantic Ocean includes the Eastern Shore, Gloucester, Mathews, and York counties, and the big rural cities of Chesapeake, Suffolk, and Virginia Beach that stretch southward from the Chesapeake Bay to the North Carolina line.

Saxis Wildlife Management Area is on the western coast of the Eastern Shore and accessible off U.S. Highway 13. This area offers good hunting for clapper rail and waterfowl. (Photograph by L. G. Kesteloo, Virginia Commission of Game and Inland Fisheries)

Generally, this area offers waterfowl for the most part, but also rails, snipes, and a few woodcocks. There is also some excellent but limited hunting for deer, quail, and rabbits. Turkeys are all but nonexistent in the Tidewater region, but there are a few black bears in the Dismal Swamp area, and the deer herds are expanding throughout the flat coastal country of marshes and broad beaches. This region also can boast a huntable population of sika deer, actually a member of the elk family, imported to the Eastern Shore generations ago.

There is also some small game hunting, mostly for cottontail rabbits and squirrels, and bird hunters enjoy both dove and quail shooting. Most bird and small game hunting is on private lands, however. The Tidewater climate is milder than it is in most of Virginia, and snow is less likely to interrupt quail hunting. The quail is the only game in Virginia that cannot be hunted when there is snow on the ground.

Federal lands in this region include Back Bay, Chincoteague, Fisherman's Island, Great Dismal Swamp, Mackay Island, and Plum Tree Island national wildlife refuges. Hunting is generally prohibited on these lands, though there is limited hunting on Chincoteague and in the Great Dismal Swamp national wildlife refuges.

The Back Bay hunting areas of the Commission of Game and Inland Fisheries—the Barbours Hill, Pocahontas, and Trojan wildlife management areas—provide good waterfowl hunting. So do the Mockhorn and Saxis wildlife management areas on the Eastern Shore. Mockhorn also offers good hunting for clapper rail. The Barbours Hill Area is part of False Cape State Park, occasionally opened to deer hunting as a means of controlling the expanding herds.

There is also some public hunting on the lands of the Chesapeake Corporation of Virginia, Glatfelter Pulp Wood Company, and the Weyerhauser Company. Other private lands available for public hunting include the barrier islands off the Eastern Shore owned by the Nature Conservancy.

Hunting on private lands is otherwise extremely limited in this heavily populated coastal region of Virginia. Landowners generally reserve it for family and friends, though permission can sometimes be obtained to hunt certain farms or other private holdings.

WILDLIFE MANAGEMENT AREAS

Wildlife management areas are owned by the Commission of Game and Inland Fisheries and managed solely for hunting and trapping. Those in the lower Tidewater area are often referred to as waterfowl management areas because they are managed primarily for ducks, geese, and rail. There is no charge for hunting most of these areas, the only requirement being a state hunting license and a migratory bird hunting stamp. The stamp is not required for hunting rail, however.

Maps of specific wildlife management areas and more detailed information are available from the Commission of Game and Inland Fisheries headquarters in Richmond or from its regional office at Box 1001, Tappahannock, VA 22560. There is a charge of $1 for the maps.

Barbours Hill Waterfowl Management Area

The Barbours Hill Waterfowl Management Area is actually a part of False Cape State Park, a long stretch of narrow, sandy land between big Back Bay and the Atlantic Ocean. It is bounded on the north by Back Bay National Wildlife Refuge and on the south by the North Carolina border. Wildlife management in the true sense is rather limited here as the area does not lend itself to extensive management practices.

Hunting is generally limited to waterfowl, and the Commission of Game and Inland Fisheries maintains a set of blinds for that purpose. The hunting is carefully controlled, and the shooting is limited to five blinds per day with not more than two hunters to a blind. Blinds are assigned on the basis of a drawing in October. Applications for the drawing are available from the commission office in Richmond in early September. The daily fee is $15 per blind. Each blind is furnished with a boat and decoys, but the boat is seldom used, for the water around the blinds is shallow enough to wade in hip boots.

The only other hunting in this area is a white-tailed deer season that is normally held in October. This hunt is held in cooperation with the Virginia Division of Parks to control the expanding deer populations in False Cape State Park. Hunters must travel to and from the hunting area by private boats launched at the Trojan Waterfowl Management Area on the western shores of Back Bay.

The climate here is generally mild, but it can run the gamut from freezing temperatures that seal off the blinds with ice to uncomfortably warm days—even during the waterfowl season.

LOCATION: City of Virginia Beach on eastern side of Back Bay.

TERRAIN: Mostly sand dunes covered with stunted pines and understory.

CAMPING: Camping is not allowed in this area.

ACCESS: Since vehicular travel is not permitted in the area, hunters are met by a Commission of Game and Inland Fisheries vehicle at the U.S. Coast Guard station at Sandbridge and transported to their blinds. Deer hunters who travel by boat from across Back Bay will find public launching ramps at False Cape State Park, the Barbours Hill Waterfowl Management Area, and Wash Woods. At the end of their hunt duck hunters are picked up at their blinds and transported back to Sandbridge.

GAME: The more popular species of waterfowl include Canada and snow geese, black ducks, buffleheads, gadwalls, mallard, ruddy ducks, scaup, widgeon, and coots, better known locally as blue petes. Other wildlife includes, in addition to deer, quail, marsh rabbits, muskrat, and nutria. Duck hunters usually bag a snipe or two as they wing over the blinds.

Pocahontas Waterfowl Management Area

The Pocahontas Waterfowl Management Area claims the major part of the 1,143-acre Back Bay Hunting Area owned by the Commission of Game and Inland Fisheries. This general area also includes the Trojan Waterfowl Management Area. Pocahontas covers one large island and a number of smaller ones near the western shore of Back Bay and just north of the North Carolina–Virginia line. Headquarters for Pocahontas is located at the Trojan Waterfowl Management Area on the western shore of the big bay. Hunters gather here on the morning of the hunt to meet their guides for transportation to their blinds.

This is the most popular and usually most productive of the three waterfowl-hunting areas at Back Bay owned and managed by the Commission of Game and Inland Fisheries. During good waterfowl years limits can come quickly. These hunts are completely outfitted, with the commission furnishing blinds, boats, decoys, and guides. The daily fee is $90 per blind, but each blind will accommodate three hunters. This area offers a unique opportunity for first-class hunting in an area where most of the best hunting is tied up by hunt clubs and privately owned blinds.

Blinds are assigned on the basis of a drawing held in October. Applications for the drawing are available in early September from the commission headquarters in Richmond.

LOCATION: City of Virginia Beach near North Carolina line.

SIZE: 737 acres.

TERRAIN: A marshy area of grass, tidal flats, and shallow water.

CAMPING: There is no camping in this area.

ACCESS: Reached by Back Bay Landing Road off Secondary Route 615 south of Creeds in the City of Virginia Beach.

GAME: Waterfowl is the only hunting allowed, but during the course of the season hunters get opportunities at just about every species of duck or goose that uses the Atlantic Flyway. Most abundant are Canada and snow geese, black ducks, buffleheads, gadwalls, mallard, ruddy ducks, teal, scaup, and widgeon. Coots are usually abundant. The hunter also will see an occasional marsh rabbit, muskrat, or nutria. He also will get chances at snipes that wing over his blind.

Trojan Waterfowl Management Area

The Trojan Waterfowl Management Area and the Pocahontas Waterfowl Management Area make up the 1,143-acre Back Bay Hunting Area owned and managed by the Commission of Game and Inland Fisheries. It is a rich area of marshes, ponds, and tidal flats along the western shore of Back Bay.

The commission owns six shore blinds that are available on a first-come, first-served basis, and hunters are advised to arrive early, not later than 6 A.M., if they hope to get a blind. While the commission furnishes a comfortable blind which will accommodate three hunters and a boat, the hunter must furnish his own boat and decoys. Hunters are required to check back through the Trojan headquarters by 4 P.M. There is an excellent launching ramp at the headquarters for the use by hunters who rent these blinds.

The cost per day for the blind is $5.

LOCATION: City of Virginia Beach near the North Carolina line.

SIZE: 406 acres.

TERRAIN: Marshy shoreline and tidal flats with some ponds.

CAMPING: Camping is not permittted on the area.

ACCESS: Reached by Back Bay Landing Road off Secondary Route 615 south of Creeds in the City of Virginia Beach.

GAME: The hunting can be good at times, but it is not consistently so. Waterfowl hunting is the only hunting available. Most of the ducks and geese that use the Atlantic Flyway appear at one time or another during the long waterfowl season, but Canada geese, snow geese, black ducks, buffleheads, gadwalls, mallard, ruddy ducks, teal, scaup, widgeon, and coots are the most abundant.

Mockhorn Island Wildlife Management Area

Mockhorn Island Wildlife Management Area is one of two wildlife management areas on the Eastern Shore of Virginia. It is also one of a number of islands off the ocean side of the Eastern Shore, and it is separated from the mainland by Magothy and Mockhorn bays. Geographically, it is 6 miles east of Cape Charles and 31 miles northeast of Norfolk. The average temperature varies considerably during the fall and winter hunting season. There will be many freezing days but also some summerlike ones. The hunter must be prepared for a wide range of weather conditions that include storms which sweep in from the Atlantic Ocean.

LOCATION: Southeastern Northampton County.

SIZE: Approximately 9,000 acres.

TERRAIN: An island of marshes and tidal flats with only 5 percent of the island being high ground. The vegetation includes greenbrier, honeysuckle, loblolly pine, poison ivy, red cedar, and wax myrtle.

CAMPING: There are no camping facilities, but self-contained camping units are allowed.

ACCESS: Boat-launching ramp at Oyster is reached by Virginia Secondary Route 639 off U.S. 13 at Cheriton. Hunters take boats to wildlife management area. This is the only access.

GAME: This is an excellent clapper rail-hunting area. A few black ducks nest here, and the island hosts some Atlantic brant. A few buffleheads and goldeneyes can usually be found on the open waters just offshore. This is the only public hunting area in Virginia that offers hunting sea ducks such as old-squaws and scoters. Rail and waterfowl hunting are the only hunting permitted, but the hunter may see marsh rabbits, muskrat, otters, and raccoon.

Saxis Wildlife Management Area

The Saxis Wildlife Management Area is located far up the Eastern Shore of Virginia near the Maryland line. Much of it is a broad peninsula that extends westward into Pocomoke Sound of the Chesapeake Bay. It is approximately 75 miles north of Norfolk.

This is the smaller of the two wildlife management areas on the Eastern Shore, but even so it offers 5,255 acres of unique public hunting. Except for a refuge area which is clearly marked, the entire area is open to hunting.

LOCATION: Accomack County.

SIZE: 5,255 acres.

TERRAIN: The basic terrain is tidal marshes and high spots or hammocks, many of which are covered with loblolly pines and other vegetation. Brackish-water Messongo Creek probes deep into the area, separating Michael Marsh on the south and Freeschool Marsh on the north. Michael Marsh is a refuge area, but the remainder of the wildlife management area is open to public hunting. In addition to Messongo Creek there are countless creeks, guts, and ponds in the area. Those farthest inland are freshwater, but the water generally ranges from brackish to salt.

CAMPING: There are no camping facilities, but self-contained units are allowed.

ACCESS: The Commission of Game and Inland Fisheries maintains a boat-launching ramp on Messongo Creek near the little village of Marsh Market at the end of Virginia Secondary Route 698. There is also a launching ramp at Dicks Point at the end of Route 788 on Messongo Creek. Secondary Route 695 provides good access to other parts of the wildlife management area, and Route 719 leads to the northeastern corner near Fig and Persimmon points. Both Routes 692 and 695 off U.S. 13 near Temperanceville lead to the general area.

GAME: Black ducks use the Saxis Wildlife Management Area for both nesting and wintering. Normally the winter black duck population ranges from 2,000 to 3,000 birds, and it is a popular area for hunting these ducks. Upwards of 1,000 Canada geese also winter in this area, and it is a good public hunting area for geese, a bird for which there is limited public hunting in the state. In addition to black ducks, other puddle ducks include mallard, pintail, both green-winged and blue-winged teal, and widgeon. Diving ducks such as buffleheads, canvasbacks, goldeneyes, redheads, scaup, and mergansers use the open waters adjacent to the area, and so do a few sea ducks. Both deer and rabbits are common in this interesting land of marshes and water, and there are good populations of gray and red foxes, raccoon, and opossums.

FEDERAL LANDS

Federal lands do not furnish much public hunting in the lower Tidewater area, though there are a number of national wildlife refuges including Back Bay, Chincoteague, Fisherman's Island, Great Dismal Swamp, Mackay Island, and the Plum Tree Island. There is limited hunting on Chincoteague and in the Great Dismal Swamp, but generally these areas serve as refuges for feeding and resting waterfowl and other wildlife. Those who hunt Barbours Hill Waterfowl Management Area on the eastern shore of Back Bay will pass through Back Bay National Wildlife Refuge, but there is no hunting there.

Chincoteague National Wildlife Refuge

Assateague Island off the Eastern Shore in Accomack County is mostly in Virginia, but a portion of it juts north into Maryland. The entire island is owned by the U.S. Fish and Wildlife Service. The Maryland portion is called the Assateague Island National Seashore, and the Virginia section, 9,460 acres, is known as Chincoteague National Wildlife Refuge.

This is a wild land of sand dunes, stunted pines, wide sandy beaches, and fertile marshlands. The entire island is 37 miles long but only 3 miles wide at the widest point.

The primary purpose of the wildlife refuge is to serve as a resting ground for waterfowl using the Atlantic Flyway during the spring and fall migrations. It is managed for that purpose. In addition to the migrating birds that stop there, many black ducks, gadwalls, mallard, teal, and wood ducks nest there and bring off their young.

The rare Delmarva fox squirrel has also been established on the refuge, and a strong population now lives there. Other game animals include opossums, rabbits, raccoon, red foxes, white-tailed deer, and sika deer, an Oriental elk released there in 1923.

Hunting on the island is limited to sika and white-tailed deer. Because of near ideal living conditions, the sika, particularly, tend to become overpopulated and a threat to waterfowl that rest and feed there. The sika population is in excess of 1,000 animals, and limited hunting is allowed to control the little elk. Both sika and whitetails are legal during the October and November archery season, and a firearms hunt is held later, usually in late November. For safety reasons the firearms hunters must be limited, and hunters are selected on the basis of a drawing.

The Chincoteague National Wildlife Refuge provides an unusual opportunity to bag a different kind of big game in Virginia. The area is easy to hunt, and a good system of trails provides access to all parts of it. The weather is mild during the fall hunting season. In fact, it can be too warm during the early days of the bowhunting season, and mosquitoes can be a problem.

There are no living accommodations on the island, but the nearby town of Chincoteague offers campgrounds, motels, and restaurants.

Hunters interested in entering the drawing for the firearms hunting or hunting during the archery season should contact the refuge office in late summer. Write or call the Refuge Manager, Chincoteague National Wildlife Refuge, Box 62, Chincoteague, VA 23336.

Great Dismal Swamp National Wildlife Refuge

The Great Dismal Swamp National Wildlife Refuge, located in the cities of Suffolk and Chesapeake, Virginia, is almost 50,000 acres of vast swamp country covered mostly with virgin cypress and juniper. Lake Drummond, a shallow, saucer-shaped freshwater lake is the heart of the refuge, but its highly acidic waters do not attract waterfowl to any degree.

For many years before its designation as a wildlife refuge by the U.S. Fish and Wildlife Service, the swamp was a popular big game hunting area. Hunting with trail hounds was popular, and hunters bagged both bears and white-tailed deer. The special swamp season opened early, usually by the first of October. This kind of hunting is still done in the general swamp area, but on private lands outside of the refuge. Both Chesapeake and Suffolk produce good deer kills and a bear or two just about every season.

Hounds are no longer allowed in the refuge, and special deer hunts set up by the Commission of Game and Inland Fisheries and the U.S. Fish and Wildlife Service have drawn little interest. Such hunts may be held in the future if public demand warrants them. Bowhunting is growing in popularity.

Travel within the refuge is difficult, and it is easy to get lost. There is a fair network of roads in the refuge, but their use is generally limited to foot travel or bicycles. Boat access to Lake Drummond is possible by way of the Feeder Ditch that connects the lake with the Dismal Swamp Canal to the east of the refuge. The canal follows U.S. Highway 17, and the boat-launching ramp is well marked. Several ditches including the Jericho and Washington ditches can be navigated by canoe.

The weather is mild in the refuge during the early fall hunting seasons, and mosquitoes can be a problem.

Maps of the Great Dismal Swamp National Wildlife Refuge and information on possible special hunts can be obtained from the Refuge Manager, Great Dismal Swamp National Wildlife Refuge, Box 349, Suffolk, VA 23434.

PRIVATE LANDS

Private land available for public hunting is extremely limited in the lower Tidewater area. There is, of course, farm hunting on the Eastern Shore, in the counties along the western shores of the Chesapeake Bay, and in the big rural areas of Chesapeake, Suffolk, and Virginia Beach. Hunters who can gain access to some of this land are likely to enjoy excellent dove, quail, and rabbit hunting. The farmlands also offer good field shooting for both Canada and snow geese, particularly on the Eastern Shore. Some commercial waterfowl guides have access to farms, but much of the hunting is reserved for the farm families and their friends.

As is true in other parts of Virginia, private timber corporations own land in the lower Tidewater area that has been made available for public hunting. It does not approach the acreage available in the Piedmont and Southside regions, but it does offer another hunting opportunity.

Chesapeake Corporation of Virginia

The Chesapeake Corporation of Virginia owns land in the counties of Accomack, Gloucester, and Mathews that is made available for public hunting at a modest fee. This is, of course, primarily timberland, and it offers primarily forest hunting.

Both Accomack and Gloucester are good deer-hunting counties, and the deer population is expanding in Mathews County. Generally, however, these flat coastal counties provide hunting for doves, quail, and rabbits. Hunting for all three species is best on clear-cut areas or young pine plantations. The hunting is good for the first three to five years after the timber is harvested, and the rabbit hunting may last even longer. The more mature stands of timber offer some squirrel hunting, and Accomack, particularly, can produce some good woodcock hunting late in the season.

Annual permits are available for $5 from the company. Maps of specific counties are also available, but requests for maps of all counties will not be honored. Write the Chesapeake Corporation of Virginia, West Point, VA 23181.

Glatfelter Pulp Wood Company

The Glatfelter Pulp Wood Company owns land in Accomack County that is available for public hunting.

Game includes a good deer population, doves, quail, rabbits, squirrels, and migrating woodcocks. The dove and quail hunting is best on cutover areas during the first three to five years after the harvesting has been completed. Rabbit hunting lasts awhile longer, and the squirrel hunting is best in mature stands of timber.

An annual hunting permit costing $7 is available from Glatfelter Pulp Wood Company, P.O. Box 868, Fredericksburg, VA 22401. Also ask for a map showing details of the company's lands in Accomack County.

Weyerhauser Company

The Weyerhauser Company owns over 11,000 acres of timberlands in Virginia, many of which are located in the county of Accomack and the rural cities of Chesapeake, Suffolk, and Virginia Beach. Most of these lands are open to public hunting, though some are leased to hunt clubs, whose members have exclusive hunting rights. Such land is posted. The company does not charge a fee for hunting, nor does it furnish maps.

There is good deer hunting in Accomack County, but the small game and bird hunting is best. The woodlands offer rabbit and squirrel hunting, and the young pine plantations provide some hunting for doves and quail. The bird hunting is good for only the first three to five years after an area has been harvested and reseeded, but rabbit hunting may last longer. Squirrels favor uncut hardwoods, but they will also use mature pine forests where they feed on the seeds in pinecones.

The hunting in the rural cities of Chesapeake, Suffolk, and Virginia Beach is much the same as that found in Accomack County, but Chesapeake also gives up a few bears just about every year, usually less than half a dozen. These come from the western part of the city, near the Great Dismal Swamp National Wildlife Refuge. Details are available from the Weyerhauser Company, Plymouth, NC 27962.

The Nature Conservancy

The Virginia Coast Reserve of the Nature Conservancy owns thirteen barrier islands off the ocean side of the Eastern Shore.

They extend from the very tip of the peninsula near Cape Charles for 45 miles up the coast. Reading south to north, they are Smith, Mink, Myrtle, Ship Shoal, Godwin, Cobb, Rogue, Hog, Sandy, Revel's, Parramore, Cedar, and Metomkin islands. These islands were purchased by the privately funded conservation organization in 1977 to protect their unique beauty and fragile nature from commercial development.

Public hunting for deer and ducks is allowed where it does not pose a threat to the fragile environment of water, marshes, and lowlands. Waterfowl hunting is limited in the intertidal marshes between the islands and the mainland. Both deer and waterfowl hunting permits are available free from the Virginia Coast Reserve of the Nature Conservancy, Brownsville, Nassawadox, VA 23413.

A cooperative agreement between the Nature Conservancy and the Commission of Game and Inland Fisheries is being considered. If it is drawn up, hunting here would be under the jurisdiction of the commission.

PUBLIC LAKES

Public lakes are almost nonexistent in Tidewater Virginia, Lake Drummond in the Great Dismal Swamp National Wildlife Refuge being a major exception. Lake Drummond, because of the acid content of its waters, does not attract many ducks or geese.

Back Bay, 25,000 acres of brackish waters in the City of Virginia Beach, is a major waterfowl-hunting area. It is actually a northward extension of Currituck Sound in North Carolina, but it is not affected by the usual ocean tides. In addition to the three waterfowl management areas managed by the Commission of Game and Inland Fisheries, there is a good deal of waterfowl hunting on the big body of water. It has been a top waterfowling area since the distant days of market hunting. Canada and snow geese, snipes, and just about every duck that flies the Atlantic Flyway can be found on the Back Bay waters. Back Bay is a public waterway, but there are over 300 licensed blinds on the big bay, all privately owned. Many have been handed down from generation to generation. Most are held to serve their owner's personal hunting, but some are for rent on a day-to-day basis.

Chesapeake Bay and the ocean waters off Virginia Beach are public, of course, but the riparian landowner's rights extend to the low-tide mark. All kinds of waterfowl use these big waters, and innovative hunters learn to hunt them on their own. Even the fast-flying sea ducks that skim the crests of the ocean swells offer shooting for those with boats big enough to handle the open waters.

On Back Bay the Commission of Game and Inland Fisheries maintains public boat-launching ramps at Knott's Island, the Game Warden Headquarters at Redhead Bay, and the Trojan Waterfowl Management Area. On the Atlantic Ocean it maintains public launching ramps at Rudee Inlet in Virginia Beach, at Oyster and Red Bank in Northampton County, and at Chincoteague, Chincoteague Park, Folly Creek, Greenbackenville, Queen Sound, and Wishart Point in Accomack County. These access points are not on the ocean, but they offer quick access to it.

On the Chesapeake Bay side of the Eastern Shore, the commission owns and maintains boat-launching ramps at Chesconessex, Onancock, Saxis, and Shad in Accomack County and at Cape Charles and Morley's Wharf in Northampton County. On the western side of the Chesapeake Bay the commission owns and maintains boat-launching ramps at Gwynn's Island and Town Point in Mathews County, at Warehouse in Gloucester County, and at Messick and Tide Mill in York County. The Commission of Game and Inland Fisheries also owns public boat-launching ramps at Willoughby in the Hampton Roads Area and in Seashore State Park near Virginia Beach. Both provide quick access to the Chesapeake Bay.

PUBLIC RIVERS

Two big tidal rivers, the James and York, and the Nansemond River in the City of Suffolk, the South Branch of the Elizabeth River in Chesapeake, and the North Landing River, which flows through the cities of Chesapeake and Virginia Beach before entering North Carolina and the Currituck Sound, also offer a great deal of waterfowl hunting. These are all public waterways, and the access to all of them is good.

The Commission of Game and Inland Fisheries maintains public boat-launching ramps at Gloucester Point on the York River and at Denbigh on the Warwick River, which flows into the James. It also maintains launching ramps at Bennett's Creek, which enters the Nansemond River in the City of Suffolk, and at Great Bridge on the South Branch of the Elizabeth River in the City of Chesapeake.

There are, of course, numerous private marinas and docks in the Tidewater region that may often present quicker and more convenient access to the Atlantic Ocean, the Chesapeake Bay, or the numerous tidal rivers.

That's hunting in the Tidewater, quite different than in any other region of Virginia, but just as interesting.

Southside Virginia

Southside Virginia is generally considered that part of the Old Dominion lying south of the James River, east of the Blue Ridge Mountains, and west of the Great Dismal Swamp. A transitional zone, it ranges from the flat coastal plains of Isle of Wight County to the eastern slopes of the Blue Ridge Mountains. It is an interesting region with an economy that enjoys a stable agricultural base. Farming is strong in all of those southern counties, and the hunting reflects that kind of land use.

Hunting in Southside Virginia is much as it was a half century ago, and as it was in most of Virginia before World War II.

White Oak Mountain and other wildlife management areas in Southside Virginia are managed for public dove hunting.

This is not to say that the region is behind the rest of the state. It is not, but whereas farmers elsewhere have turned to cattle and grazing, crops are still the heart of Southside Virginia farming. This means doves and quail and rabbits and squirrels, game that young Virginians have cut their hunting teeth on since before the Civil War. The very best bird hunting in the state is found here, and there are enough farm woodlots and timberlands to nourish a continuing supply of gray squirrels. Rabbits seem to suffer population cycles, but when the populations are up, there is no better rabbit hunting anywhere than on the big Southside Virginia farms.

The mourning dove does not enjoy the rich tradition that is afforded the bobwhite quail, but a September dove shoot over a big southern Virginia grainfield is a rare hunting experience, the kind of shooting that has sent the dove to the top as possibly the number one game bird in the state.

Buggs Island Lake, the largest reservoir in Virginia, rests astride the Virginia–North Carolina border in Southside Virginia, and just below it is big Gaston Lake. To the west in the Blue Ridge foothills are Smith Mountain Lake and Leesville Lake, and to the north in Chesterfield County is Lake Chesdin. Most of these bodies of water offer some waterfowl hunting. The Buggs Island and Lake Gaston waterfowlers enjoy good shooting at times, and so do those who hunt the Smith Mountain Lake waters.

In the western part of the region are the Dan and Roanoke rivers and the Banister River, and to the east the Meherrin, Nottoway, and Blackwater rivers wind south into North Carolina. To the north the Slate, Willis, and Appomattox rivers drain into the mighty James. All offer jump shooting for ducks, as does the James River itself. The James is one of the best waterfowling rivers in this part of the state.

Bedford County in the west and Isle of Wight in the east furnish the extremes of bear hunting as it is known in Virginia, rugged mountains and almost impenetrable swamps. Hunting is reasonably good in Bedford, but almost nonexistent in Isle of Wight even though there is a season there. Except for these two counties there is no bear hunting in Southside Virginia.

Deer hunting is a different story. At least a dozen counties in this area produce annual harvests in excess of 1,000 animals. Many top 2,000, and Southampton is traditionally the best deer county in the state. Other good ones include Amelia, Bedford, Brunswick, Buckingham, Chesterfield, Cumberland, Dinwiddie, Isle of Wight, Nottoway, Pittsylvania, Powhatan, Prince Edward, and Sussex counties. The seasons are long here, and hunting with hounds is popular, though many eastern hunters prefer still hunting.

Turkeys are also making a comeback in the southern counties, but the turkey hunting in most of them does not compare with that in other parts of the state. Good counties include Amelia, Appomattox, Bedford, Buckingham, Charlotte, Cumberland, and Powhatan.

Except for a small section of the Jefferson National Forest in western Bedford County, there is no national forest land in Southside Virginia, the federal lands otherwise being limited to the Fort Pickett Military Reservation and the U.S. Army Corps of Engineers lands around Buggs Island Lake and Philpott Reservoir.

State lands are more abundant. There are ten wildlife management areas owned and managed by the Commission of Game and Inland Fisheries, all of the state forests in the state, and several state parks on which hunting is permitted.

Equally as important to hunters in this big region are the many thousands of acres of private land, mostly timberlands, made available to the hunting public. Much of this land is managed for hunting by the Commission of Game and Inland Fisheries under cooperative agreements. In total acreage this hunting land approaches the big blocks of national forest lands in the western part of Virginia. Some of the corporations that own this land charge modest fees for hunting permits, but others do not. Some lease portions of their land to hunt clubs, and the members have exclusive hunting rights on the leased land.

Located as they are far from the big population centers, farmers and private landowners have not been subjected to the hunting pressure that exists in other parts of Virginia. A polite inquiry and common courtesy will open up some good hunting on private lands. Deer-hunting clubs lease many farms and timberlands, and often the bird or small game hunter can get permission to hunt such land once the deer season closes in early January.

WILDLIFE MANAGEMENT AREAS

Southside Virginia can boast the largest number of wildlife management areas of any region in Virginia. There are ten of them, all owned and managed by the Commission of Game and Inland Fisheries for wildlife and public hunting. There is no charge for hunting these lands, the only requirement being a state hunting license, a big game stamp for bears, deer, and turkeys, and a migratory bird stamp for waterfowl.

Maps of the wildlife management areas and more detailed information are available from the Commission of Game and Inland Fisheries headquarters in Richmond or from its regional office at Box 1001, Tappahannock, VA 22560, for Elm Hill, Hog Island, and Ragged Island or its regional office at HCO2, Box 238, Buckingham, VA 23921, for Amelia, Briery Creek, Fairystone, Horsepen, Powhatan, Turkeycock Mountain, and White Oak Mountain. The cost of a set of maps is $1.

Amelia Wildlife Management Area

The land now within the boundaries of the Amelia Wildlife Management Area was once prime farmland and among the earliest settled regions of Virginia. A nineteenth-century farmhouse and barns still stand. Over several generations, the land use changed from crops and the tilling of the soil to cattle and grass farming, and eventually much of it was allowed to revert to forest. As part of the management plan, many of the fields are leased to local farmers, and the commission once produced its game bird seed here.

Adding to the attractiveness of this wildlife management area are two big tracts of private land, both of which are open for public hunting. Directly across the Appomattox River is a Westvaco tract of managed woodlands, and adjoining the southern corner is a woodlot of the Chesapeake Corporation of Virginia.

The proximity of this big wildlife management area to the Richmond metropolitan area makes it highly attractive.

LOCATION: Entirely within Amelia County.

SIZE: 2,217 acres.

TERRAIN: The land rolls gently, but the elevation is relatively low, ranging from 200 to 500 feet. The Appomattox River forms the northern boundary of the wildlife management area, and there is a 100-acre lake with a boat-launching ramp and one small pond.

CAMPING: There are no developed campgrounds, but camping in self-contained vehicles is permitted.

ACCESS: Located 10 miles northeast of Amelia Courthouse and 7 miles south of U.S. Highway 360, the area is reached by Virginia Secondary Route 604 off U.S. 360, Secondary Route 616 west from

Route 604 at Masons Corner, and Secondary Route 652, which leads into the area.

GAME: When the Commission of Game and Inland Fisheries first acquired the area and assumed the management of wildlife, there were good populations of doves, quail, rabbits, and squirrels, and the management plan favors the future of this kind of hunting. Dove hunting is limited to Wednesdays and Saturdays, as is typical of public dove-hunting areas. The populations of both foxes and raccoon were high when the land was converted to wildlife management, and the area still offers good night hunting.

The Appomattox River offers good jump shooting for black ducks, mallard, and wood ducks, but access to the river is poor. There are no developed boat-launching ramps. The lake and pond also attract ducks, as do the beaver ponds and wooded marshes.

Though down considerably when the area was acquired, the deer populations are now high. Amelia County has one of the best deer harvests in the state. Turkeys are also present and reproducing annually, but the quality of the hunting does not approach that of the deer hunting.

Small game hunters also kick up an occasional woodcock, but the hunting is spotty at the best.

The area is a popular one for field trials; the events are held in the early fall and again in the spring.

Briery Creek Wildlife Management Area

The Briery Creek Wildlife Management Area, located in gently rolling farm and woodland country, is considered one of the most productive management areas owned by the Commission of Game and Inland Fisheries. Thirty-three separate parcels of land were put together to form it, and they make up its character. Previous owners were dairy and livestock farmers, tobacco farmers, grain producers, timber and forest managers, and pine growers. All made their impact on the land.

The rich and diverse wildlife populations in the area have been increased by commission management plans, which include limiting vehicle access and leasing fields to farmers for the production of crops. The commission's share of such crops is usually left standing for wildlife.

The 800-acre lake under construction on the wildlife management area will have a profound effect on this land, changing its nature and the hunting on at least half of it. The target date for its completion is 1985, and the area is now closed to hunting until the construction has been completed.

LOCATION: Western Prince Edward County.

SIZE: 2,775 acres.

TERRAIN: Gently rolling hill country of forests and open fields. Elevations range from 350 feet along the creek bottoms to 750 feet at the top of the hills. Briery and Little Briery creeks run northeasterly the entire length of the area.

CAMPING: There are no camping facilities, but camping in self-contained vehicles is permitted.

ACCESS: U.S. Highway 15 skirts the northeastern boundary and Virginia Secondary Route 630 and other such roads off U.S. 15 provide easy access. Secondary Routes 604 and 666 provide access from the west. There are also three miles of all-weather roads within the area.

GAME: The wildlife management plan favors dove, quail, and rabbit populations, and these species along with deer and turkeys receive most of the attention. Both deer and turkeys are on the increase in Prince Edward County. There are also good populations of squirrels in the mixed pine and hardwood forests, and frequently good concentrations of woodcocks provide good shooting for those who concentrate on this kind of hunting. Night hunters enjoy opossum and raccoon hunting, and there is limited waterfowl shooting on Briery Creek and over beaver ponds and marshes. The new lake will no doubt have some influence on the waterfowl populations.

Elm Hill Wildlife Management Area

Dove hunting on Wednesday and Saturday afternoons, numerous field trial events, and development as a waterfowl refuge are the major uses of this wildlife management area near the North Carolina line. Located just below Buggs Island Lake on the Roanoke River and Gaston Lake, it is being developed as a winter feeding area for the duck and goose populations that can be hunted on those lakes.

LOCATION: Mecklenburg County.

SIZE: 1,330 acres.

TERRAIN: This is gently rolling hill country in the heart of one of Virginia's richest farming regions. Much of the land that is now the management area was once a large cattle farm, and approximately 850 acres are still used for agricultural purposes. The remainder is hardwood forests and marshlands. The open lands are leased to farmers on a share-crop basis, and the commission's share is left standing for wildlife. The dove fields are planted in millet. Other plantings include lespedeza and autumn olive. Water is abundant, with the Roanoke River and Gaston Lake forming its southern border. Coleman's and Kettle creeks flow through the area, and bigger Allen Creek winds through the northeastern corner to skirt the eastern border. There are also several waterfowl feeding ponds that total approximately 60 acres.

CAMPING: There are no developed campgrounds, but camping in self-contained vehicles is allowed, and the U.S. Army Corps of Engineers operates a large campground on the shores of nearby Lake Gaston.

ACCESS: Virginia Secondary Routes 815, 615, and others off Primary Route 4 provide good access. There is a good network of all-weather roads in the area.

GAME: While the managed dove fields are the major hunting attraction, there is also hunting for quail, rabbits, and a few woodcocks. There is also limited squirrel hunting in the hardwoods and a few opossums and raccoon. The dove hunting can be good at times, but there is always the possibility that a nearby farmer might harvest a field and draw the birds off the public fields for a day or so. The share-crop farming should assure the future of quail and rabbit hunting, but this wildlife management area is popular for field trials, and except for doves, there is no hunting until after the field trials end in early December. The trials are open to the public.

Fairy Stone Farms Philpott Reservoir Wildlife Management Area

The Fairy Stone Farms Philpott Reservoir Wildlife Management Area includes, in addition to the Commission of Game and Inland Fisheries lands, blocks of U.S. Army Corps of Engineers land adjacent to Philpott Lake and Fairy Stone State Park lands that are open to hunting. The entire block is managed by the commission as Fairy Stone Farms Philpott Reservoir Wildlife Management Area.

LOCATION: Mostly in Patrick County but also some land in Franklin and Henry counties.

SIZE: 5,286 acres, but lands of Fairy Stone State Park and Philpott Reservoir expand the total to 12,000 acres.

TERRAIN: This is foothills country along the eastern slopes of the Blue Ridge Mountains, steep and rugged with narrow stream valleys. Elevations range up to 1,500 feet. Before the commission bought the land, much of the timber was removed, but good stands of second-growth hardwoods and pines now cover much of it. There are also a few open plots planted in corn and tobacco.

CAMPING: There is limited camping in Fairy Stone State Park, but only primitive facilities are available during the hunting seasons. There are also good camping facilities on the Corp of Engineers lands.

ACCESS: Virginia Primary Highway 57 off U.S. Highway 58 provides the major access to the area. Route 57 also leads west off U.S. 220 into the area. Approximately five miles of roads and ten miles of trails provide access within the area, and Philpott Lake offers access to the more remote regions.

GAME: The terrain and forest cover favor deer and squirrels primarily, but there are a few turkeys plus some night-roaming opossums and raccoon. The deer herds are expected to expand, and there are plenty of den trees for squirrels. Fields leased to farmers attract some doves, and there is some waterfowl hunting on Gobblingtown Creek above Fairy Stone State Park. Duck hunting on Philpott Lake is generally poor.

Hog Island Waterfowl Management Area

The Hog Island Waterfowl Management Area is a flat, coastal region on the James River. Much of it is a peninsula jutting into the river, but the Carlisle tract extends inland from the water. Hog farming was popular here during the seventeenth-century; hence the name Hog Island. This is a carefully controlled waterfowl management area, planted in milo and winter wheat. Power and pipeline right-of-ways on the inland tract are planted in wildlife patches. Cutover hardwoods planted in pines provide some deer and quail hunting.

LOCATION: Mostly in Surry County but a small tract in Isle of Wight County.

SIZE: 3,200 acres.

TERRAIN: Of the 3,200 acres, 2,485 are on the tip of the peninsula, approximately 200 acres of which are open farmland and 600 acres in pine forest. The remainder is tidal marshlands and open ponds. This is Hog Island proper. Inland near the base of the peninsula are the Boyce and Carlisle tracts in Surry County and the Stewart tract in Isle of Wight County. The Hog Island tract ranges from sea level to 8 to 10 feet above sea level, and the inland tract rises to 35 feet, though the Stewart tract is mostly marshlands.

CAMPING: There are no developed campgrounds, but camping in self-contained vehicles is permitted.

ACCESS: Virginia Secondary Route 650 off Primary Route 10 leads to the main gate. There are several miles of gravel roads leading into the Hog Island, Boyce, and Carlisle tracts, and a boat-launching ramp on the Carlisle tract provides access by water to the Stewart tract.

GAME: The major attraction on this area is the waterfowl hunting, mostly for Canada geese. Hog Island probably offers the best goose hunting of any public hunting area in Virginia. Interested hunters draw for blinds, and five parties of two each are allowed to hunt on Monday, Tuesday, Thursday, and Friday during the waterfowl season. The drawing for blinds is held in October, and applications are available from the commission headquarters in Richmond after Labor Day. Lucky hunters pay $15 for the blind. The only other hunting allowed on Hog Island proper is for deer during the archery season. Deer are reasonably abundant, and hunting is a means of controlling the population. The Carlisle tract, on the other hand, is open to all kinds of hunting. Much of it is done along the two power line right-of-ways and the one pipe-line right-of-way. Doves, quail, and rabbits are the most popular species. There is also excellent deer hunting, with the harvest in both Isle of Wight and Surry counties running consistently above 1,000 animals. The young pine plantations offer good hunting for deer and quail. Creeks and ponds in the Stewart tract provide limited hunting for ducks and rail.

Horsepen Lake Wildlife Management Area

Located near the geographical center of Virginia, Horsepen Lake Wildlife Management Area is the home of one of the four regional offices of the Commission of Game and Inland Fisheries. The land now included in the wildlife management area was once under the ownership of the U.S. Forest Service and was used as a forest research area.

LOCATION: Buckingham County.

SIZE: 2,688 acres.

TERRAIN: Rolling hill country in the Slate River drainage with numerous springs and streams including Horsepen Creek on which is located 18-acre Horsepen Lake. Most of the area is well forested with a mixture of hardwoods and pines. Approximately 800 acres of pine forest became infested with bark beetles in the late 1970s, and this area was clear-cut, creating excellent quail cover.

CAMPING: There are no developed campgrounds, but camping in self-contained vehicles is allowed.

ACCESS: Virginia Secondary Route 638 off U.S. Highway 60 at Buckingham Courthouse leads deep into the area. Secondary Route 665 off U.S. Highway 15 also provides access. Within the area a good network of all-weather and secondary roads provides good access.

GAME: The area is best known for its deer hunting. The population is high, with an estimate placing it at twenty deer per square mile. Turkeys and squirrels are also plentiful. The area is near the extreme eastern limit of the range of the grouse, and the clear-cut areas offer good quail hunting. Other game includes a few doves, foxes, opossums, rabbits, raccoon, waterfowl, and woodcocks.

Powhatan Wildlife Management Area

Gently rolling country located just 30 miles west of Richmond, the Powhatan Wildlife Management Area offers good hunting convenient to a large metropolitan area. Generations ago this area was cleared of most of its rich forests and planted in corn, tobacco, and wheat. Later much of the land was permitted to revert to forests, and during the 1930s and 1940s the emphasis changed to pastures for beef cattle. When it was purchased by the Commission of Game and Inland Fisheries, the area supported five beef cattle farms and one dairy operation.

Modern wildlife management plans include the leasing of open fields to farmers on a share-crop basis with the commission's share of the crops left standing for wildlife.

LOCATION: Powhatan County.

SIZE: 4,171 acres.

TERRAIN: Elevations range up to 500 feet above sea level, but the country rolls gently. The area holds an abundance of water for wildlife, with numerous springs, small streams, and a half dozen ponds or small lakes. Salee Creek, which flows north through the area, is the major stream, but others include Beaver and Salmon creeks. The lakes and ponds range in size from one to 35 acres.

CAMPING: There are no developed campgrounds, but camping in self-contained vehicles is permitted.

ACCESS: U.S. Highway 60 bisects the wildlife management area, and Secondary Route 627 off this highway provides the main access. It also provides access from the south, and other secondary routes lead into the area from the north and east. Virginia Primary Route 13 skirts the southern border. A good system of trails provides access throughout the area.

GAME: Powhatan County has one of the best deer harvests in Virginia, and its turkey flocks are on the increase. This was once the best turkey range in the state. The wildlife management area gives up approximately fifty deer per season, and there are at least a half dozen flocks of turkeys. The rabbit and squirrel hunting is good, though the cottontail population tends to fluctuate considerably. There are a few quail, and ducks use the ponds and beaver swamps. The night hunter will find fair populations of opossums and raccoon, and there is dove hunting on Wednesdays and Saturdays.

Ragged Island Wildlife Management Area

The Ragged Island Wildlife Management Area is a unique region of brackish-water marsh and small pine-covered islands in the James River. It is located at the southern end of the James River Bridge. Most of the area lies south of U.S. Highway 17. Though close to a major metropolitan area, it has seen little use by man. It is generally unspoiled.

LOCATION: Isle of Wight County.

SIZE: 1,475 acres.

TERRAIN: Much of this wildlife management area is inundated during unusually high tides or storms. The mainland is primarily a brackishwater marsh, but the islands are covered with loblolly pines and greenbrier and almost impossible to walk on. There are three major creeks, Cooper and Ragged creeks to the south of U.S. 17 and Kings Creek to the north. There are also several smaller creeks plus a number of both brackish and freshwater ponds.

CAMPING: There are no developed campgrounds, but camping in self-contained vehicles is permitted.

ACCESS: U.S. Highway 17 passes through the area, and it is the only access except by water. There is no boat ramp at the present, however. A parking lot near U.S. Highway 17 is in the planning stages.

GAME: The duck hunting can be good for those willing to look for it. It includes jump shooting on the creeks and ponds and hunting over decoys along the river shoreline. Waterfowl include black ducks, canvasbacks, gadwall, mallard, ruddy ducks, and scaup. Hunting for other game is limited, though there are deer, foxes, rabbits, raccoon, and squirrels on the higher ground, including some of the islands.

Turkeycock Mountain Wildlife Management Area

Turkeycock Mountain Wildlife Management Area is a new one just acquired by the Commission of Game and Inland Fisheries. It is a woodland area on top of Turkeycock Mountain approximately halfway between the Fairy Stone Farms Philpott Reservoir Wildlife Management Area and the White Oak Mountain Wildlife Management Area.

LOCATION: Franklin and Henry counties.

SIZE: 1,789 acres.

TERRAIN: Mountainous and scenic with limited water, though there are a number of wet-weather streams and one small pond.

CAMPING: There are no developed campgrounds, but camping in self-contained vehicles is permitted.

ACCESS: The area can be reached by Secondary Route 890 south from Snow Creek in Franklin County, and an old Civilian Conservation Corps road passes through the area providing good access.

GAME: Being a high mountain forestland, this is primarily a deer, turkey, and squirrel hunting area. Squirrels rate as the most popular at the present.

White Oak Mountain Wildlife Management Area

The White Oak Mountain Wildlife Management Area stretches along a high plateau and up the north and south slopes of

800-foot White Oak Mountain. Two-thirds of it is forested. These hardwood forests and some pine are interspersed with open fields, and there are a dozen old farm ponds ranging in size from a half acre to about six acres. The Banister River forms the northern boundary of the popular public hunting area.

Practically all of the open land was used to grow tobacco before its purchase by the Commission of Game and Inland Fisheries.

Facilities include a dozen parking areas and toilets.

LOCATION: Pittsylvania County.

SIZE: 2,700 acres.

TERRAIN: Generally rolling hill country with forests and open fields. Numerous small streams and springs.

CAMPING: There are no developed campgrounds, but camping in self-contained units is allowed.

ACCESS: Virginia Secondary Route 823 off U.S. 29 at Chatham leads to the area, and so does Secondary Route 640 off U.S. 29 south of Chatham. Secondary Routes 649 and 706 pass through the area also. There are also five miles of all-weather roads within the area and several trails.

GAME: Hunting here is mostly for small game, though both deer and turkeys are on the increase. Doves, quail, and rabbits are more abundant here than on most wildlife management areas as the habitat favors them. The forests, of course, hold good squirrel populations and some opossums and raccoon. Agricultural leases to local farmers help create a nearly ideal small game habitat. Dove hunting is popular but limited to Wednesdays and Saturdays. Nesting boxes placed on the farm ponds are increasing the populations of wood ducks, but the shooting is very limited at the present. There is some jump shooting for waterfowl on the Banister River.

FEDERAL LANDS

There are no vast national forest lands here, but the Fort Pickett Military Reservation, the U.S. Army Corps of Engineers lands adjacent to the John H. Kerr and Philpott reservoirs, a small section of the Jefferson National Forest, and the Presquile National Wildlife Refuge in the James River provide a rich variety of hunting opportunities, some of which are quite good.

Jefferson National Forest

A small section of the Jefferson National Forest stretches across the Blue Ridge Parkway into western Bedford County. It includes the popular Peaks of Otter Recreation Area.

The Jefferson National Forest is described completely in the next chapter and is mentioned here mainly because this small patch of the big national forest offers the only significant bear hunting in Southside Virginia. Hunters take ten or twelve bears annually in Bedford County, and many of them come from this section of the Jefferson National Forest.

Bedford County is also one of the better deer and turkey counties in Virginia. Other game includes grouse, squirrels, a few woodcocks, opossums, raccoon, and a few bobcats.

Headquarters for the Jefferson Naional Forest is located in Roanoke. This section of the national forest is in the Glenwood Ranger District, where maps are available at $1 each.

Glenwood Ranger District

ADDRESS: Box 10
                 Natural Bridge Station, VA 24579
                 Telephone 703-291-2189
LOCATION: Bedford County.
ACCESS: Access is reasonably good. The Blue Ridge Parkway, where hunting is prohibited, passes through the national forest, and secondary roads leading off the parkway head down the eastern slope of the mountains. They may be gated at times, and it is best to check with parkway officials regarding their use for hunting access. Secondary Routes 602, 764, and 765 lead into the forest from the south. There are also a number of forest service roads that provide access.
CAMPING: Developed campground at Peaks of Otter Recreation Area, and rough camping permitted in national forest.

Fort Pickett Military Reservation

Fort Pickett, a U.S. Army installation, is the largest and possibly the most popular public hunting area in Southside Virginia. Most of the land is open to public hunting under a long-standing cooperative agreement between the military authorities and the Commission of Game and Inland Fisheries. This agreement between a state game agency and a military establishment is the oldest in America, and it has been copied all over the United States. Under the agreement, military operations take top priority, but there is limited military activity during the fall and winter hunting months. This, of course, could change drastically in the event of a national emergency.

Hunting and wildlife management are under the supervision of a wildlife manager and his staff, and they are responsible for the handling of hunters. Hunters are required to check in and out, and for safety reasons the number assigned to any one area is limited. This also assures a quality hunt. Daily permits are required, but at the present there is no charge for them. They are available at the Game Checking Station in Building T-420 and are not available by mail. Hunters are also required to fill out game reports and turn them in at the conclusion of their hunt.

The reservation can support several hundred hunters daily, but on many weekdays there are less than a dozen.

Before World War II what is now Fort Pickett was a patchwork of farms and woodlots. Crop farming, typical of Southside Virginia, was the agricultural pattern. Most of the land was acquired as America geared up for World War II. The pattern of mixed fields and woodlots has been continued, and the military reservation has helped protect a style of hunting traditional in Virginia for many generations.

LOCATION: Brunswick, Dinwiddie, and Nottoway counties.

SIZE: 45,198 acres.

TERRAIN: Flat to slightly rolling with a good mixture of open fields and mixed hardwood and pine forests. There are numerous small streams, springs, beaver ponds, old farm ponds, and several lakes. There is also a fair amount of marsh or swamp land.

CAMPING: Camping in self-contained units only.

ACCESS: Few public hunting areas have better access than Fort Pickett. Virginia Primary Routes 40 and 46 pass through the reservation, and U.S. Highway 460 skirts its northern border. Most hunters enter the reservation through the main gate near the city of Blackstone. Numerous military roads, old farming roads, and trails offer access to just about every part of the reservation. Hunters should ask for maps when they pick up their hunting permits. They are available at no cost. Some areas such as the impact area are off limits to hunting, but they are well marked and shown on the hunting maps.

GAME: The quail, rabbits, and squirrels of prewar years still flourish, but today deer and turkeys are just as popular. There are also ducks, snipes, and woodcocks and usually an abundance of doves. Opossums and raccoon are present, but night hunting is not allowed. There are also plenty of woodchucks, but the best woodchuck hunting conflicts with the busy summer training season, when thousands of reservists do their annual active duty.

The quail hunting may well be the best of any public hunting area in Virginia. Acres of open fields and unkempt edges take the veteran bird hunter back to yesteryear. The area is popular for field trials because the dogs are easy to observe in the big open fields. During good quail years hunters may bag in excess of 2,000 birds.

Dove hunting is limited to Wednesdays and Saturdays because too much shooting will cause the birds to avoid the managed dove fields. At times the dove shooting can be fast, but Fort Pickett is in the heart of good farming country, and the birds may be temporarily attracted elsewhere if a freshly harvested field offers better feeding.

The white-tailed deer may offer the most popular hunting at Fort Pickett, and it can be good. During a typical season, one out of eight hunters is successful and the bag approaches 1,000 animals. Rifles are prohibited; most hunters use shotguns and buckshot, but archery tackle is also popular. Archers take a number of whitetails every season. Because hunting with hounds is so popular in Southside Virginia, dogs are permitted on Fort Pickett, and this is the most popular deer-hunting method.

Squirrel hunters probably reap the richest harvest. During a good year they may bag in excess of 2,000 bushytails. The season is long, usually opening in mid-October to run through January. Forestry management includes the sparing of den and mast-bearing trees such as hickory and oak. The gray is the only squirrel present.

The planting of autumn olive, winter wheat, and sawtooth oaks is part of a productive wild turkey management plan that has seen turkey hunting flourish. Most of the hunting emphasis is on the spring season when only gobbblers are legal, but there is usually a brief fall season when hens are also legal.

The wildlife management plan favors the cottontail rabbit, long the very heart of Southside Virginia hunting, and when the rabbit populations are up, the hunting is usually good, better than on most public hunting lands. The cottontail harvest has occasionally topped the 3,000 mark, but at the present it does not approach that lofty figure.

Hunters who keep abreast of the woodcock migrations will enjoy good hunting in the Fort Pickett wetlands. The numerous bogs and swamps favor the woodcock, but most of the birds are taken by quail or rabbit hunters. Those same bogs and swamps also favor the snipe, another migrant that offers some good shooting every season. As is the case with the woodcock, most snipes are taken by hunters in pursuit of other game.

The Fort Pickett waterfowl hunting is usually good, but few hunters take advantage of it. Old farm ponds, beaver ponds, and swamps, wildlife ponds built by game management people, and numerous streams, marshes, and bogs support good populations of black ducks, mallard, ringnecks, and wood ducks, and a few buffle-heads and scaup. Many of the ponds are seeded with millet to attract the birds.

While there is no night hunting, Fort Pickett hunters take a few daytime-roaming foxes, opossums, and raccoon. Limited trapping is permitted to control these and other furbearing species.

John H. Kerr Reservoir and Dam

The John H. Kerr Reservoir, better known as Buggs Island Lake in Virginia, is a U.S. Army Corps of Engineers impoundment on the Roanoke River near the Virginia–North Carolina border. After Fort Pickett, the land around the lake is the second largest block of public hunting land in Southside Virginia.

Early in the life of the project the Commission of Game and Inland Fisheries was granted over 700 acres of federal land for the development of wildlife management areas, and the result was over 100 upland game feed plots of lespedeza, milo, and other plantings. Over 50 waterfowl pastures were also established during those early years.

Back in 1954, when the big lake was just beginning to fill with water, the waterfowl count was estimated at over a million birds, but this bonanza did not continue. The waterfowl hunting is still good, however. Early estimates also placed the deer harvest at 54, squirrels at 3,500, rabbits at 7,600, turkeys at 60, and quail at 7,000. This general pattern of game resources has continued, though the deer harvest is up considerably, and the quail and rabbit kill is down from those peak years.

LOCATION: Mostly in Mecklenburg County, but small part in Halifax.

SIZE: The total area is 117,300 acres, some of which extends into North Carolina. Of these acres the lake claims 50,000, and 75 percent of the water is in Virginia. There are also 38,000 acres of public hunting land in Virginia.

TERRAIN: Much of the land is flat and covered with mixed pines and hardwoods, but there is some gently rolling hill country as well as many open fields. There are numerous creeks, beaver ponds, bogs, and marshes, particularly close to the lake. The lake itself is usually low during the fall and winter hunting seasons.

CAMPING: There are several well-developed campgrounds on the shores of the lake. Good maps showing the location of the campgrounds are available from the Reservoir Manager, John H. Kerr Reservoir and Dam, Route 1, Box 76, Boydton, VA 23917.

ACCESS: U.S. Highways 15 from the north and south and 58 from the east and west provide access to the area, and numerous secondary roads off these major highways lead to various parts of the area. The lake itself provides access to much of the public hunting land and to remote areas otherwise inaccessible. The big lake rarely freezes.

GAME: Much of the hunting interest centers around the big lake and waterfowl. Floating blinds are permitted upon application to the reservoir manager, but many waterfowlers hunt by boat, using the points for concealment to sneak up on the ducks in the creeks and coves. The major species are black ducks, mallard, pintail, teal, and Canada geese, but ringnecks, scaup, and other Atlantic Flyway birds use the lake. Some hunters have blinds on the shore.

The Mecklenburg County deer herds are continuing to expand, and the Kerr Lake lands offer good deer hunting. The wild turkey is continuing its comeback here as it is statewide, but the harvest is still low. Currently, turkey hunting is limited to the spring season.

The squirrel is undoubtedly the most abundant game species, and the mixed pine and hardwood forests around the lake offer good hunting. The quail and rabbit hunting is fair in a part of the state known for this kind of hunting. Night hunters find fair populations of opossums and raccoon, and bird hunters flush an occasional woodcock.

Philpott Dam and Reservoir

Located along the eastern slopes of the Blue Ridge Mountains, this U.S. Army Corps of Engineers lake and surrounding land adjoins Fairy Stone State Park and the Fairy Stone Farms Philpott Reservoir Wildlife Management Area. All three are managed as a block by the Commission of Game and Inland Fisheries.

LOCATION: Franklin, Henry, and Patrick counties.

SIZE: 4,570 acres.

TERRAIN: Rugged mountain country surrounding 2,880-acre lake.

CAMPING: Camping in Fairy Stone State Park and in Corps of Engineers developed campgrounds. A map of lake and surrounding land is also available from the Reservoir Manager, Philpott Reservoir, Route 6, Box 140, Bassett, VA 24055.

ACCESS: Can be reached by Virginia Primary Highway 57 off U.S. Highways 59 and 220. Also accessible by various secondary roads leading off Secondary Route 605 on the north side of the lake. There is a good network of secondary roads in the area, and the lake provides access to much of the public hunting land. The lake rarely freezes completely over.

GAME: The gray squirrel is by far the most abundant game species, and squirrel hunting is extremely popular in this part of Virginia. There is also good deer hunting, and the turkeys are coming back. Both Franklin and Patrick counties produce good deer harvests. There is limited duck hunting on the lake, but the steep, wooded shorelines and scarcity of shallow water do not attract many ducks. Duck blinds are permitted upon application to the reservoir manager. A few grouse, opossums, and raccoon get some attention.

Presquile National Wildlife Refuge

The Presquile National Wildlife Refuge claims a large island in the James River near Hopewell, and it is owned and managed by the U.S. Fish and Wildlife Service. It is actually a waterfowl feeding and rest area, and hunting is normally not allowed. The waterfowl management work, however, attracts an ever-growing deer herd to the island, and unless controlled, the animals would destroy the crops planted for ducks and geese. Hunting is the tool used to control the deer population.

LOCATION: Prince George County.

SIZE: 2,336 acres.

TERRAIN: River island, flat and rich in vegetation. Mixture of pine forests and open fields managed for waterfowl. Much bog and marsh area.

CAMPING: No camping facilities.

ACCESS: Hunters are ferried to island from Hopewell.

GAME: Only deer are hunted, and there is normally an annual archery hunt in October. Hunters are selected on the basis of a drawing held in late September. If the archery hunt does not reduce the population to the desired level, a gun hunt is sometimes held later, usually in November. A drawing also is used to select hunters for the gun hunt. Shotguns only are allowed during the gun hunt. Hunters interested in this unique white-tailed deer hunting should contact the Refuge Manager, Presquile National Wildlife Refuge, P.O. Box 620, Hopewell, VA 23860.

OTHER STATE LANDS

Unique to Southside Virginia are several classes of state lands other than wildlife management areas that offer good public hunting. The various state forests are the major ones, but there is also hunting in several state parks. The Buckingham-Appomattox, Cumberland, Pocahontas, and Prince Edward-Gallion state forests all provide land for public hunting, and there is some hunting on Fairy Stone and Saylor's Creek Battlefield state parks. Maps of the state forests are available from the Virginia Division of Forestry, P.O. Box 3758, Charlottesville, VA 22903, from the Commission of Game and Inland Fisheries in Richmond, or from its regional office at HCO2, Box 238, Buckingham, VA 23921. Maps of the state parks are available from the Virginia Division of Parks, State Office Building, Capitol Square, Richmond, VA 23219.

Buckingham-Appomattox State Forest

Though the management of timber is the primary reason for the public ownership of the Buckingham-Appomattox State Forest, wildlife is managed by the Commission of Game and Inland Fisheries under a cooperative agreement between the commission and the Virginia Division of Forestry.

LOCATION: Appomattox and Buckingham counties.

SIZE: 18,534 acres.

TERRAIN: Rolling, well-forested hill country with a good mixture of pine and hardwood forests. There are numerous small streams, and the headwaters of the Appomattox River gather here. Holiday Lake straddles the Appomattox-Buckingham county line near the southern edge of the forest. Some fields are leased to local farmers.

CAMPING: No camping in the forest, but it is permitted at Holiday State Park adjacent to forest.

ACCESS: The main entrance to the forest is off Virginia Primary Route 24 between Appomattox and Mount Rush. A network of state forest roads offers good access to most areas, though some of them may be closed during wet weather.

GAME: This is the very heart of what was once Virginia's best turkey range, and the turkey hunting is still good. There are also deer, quail, rabbits, squirrels, and a few grouse and woodcocks. Ducks use the lake, beaver ponds, and streams, and opossums and raccoon offer night hunting.

Buckingham has long been one of the top deer-hunting counties in the state, and the hunting is good in Appomattox County, although not in the class with Buckingham. The turkey populations, once down, are on the increase in both counties.

Squirrels are reasonably abundant, particularly in good mast years.

The quail hunting is limited, but a few birds can be found in the clearings and cutover areas that have been planted with young pines. The leased fields also support both quail and rabbits. Both grouse and woodcocks are present, but the forest is near the eastern edge of the grouse range. The woodcock hunting can be good at times.

The waterfowl hunting is extremely limited, but beaver ponds and streams support some wood ducks and a few blacks. There is some jump shooting on the Appomattox River, but very little of the river is in the state forest.

Cumberland State Forest

A cooperative agreement between the Commission of Game and Inland Fisheries and the Virginia Division of Forestry has opened the Cumberland State Forest to public hunting. The land surrounding Bear Creek Lake in the forest is part of the state park system, and hunting is not permitted. There is also a small game sanctuary where hunting is prohibited, but the rest, including other lakes in the forest, is open to hunting.

LOCATION: Western Cumberland County with a small section jutting into Buckingham County.

SIZE: 15,015 acres.

TERRAIN: This is rolling hill country with good stands of hardwoods, though much of it has been converted to pine plantations. The Willis River winds through the forest, and there are five small lakes, Bear Creek Lake being the best known. Numerous small streams and beaver ponds add to the attractiveness of the forest. Some open fields are leased to local farmers.

CAMPING: Camping is not permitted in the forest, but there is a developed campground in Bear Creek State Park, which adjoins the forest.

ACCESS: Virginia Secondary Route 622 off both U.S. Highways 15 and 60 passes through the forest, and a good network of forest roads provides access within the forest. Some of these may be closed during wet weather. A pair of boat-launching ramps on the Willis River provides access to the river. One is located near the northern edge of the forest, and the other near its southern edge.

GAME: Deer, doves, quail, rabbits, squirrels, turkeys, and raccoon are the major game species. Cumberland County has long been one of the top in the east for deer, and the turkey hunting is good. Turkey hunting draws many hunters to the forest, where there is both fall and spring hunting.

Squirrels are probably the most abundant game species, but there is no early season as there is in so many counties.

Land leased to local farmers, wildlife clearings, and young pine plantations support good quail and rabbit hunting. The Cumberland State Forest is one of the better public hunting areas for quail. The farming operations also support reasonably good dove hunting, with the shooting limited to Wednesdays and Saturdays.

Night hunters enjoy fair opossum and raccoon hunting, and the Willis River and some of the lakes and ponds offer limited waterfowl hunting.

Pocahontas State Forest and Park

Pocahontas State Forest completely surrounds Pocahontas State Park. The park is off limits to hunting, and some of the forest is a game sanctuary, but much of it is open to hunting thanks to a cooperative agreement between the Commission of Game and Inland Fisheries and the Virginia Division of Forestry. Located on the western fringe of the heavily populated corridor between Petersburg and Richmond, the forest receives heavy pressure, but the hunting remains good.

LOCATION: Chesterfield County.

SIZE: 7,605 acres, of which 5,500 are open to public hunting.

TERRAIN: Generally flat with a few small hills and a forest covering of hardwoods and pines with numerous clear-cut areas. Most of the cutover land is planted with pine seedlings. Many small streams and beaver ponds provide good water for wildlife. Beaver and Swift Creek lakes are in the state park where hunting is prohibited, and most of Swift Creek is in the sanctuary.

CAMPING: No camping in the forest, but the state park offers camping in its developed campgrounds.

ACCESS: Secondary Routes 603, 604, 621, and 653 provide access off U.S. Highway 360, and Secondary Routes 604 and 655 offer access of Virginia Primary Highway 10. A good network of roads provides access within the forest, but some may be closed during wet weather to protect them from rutting. Walk-in hunting is encouraged, and parking areas are provided for hunting vehicles.

GAME: The area offers surprisingly good hunting for deer, squirrels, and turkeys and fair hunting for doves, quail, and rabbits. The young pine plantations support the dove, quail, and rabbit hunting. Both Beaver and Swift Creek lakes draw some ducks, and so does Swift Creek, but all are closed to hunting. Birds from these waters range out to beaver ponds and smaller streams, however, and there is some shooting for wood ducks and other species.

Chesterfield County, despite its proximity to one of the heaviest populated regions in the state, produces good deer hunting year after year, with the kill consistently above the 1,000-animal level. There is both fall and spring hunting, but the fall season is usually a very brief one. Night hunters enjoy the opossum and raccoon populations.

Prince Edward–Gallion State Forest

Most of Prince Edward–Gallion State Forest is open to public hunting under a cooperative agreement between the Commission of Game and Inland Fisheries and the Virginia Division of Forestry. Off limits to hunters is Prince Edward State Park, a small area surrounding Goodwin and Prince Edward lakes. There is also a small game sanctuary in the southwestern corner of the state forest, just west of Virginia Secondary Route 696 between Farmville and Green Bay.

LOCATION: Eastern Prince Edward County.

SIZE: 6,365 acres, most of which is open to hunting.

TERRAIN: This is rolling hill country, and much of the forest is in mature hardwoods. There are also many acres of original pine, but these are gradually being logged and reseded in pine seedlings. Open areas are leased to local farmers or managed as wildlife clearings.

CAMPING: No camping in the forest, but there are developed campgrounds in the state park adjacent to Goodwin and Prince Edward lakes.

ACCESS: Virginia Secondary Route 696 off U.S. Highways 360 and 460 passes through the forest and provides good access. Most of the state forest land is east of Route 696, but there are three small patches west of the road. Secondary Route 696 skirts two of them, and the other is accessible by Secondary Routes 632 off 696. Forest service roads provide access within the area, but they may be closed in wet weather.

GAME: The Prince Edward County deer herds are growing, and the annual harvest exceeds 1,000 animals every season. It was once one of the top turkey counties, but the turkey hunting today is better in other parts of the state.

The mixed pine and hardwood forests support a good population of squirrels, and night hunters enjoy going after opossums and raccoon. The wildlife clearings and leased fields attract fair numbers of doves, quail, and rabbits.

While Goodwin and Prince Edward lakes hold small populations of waterfowl, hunting is prohibited on these recreational lakes. There is limited hunting, however, on the beaver ponds and small streams in the forest.

Fairy Stone State Park

Nestled in the foothills of the Blue Ridge Mountains, 2,400 acres of the 4,500-acre Fairy Stone State Park are managed for public hunting under a cooperative agreement between the Virginia Division of Parks and the Commission of Game and Inland Fisheries. It is part of the complex which also includes the U.S. Army Corps of Engineers lands around Philpott Lake and Fairy Stone Farms Wildlife Management Area, all of which are managed for public hunting as the Fairy Stone Farms Philpott Reservoir Wildlife Management Area. The state park lands swell the total to more than 12,000 acres.

The park is located in the southwestern corner of the complex, and a long arm of Philpott Lake extends westward to the eastern fringes of the park. Fairy Stone Lake is an integral part of the park.

LOCATION: Henry and Patrick counties.

SIZE: 2,400 acres.

TERRAIN: Mountainous and covered for the most part with mixed pine and hardwood forests. Some foothills country with streams and lakeshore on Fairy Stone and Philpott lakes.

CAMPING: Developed campgrounds in park.

ACCESS: Virginia Primary Highway 40 off both U.S. Highways 58 and 220 passes through the park. Secondary Routes 623 and 704 off Primary Highway 40 also provide access. Hiking trails and service roads provide access within the park.

GAME: The gray squirrel is the most popular animal in this area, but the deer population is increasing. The park straddles the Henry-Patrick county border, and the deer harvest in both counties is modest though better in Patrick. The turkey population is also increasing, and both fall and spring seasons are held.

The grouse hunting is fair, and the land managed by the commission provides some hunting for doves, quail, and rabbits. Night hunting for opossums, raccoon, and bobcats is fair, and Fairy Stone Lake attracts a few ducks, though it is closed to hunting. Some duck hunting is available when the birds use Gobbblingtown Creek above the park land, but it is spotty at the best.

Saylor's Creek Battlefield State Park

The last major battle of the Civil War took place at the site of this park, and three days later General Lee surrendered at nearby Appomattox. This is a relatively small area spread along the Amelia–Prince Edward county line, but hunting in much of it is open under a cooperative agreement between the Commission of Game and Inland Fisheries and the Virginia Division of Parks.

LOCATION: Amelia and Prince Edward counties.

SIZE: 240 acres.

TERRAIN: The terrain rolls gently beneath a cover of mixed hardwood and pine forests and open fields. Fields not used for park purposes are leased to local farmers, and they provide farm hunting.

CAMPING: No camping in this park.

ACCESS: Virginia Secondary Route 617 between Jetersville and Rice provides access. The park is approximately 10 miles east of Farmville.

GAME: The fields leased to farmers offer limited hunting for doves, quail, and rabbits, and the hardwood forests provide good squirrel hunting. There is also fair deer and turkey hunting. Amelia County is one of the best deer-hunting regions in the state, and the Prince Edward County herds are increasing. Both counties are in the historic range of the wild turkey in Virginia.

PRIVATE LANDS

The sprawling farmlands of Southside Virginia provide almost unlimited hunting opportunities, and permission to hunt private lands is a bit easier to secure here than in other parts of the state. Much of the land is tied up in hunting leases, however, and many farmers reserve the hunting for their families and friends.

The large timber corporations, however, open their vast lands to public hunting, and the total acreage made available equals that of the big Jefferson National Forest in Southwest Virginia. These lands are managed primarily for the production of fast-growing pine, and where there is wildlife management it is a secondary goal. By its nature the management and harvesting of timber favors certain kinds of hunting, but it is contrary to the best interests of other game species. Clear-cutting a stand of hardwoods eliminates mast and den trees, the kind of food and cover squirrels prosper on. The little animals move to a more friendly environment once a woodlot has been clear-cut.

But modern forest management dictates that no timber be cut along streams, and most cliffs are too rugged to log. Even in clear-cut areas there are usually stands of hardwoods left to support modest squirrel populations, and squirrels feed on those berries and seeds that sprout up in the clear-cuts. Grouse find the new growth of briers, vines, and weeds a bountiful source of food, and old ruff may prosper, particularly if there is good hardwood cover not too far away. Logging also favors the white-tailed deer because of the browse and cover it creates. Quail hunters enjoy hunting young pine plantations for the first three to five years after they have been planted, but eventually the young pines grow to the point that the forest canopy chokes out the rich ground cover the birds thrive on.

The upshot of all of this is that regardless of whether lands are managed for wildlife, certain game species are going to fit into the pattern—and they provide good hunting. This is what the big corporate timberlands offer the hunters of Southside Virginia.

Most companies charge a modest fee for hunting permits, and hunters writing them for permits should include a stamped, self-addressed envelope, the number of their Virginia hunting license, and their complete name and address.

Appalachian Power Company

The Appalachian Power Company of Roanoke has 13,000 acres of Virginia land available for public hunting, and some of them are in the Southside Virginia counties of Campbell and Franklin where they adjoin Smith Mountain Lake. Both counties offer fair deer and turkey hunting, a few grouse, and small game.

No permit is required to hunt these lands.

This land is mostly idle. It is not well marked, nor are there any maps.

More information is available from the Appalachian Power Company, P.O. Box 2021, Roanoke, VA 24022.

Champion International Corporation

The Halifax Timber Division of the Champion International Corporation, P.O. Box 309, Roanoke Rapids, NC 27870, owns 34,000 acres of land available for public hunting, all in Southside Virginia. Most of its holdings are fairly well concentrated in the southeastern corner of the state in the counties of Brunswick, Charlotte, Dinwidde, Greensville, Halifax, Lunenburg, Mecklenburg, Prince Edward, Southampton, and Sussex. This is quail-hunting country, possibly the best in Virginia, and the young pine plantations offer good hunting for the first three to five years after the land has been cleared and prepared for planting the seedlings.

Brunswick, Dinwidde, Prince Edward, Southampton, and Sussex are among the top deer-hunting counties, with Southampton and Sussex being possibly the best in Virginia. All offer turkey hunting, but Charlotte and Dinwiddie are the best bets.

Permits good in a single county are available for $2, but one covering all company lands can be purchased for $5. Write the company at the above address. There are no maps, but the company's lands are well marked.

Chesapeake Corporation of Virginia

The Chesapeake Corporation of Virginia, West Point, VA 23181, has approximately 2,700 acres of land in Amelia, Bedford, and Campbell counties that are open to public hunting under a cooperative agreement with the Commission of Game and Inland Fisheries. This land is well marked, and no permit is required to hunt it.

This, however, is a drop in the bucket when compared to the almost 200,000 acres of other land scattered throughout eastern Virginia, mostly in Southside, that are open to public hunting by permit. Southside Virginia counties in which such land is located include Amelia, Appomattox, Bedford, Buckingham, Campbell, Charlotte, Chesterfield, Lunenburg, Nottoway, Pittsylvania, Powhatan, Prince Edward, and Surry.

These counties are in the heart of some of Virginia's best quail hunting, and the young pine plantations offer good hunting. Amelia, Bedford, Buckingham, Chesterfield, Nottoway, Pittsylvania, Powhatan, and Prince Edward are among the best deer-hunting counties in the state. Bedford offers bear hunting, and Amelia, Appomattox, Bedford, Buckingham, Charlotte, and Powhatan are top turkey counties.

Hunting permits costing $5 are available from the company

at the above address. Maps are available for specific counties, but blanket requests for all counties will not be honored.

Continental Forest Industries

Continental Forest Industries, P.O. Box 1041, Hopewell, VA 23860, is one of the largest landowners in Virginia, with over 300,000 acres of land open to public hunting. Much of it is in Southside Virginia.

Good counties include Amelia, Appomattox, Brunswick, Buckingham, Campbell, Charlotte, Chesterfield, Cumberland, Dinwiddie, Halifax, Lunenburg, Mecklenburg, Nottoway, Powhatan, Prince Edward, Prince George, Southampton, Surry, and Sussex.

All offer prime quail hunting, and the young pine plantations are well worth checking out.

The big game hunter will find good deer and turkey hunting in most of these counties, with Amelia, Buckingham, Cumberland, and Powhatan among the best Southside Virginia counties for both species. Brunswick, Chesterfield, Dinwiddie, Nottoway, Prince Edward, Southampton, and Surry are top deer counties, with Southampton the best in the state. Appomattox and Charlotte are also good turkey-hunting counties.

The Continental lands are well marked with metal signs, and a map of the various lands is available at a modest cost. Ask for it when writing for a permit. Hunting permits costing $8 are available at the above address in early October.

Glatfelter Pulp Wood Company

The Glatfelter Pulp Wood Company, P.O. Box 868, Fredericksburg, VA 22404, owns land in a number of Virginia counties, but its Southside Virginia land is limited to Buckingham, Cumberland, and Lunenburg counties.

Both Buckingham and Cumberland are top deer and turkey-hunting counties. Both species are also reasonably abundant in Lunenburg, but not to the extent that they are in the other counties.

Some of the company's land is leased to hunt clubs, and this is not open to permit holders. Such land is well marked.

Hunting permits costing $7 are available at the above address. Location maps for specific counties are also available, but blanket requests for all maps will not be honored.

Lester Properties

The Forestlands Division of Lester Properties, Box 4784, Martinsville, VA 24115, makes available 20,000 acres of public hunting land in Virginia. All of it is in the Southside counties of Franklin, Halifax, Henry, and Pittsylvania.

Pittsylvania is the best deer-hunting county in this group, and Halifax takes the top spot for turkeys. All offer deer hunting, however, and Halifax and Pittsylvania both offer fair turkey hunting. Primarily, though, these counties are best for small game hunting.

Hunting permits are available at no cost from the above address. There are no location maps.

Owens-Illinois Company

The Owens-Illinois Company, P.O. Box 28, Big Island VA 24526, owns 82,000 acres of land in Virginia, all of which is open for public hunting. Much of this land is located in the Southside Virginia counties of Bedford and Buckingham. Both of these counties offer excellent deer and turkey hunting, and there is good bear hunting in Bedford County.

Both counties also offer good small game and bird hunting, and night hunting for opossums and raccoon.

Hunting permits are available at the above address. The cost for Virginia hunters is $4, but nonresident hunters pay $10.

Westvaco

Westvaco, Virginia Woodlands, Route 3, Box WV, Appomattox, VA 24522, though primarily engaged in growing pulpwood for its mills in Covington, Virginia, has one of the most modern wildlife management programs of any timber corporation in the state. In addition to planting wildlife patches, seeding road shoulders, and protecting streams, it also leaves hardwood corridors that permit deer, turkeys, and other game to travel under cover from one tract of timber to another.

Of the company's 135,000 acres of Virginia land, 102,000 acres are open to the public for hunting and other recreation. The individual tracts, scattered over sixteen Virginia counties, range in size from 50 to 7,000 acres. Many are in the Southside, with hunting land available in Appomattox, Bedford, Buckingham, Campbell, Cumberland, Franklin, Halifax, Henry, and Pittsylvania counties.

There is bear hunting in Bedford, and fair to excellent deer and turkey hunting in all of them. Appomattox, Bedford, Buckingham, and Cumberland are the top turkey counties, and Bedford, Buckingham, Cumberland, and Pittsylvania counties lead in the deer kill.

There is fair grouse hunting in the western part of Buckingham, Campbell, and Franklin counties, and quail in the clearcuts and young pine plantations in Appomattox, Cumberland, Halifax, and Pittsylvania counties. Company personnel will direct prospective hunters to these areas, which change from year to year, and sketch them in on maps.

Annual hunting permits costing $5 are available at the above address. Location maps are available, but hunters are requested to specify what counties they plan to hunt rather than make blanket requests. There is no charge for the maps.

Weyerhauser Company

The Weyerhauser Company, Plymouth, NC 27962, owns over 11,000 acres of land in Virginia, most of which is open to public hunting. Much of this land is in Appomattox, Southampton, and Surry counties. Appomattox is a good turkey-hunting county, and Southampton produces the largest deer harvest in Virginia. Appomattox and Surry are also fair deer counties.

All of these counties are also in good quail-hunting country, and the cutover areas and young pine plantations offer good hunting for the first three to five years after the timber has been harvested.

Some of the Weyerhauser land has been leased to hunt clubs, but most is open to public hunting. No permit is required, and there are no maps.

Hunting Leases

Hunters interested in leasing the exclusive hunting rights to company property should contact Lester Properties, Chesapeake Corporation of Virginia, or Westvaco at the above addresses. While all three companies have land open to the general public under their permit system, they also hold land for lease. Such land is not open to permit holders.

Private Land under Cooperative Agreements

In addition to the privately held lands available to the hunting public under the permit system or hunting leases, there are also big chunks open under cooperative agreements between the owners and the Commission of Game and Inland Fisheries. Such lands are available for hunting without the necessity of obtaining a permit. All such lands are marked with commission signs, and the only requirement is a hunting license.

Such is the arrangement for a 6,000-acre Smith Mountain tract in Bedford and Pittsylvania counties owned by the Appalachian Power Company. Maps of the area are available from the Regional Planning Commission, P.O. Box 456, Chatham, VA 24531. This land offers deer and turkeys for the big game hunter and possibly a few bears, grouse, and squirrels.

The commission manages a 2,700-acre tract of Chesapeake Corporation of Virginia land in Bedford and Campbell counties. The land is adjacent to the Leesville Reservoir and offers hunting for bears, deer, turkeys, grouse, and other small game. The commission also manages a big 16,000-acre Union Camp Corporation tract in Brunswick and Dinwiddie counties. Both are good deer and turkey counties, and they are in the heart of Virginia's best quail-hunting country.

PUBLIC LAKES

Aside from the dozens of small lakes and ponds already discussed in connection with the various public hunting lands, there are the big flood control and hydroelectric lakes. There are a half dozen of them—Buggs Island and, just below it on the Roanoke River, 20,000-acre Lake Gaston; Smith Mountain Lake and, immediately below it on the same river, Leesville Lake; Philpott Lake deep in the Blue Ridge Mountains; and Lake Chesdin across the state near Petersburg. All offer waterfowl hunting of varying degrees of quality. Philpott is probably the poorest for waterfowl hunting, and 50,000-acre Buggs Island the best.

All have excellent public launching ramps, so access to them is no problem.

A variety of ducks and geese use these lakes. Most are good for a few Canada geese, and all host a mixture of black, mallard, and wood ducks, plus some pintail, ringnecks, scaup, and teal.

Hunting waterfowl on these lakes takes a variety of forms. Many hunters simply run their boats back into coves and conceal them in the weeds or other available cover. Some throw up temporary blinds or use burlap or camouflage nets to conceal their boats. Others get permits and build permanent blinds, and a great many jump shoot, attempting to sneak around points or curves in the shoreline and surprise the ducks or geese.

The waterfowling on these inland lakes will not approach that of the coastal marshes, but hunters who work at it can enjoy some good shooting.

With the possible exception of Philpott, the larger lakes in this part of Virginia are not likely to freeze over, though ice may form around the edges in very cold weather.

PUBLIC RIVERS

The many winding rivers in Southside Virginia could well offer better waterfowl hunting than the big lakes. The region is blessed with an abundance of free-flowing rivers.

The mighty James River is the best known and possibly the most popular. It is a public waterway all the way from Iron Gate where the Cowpasture and Jackson join to form its headwaters to Hampton Roads where it enters the Chesapeake Bay. From Richmond to the salt water it is a tidal stream, but west of Richmond it is a fast-flowing river with many miles of racing currents. Access is good, with boat-launching ramps at Monocan Park in Amherst County, Bent Creek in Appomattox, Wingina and Midway Mills in Nelson, Howardsville and Scottsville in Albemarle, Columbia and Cartersville in Cumberland, West View and Beaumont Ramp in Goochland, and Beaumont and Watkins in Powhatan County. On the tidal stretch of the river, there are ramps and access points at Dutch Gap in Chesterfield County and Deep Bottom in Henrico. These are all public ramps developed by the Commission of Game and Inland Fisheries. On the lower stretches of the James between Hopewell and the Chesapeake Bay, numerous marinas and other privately operated facilities offer launching ramps.

The Appomattox River, which forms in Appomattox County and flows through Farmville to form Lake Chesdin and eventually enter the James River east of Petersburg, is another popular jump-shooting river, offering blacks, mallard, wood ducks, and other species. Formal access is limited, however, and hunters must use bridges and other makeshift access points to get their boats on the river.

The Roanoke (Staunton) River, which forms first Smith Mountain Lake and then Leesville Lake before entering big Buggs Island Lake in Halifax County, is one of the better-known waterfowl-hunting rivers in Southside Virginia. The hunting is particularly good in Halifax County. There are a pair of Commission of Game and Inland Fisheries access points, one at Brookneal and the other near Clover. Jump shooting is popular, and a few hunters have blinds along the lower stretches. To the south of the Roanoke River is its twin, the Dan River, which also flows into Buggs Island Lake. It too offers good waterfowl-hunting in Halifax County, though the only public access point is near Danville. In between the Dan and Roanoke rivers is the Banister River, with limited access. It too offers good jump shooting for ducks.

A pair of Buggs Island Lake public launching ramps provide fair downstream access to all three of these rivers. There is one Commission of Game and Inland Fisheries launching ramp in the Staunton River State Park and another just off U.S. Highway 58 on the southern shore of the lake. They offer possible take-out points for hunters floating from upstream or entry points for those who want to motor up the rivers and float back. Both require several miles of travel by outboard motor.

Farther east there are the Blackwater, Meherrin, and Nottoway rivers, all offering fair to good jump shooting for waterfowl. Access to the Nottoway is fair, but it is almost nonexistent on the others. Hunters floating the Blackwater or Meherrin must rely upon public road crossings or private land where they can get permission. On the Nottoway, however, the Commission of Game and Inland Fisheries has public access points near Blackstone in Nottoway County, at Peters Bridge in Sussex County, and at Carey's and Hercules in Southampton County.

Hunting in Southside Virginia is a way of life for many of its rural residents and a joy for those who have the opportunity to visit this big country of mountain foothills, rolling hills, and flat coastal plains.

Southwest Virginia

Picturesque but rugged Southwest Virginia, wedged between West Virginia on the north and North Carolina on the south, stretches from metropolitan Roanoke to historic Cumberland Gap, through which Daniel Boone blazed his wilderness route to the West. Kentucky, Tennessee, and Virginia meet here, and Kentucky and Tennessee form Southwest Virginia's far western boundaries.

Much of Southwest Virginia is Appalachia, where guns and hunting are an important part of the colorful mountain culture. Rural youths learn to hunt at an early age, honing their skills

Clinch Mountain Wildlife Management Area in Southwest Virginia is the largest wildlife management area in Virginia.

on rabbits and squirrels initially but quickly graduating to the more challenging ruffed grouse or exciting big game.

This is mountain country, the Trail of the Lonesome Pine. The Appalachian Range claims much of it—the Cumberland and Clinch Mountains, Powell and Walker mountains, Brush Mountain, Rich Mountain, and the western slopes of the misty Blue Ridge Mountains. Mount Rogers, the highest point in Virginia, towers 5,729 feet above Grayson and Smyth counties near the North Carolina line, and 5,520-foot White Top Mountain rests in its shadow.

The newcomer will quickly learn here that mountain hunting in Virginia can be tough. The leaf-covered forest floors are deceptive, for they cover small boulders and other toe-stubbing obstacles. But there are also rich river valleys, the mighty New River that rises in North Carolina to flow north through Virginia into West Virginia, the North, South, and Middle Forks of the Holston River, and the winding Clinch and Powell rivers in the deep Southwest. Claytor, Flannagan, and South Holston are the major big lakes.

Mountains and babbling brooks, big rivers, lush valleys, and sprawling reservoirs that claim a bit of all—that is the geography of Southwest Virginia, where civilization arrived considerably later than it did at Jamestown and in the country east of the Blue Ridge Mountains. These hardy pioneers also learned to live off of the land, and many did so well into the twentieth century. Modern game management won more grudging acceptance in this rugged but beautiful country, but it is turning the corner. It is highly possible that in the not-too-distant future the very best of Virginia hunting may be found in these rugged mountains and fertile valleys.

Steadily increasing populations of deer and turkeys and a struggling black bear population support big game hunting in Southwest Virginia, and the hardy ruffed grouse is the king of the game birds. "Mountain pheasant" it is called locally, and this is the best grouse country in Virginia. Big game hunting is generally best south of the Clinch River.

The frisky and abundant gray squirrel is undoubtedly the most popular game species, but there is also limited hunting for quail and cottontail rabbits. There are also thriving populations of big fox squirrels in the Clinch Mountains and Walker Mountain areas. Bird hunters also enjoy limited dove and woodcock hunting, and night hunters roam the mountain hollows for opossums, raccoon, and an occasional bobcat. There is some waterfowl hunting on the big lakes, but beaver ponds and the winding rivers are a better choice for the duck hunter. Floating the winding streams in a canoe or john boat can provide some thrilling gunning for black ducks, woodies, and other species.

Public hunting lands are abundant in Southwest Virginia. The Jefferson National Forest, which sprawls in a patchwork pattern from east to west, is by far the largest, but other federal lands include the mountain country adjacent to the John W. Flannagan Reservoir in Dickenson County and the North Fork Pound Reservoir in Wise County.

The major state lands are the wildlife management areas owned and managed by the Commission of Game and Inland Fisheries. They include Clinch Mountain Wildlife Management Area in Russell, Smyth, Tazewell, and Washington counties, Havens in Roanoke County, and Hidden Valley in Washington County. Grayson-Highland State Park in Grayson County is also open to public hunting.

Corporate hunting lands are not nearly as abundant in Southwest Virginia as they are in other parts of the state, but the Appalachian Power Company owns land in Carroll, Giles, Grayson, Montgomery, Pulaski, and Russell counties, and the Owens-Illinois Company owns land in Roanoke and Wythe counties. All of this land is available for public hunting. From time to time mining company lands in Southwest Virginia are open to public hunting, but this varies depending upon how active the company is on its land.

Collectively, these various lands offer almost unlimited hunting opportunities. The big game hunter will find white-tailed deer scattered throughout Southwest Virginia, but his chances are highest in the counties of Bland, Craig, and Giles. During the decade ending in 1979 the average deer harvest in Craig was slightly less than 1,000 animals, and it was increasing yearly. The Giles average was approximately 600, and Bland's just under 500, but the kill in both counties was increasing. Grayson County is also a good deer area, and the Mount Rogers National Recreation Area is noted for its trophy bucks. Only in Buchanan and Dickenson counties are the populations so low that the season is closed. The use of hounds, a popular method of hunting deer in the eastern part of Virginia, is illegal in Southwest Virginia. Rifles are the choice of most hunters, but both archery tackle and primitive weapons are popular.

The counties of Buchanan, Carroll, Dickenson, Floyd, Lee, Scott, Roanoke, and Wise are closed to bear hunting at the present, but the other counties give up an occasional bruin.

During the decade ending in 1979, Bland, Craig, and Giles were head and shoulders above the other Southwest Virginia counties, but the harvest did not compare with the better bear-hunting country in the northwestern part of the state. Giles is generally considered the best bear county. Except during the brief two-week deer-hunting season, bears can be hunted with hounds in Southwest Virginia.

With intensive management and carefully regulated seasons, the wild turkey has made a dramatic comeback in the Jefferson National Forest, where vast hardwood forests favor this noble bird of the woods. Bland, Craig, Giles, and Wythe are the top turkey counties, but Grayson and Montgomery also offer good turkey hunting. While all of Southwest Virginia is open to spring turkey hunting, Buchanan and Dickenson counties are closed to fall hunting. These are counties where the birds are still in the early stages of a comeback.

Grouse hunters flush an occasional woodcock, but these popular birds are extremely limited in Southwest Virginia. There is also some dove hunting in the farming country, but it is a cut or two below that found in the eastern counties.

The gray fox is reasonably abundant, but mostly in the agricultural regions. The red fox particularly likes the farming country. The gray, incidentally, is Virginia's native fox, the red having been introduced from England.

The hunter will find plenty of opportunities in picturesque Southwest Virginia.

WILDLIFE MANAGEMENT AREAS

Wildlife management areas, owned and managed by the Commission of Game and Inland Fisheries, are the only lands in Virginia held exclusively for public hunting and trapping. Though in some states the game agencies exact a specific charge for hunting such lands, that is not the case in Virginia. There are no fees other than those for the usual licenses.

Maps of specific wildlife management areas and more detailed information are available from the Commission of Game and Inland Fisheries headquarters in Richmond or from its regional office at 712 Middle Avenue, Marion VA 24354. There is a charge of $1 for a booklet containing all the wildlife management area maps.

Clinch Mountain Wildlife Management Area

Clinch Mountain Wildlife Management Area is the largest wildlife management area in Virginia. It is a mountainous area claiming some of the most rugged country in Southwest Virginia. Once under private ownership, it was logged exclusively early in this century. Before that time it was covered with a rich virgin forest. Evidence of the logging operations still exist in the form of the beds of narrow-gauge railroads, which hunters often use for access into the more remote parts of the area.

The land was purchased from the Stuart Land and Cattle Company in 1961. Smaller purchases since have expanded the area. Most of the wildlife management area is in one solid block of mountain land just north of Saltville, but there are smaller, individual patches along the North Fork of the Holston River just to the south.

Laurel Bed Lake, a popular trout-fishing lake, is located in the north-central section near the Russell-Tazewell county line. At 3,600 feet it is a high lake for Virginia.

LOCATION: Russell, Smyth, Tazewell, and Washington counties.

SIZE: 25,477 acres.

TERRAIN: The terrain is typical of the rugged Appalachian Range, narrow valleys and steep mountains that rise abruptly from the valley floors. Flat land is extremely limited. Most of it is high country, with Whiterock Mountain peaking at 4,200 feet and Beartown on the western border reaching to 4,600. The smaller sections at the lower elevations range up to 2,200 feet.

Northern and southern forests overlap here, but the major forest species include basswood, beech, birch, hickory, locust, maple, oak, and poplar. At the highest elevation there are stands of red spruce. Approximately 1,500 acres of the area have been cleared.

CAMPING: There is a developed twenty-site campground at Jackson Gap.

ACCESS: The major access is by Virginia Primary Route 91 or 107 off Interstate Highway 81. Both lead to Saltville. From Saltville take Secondary Routes 634, 613, and 747 to the main entrance of the wildlife management area. A service road follows Big Tumbling and Laurel Bed creeks to Laurel Bed Lake and the campground. The only other access, except by foot, is a narrow road that leads off Virginia Route 91 just east of the wildlife management area. It follows the headwaters of Little Tumbling Creek but is often closed to vehicular travel. There are also spur roads off the road to Laurel Bed Lake, and many hunters walk into the area off Secondary Route 726 and Primary Route 91, which run parallel to the southeastern boundary. Various trails provide comfortable walking. Good ones follow Laurel Bed, Red Branch, and Little Tumbling creeks and Turkey Run. There is a boat-launching ramp on Laurel Bed Lake, and the lake provides access to some remote parts of the wildlife management area.

GAME: Bear, deer, and turkeys are the big game in Clinch Mountain Wildlife Management Area, and all are on the increase since the elimination of cattle grazing in 1982. The temporary grazing of cattle was a condition that came with purchase of the area. Modern forestry management practices favor the increase of big game, particularly bears and turkeys.

The ruffed grouse is the major game bird. The hunting can be quite good, and it is expected to improve with the changes in land use and better management practices. Big and Little creeks and Red Branch Creek are the major streams, and they offer eighteen miles of valley hunting.

Hunting for both fox and gray squirrels is good. The Clinch Mountain Wildlife Management Area is one of two good areas in Southwest Virginia for fox squirrels. Good squirrel hunting is dependent upon a good mast crop, an event that varies from year to year.

Big game, grouse, and squirrels dominate the hunting picture here, but there is fair rabbit hunting at times and some duck hunting on Laurel Bed Lake and numerous beaver ponds. The water freezes early, however, and it may remain frozen much of the waterfowl season.

Crooked Creek Wildlife Management Area

Though managed primarily for trout fishing, the Crooked Creek Wildlife Management Area offers some good mountain hunting. The squirrel hunting is excellent, and there is good turkey hunting. Much of the land that now makes up the wild-life management area was farmland before its purchase by the Commission of Game and Inland Fisheries, and about a third of it is in open fields. The remainder is forested with hickory, maple, red and chestnut oaks, and white pine.

LOCATION: Carroll County just east of Galax.

SIZE: 1,596 acres.

TERRAIN: The area is mountainous with elevations ranging from 2,400 feet at the beds of Crooked and East Fork creeks to over 3,000.

CAMPING: There are no developed campgrounds, but camping in self-contained vehicles is permitted.

ACCESS: Virginia Secondary Route 620 off U.S. Highway 58 goes directly through the wildlife management area, and Routes 683, 711, and 712 brush it. Trails within the area are limited, but access is generally good—better than on many wildlife management areas.

GAME: Early in the life of Crooked Creek Wildlife Management Area, the abandoned farms provided good hunting for farm species such as quail and rabbits. Such hunting still exists on a limited basis, but grouse, squirrels, and turkeys are the backbone of the hunting now. Deer were stocked along with turkeys, and huntable populations of whitetails are also present, though they are not overly abundant.

Havens Wildlife Management Area

The Havens Wildlife Management Area is one of the most inaccessible public hunting areas in Virginia. The area is visible from Interstate Highway 81, but except to those who know the area it is indistinguishable from the surrounding mountain country. It is part of Fort Lewis Mountain and is about 10 miles northwest of Roanoke and Salem.

The major portion of this management area was purchased by the Commission of Game and Inland Fisheries in 1930, but it has been expanded since by additional purchases and gifts.

LOCATION: Roanoke County.

SIZE: 7,158 acres.

TERRAIN: The terrain is mountainous and steep. There is very little water, with most streams being small and intermittent. It is high country for this part of the state with mountains reaching to 3,000 feet.

The land has been in timber since recorded time, and rich forests of hickory and oak are the dominant vegetation. Game managers seed the power lines, plant food-producing shrubs, clear wildlife openings, and establish watering holes.

CAMPING: No camping facilities.

ACCESS: Until recently the only access to the area was by foot, but a road now has been built to it. Its inaccessibility appeals to hunters who do not mind hiking to escape the crowds. Virginia Secondary Routes 311, 619, 635, and 705 off Interstate Highway 81 lead to the area, but access beyond the boundary lines is blocked by gates. From there hunters must proceed by foot. Secondary Routes 622 and 883 skirt the northern boundary, providing walk-in access from that point.

GAME: There are a few bears and fair populations of deer and turkeys, though Roanoke County is not noted for its big game hunting. A few deer and turkeys are taken every season, but bears are rare.

The grouse and squirrel hunting is reasonably good, and it promises to improve with better game management and law enforcement. Located as it is near a metropolitan center, poaching has been a problem.

There is also a fair raccoon population.

Hidden Valley Wildlife Management Area

Located between the cities of Abingdon and Lebanon, the Hidden Valley Wildlife Management Area is the westernmost one in Virginia. It claims much of Brumley Mountain, a well-known landmark in the western part of the state.

What is now the wildlife management area was land that was logged heavily around the turn of the century, but second-growth timber now covers most of the area.

Hidden Valley Lake, a 60-acre impoundment built by the previous owner, was completely renovated by the Commission of Game and Inland Fisheries in 1963 and now offers public fishing. This area also serves as a black bear refuge, and hunting for this popular animal is prohibited.

LOCATION: Washington County.

SIZE: 6,400 acres.

TERRAIN: The area is mountainous, with Brumley Mountain reaching over 4,000 feet, and mostly wooded, with forests of basswood, beech, birch, cherry, hemlock, hickory, locust, maple, oak, and poplar. Red spruce thrives at the highest elevations. There are some small clearings, however, and one area of about 30 acres is mowed periodically.

CAMPING: No camping facilities, but self-contained units are permitted.

ACCESS: Access to the area is by Secondary Route 690 off U.S. Highway 19. The road is steep but paved, and it leads to 3,600-foot-high Hidden Valley Lake. There is a boat-launching ramp on the lake. Beyond the lake the hunter has to go on foot, but there are several good trails that lead deep into the hunting country. A trail following Brumley Creek provides foot access from the east, and to the south a spur road off Secondary Route 689 through Poor Valley leads to the management area boundary.

GAME: The ruffed grouse is the top game species on the Hidden Valley Wildlife Management Area, and the hunting can be quite good. The squirrel hunting is also good, and these two species are probably the major attractions, though there are also a few rabbits. Both fox and gray squirrels are present. Introduced deer and turkeys have thrived, and they are now present in huntable numbers. Opossums are abundant, but raccoon are spotty at the best.

FEDERAL LANDS

The Jefferson National Forest and the U.S. Army Corps of Engineers lands adjacent to the John W. Flannagan Reservoir in Dickenson County and the North Fork Pound Reservoir in Wise County offer over half a million acres of public hunting land in Southwest Virginia. Most of it is mountain land, but there are many acres of valleys and stream bottoms also. All of it is managed for wildlife and public hunting under cooperative agreements between the federal agencies and the Commission of Game and Inland Fisheries.

Jefferson National Forest

Just about every county in Southwest Virginia can claim sections of the Jefferson National Forest. The only exceptions are Buchanan and Floyd counties. This sprawling chunk of federal land is the major public hunting land in mountainous Southwest Virginia. It stretches from Pennington Gap in Lee County to the James River in Botetourt County. The river divides it from the George Washington National Forest that spreads over much of the northwestern part of Virginia.

To the north of Interstate Highway 81, Bland, Craig, Giles, and Wythe are the big national forest counties, and in the far west Scott and Wise counties claim much of it. To the south of Interstate Highway 81 there is the Mount Rogers National Recreation Area, a popular section of the national forest lying mostly in Grayson, Smyth, and Wythe counties.

Of the million and a half acres of national forest lands in Virginia, the Jefferson National Forest makes up a bit over a third, roughly 686,000 acres, of which approximately 20,000 are in West Virginia and 7,000 in Kentucky. Unfortunately, much of it is along the ridges of the Appalachian Mountains, land that is inaccessible and not productive of wildlife. This is not to say, however, that there is not some good hunting land in the Jefferson National Forest. There is, in fact, some very good land, which produces bears, deer, turkeys, grouse, and squirrels.

Wildlife in the forest is managed under a cooperative agreement between the U.S. Forest Service and the Commission of Game and Inland Fisheries. This has been a highly fruitful agreement dating back to 1938. Headquarters for the Jefferson National Forest is in Roanoke, but the hunter in the field can usually get maps and general hunting information from any of the half dozen ranger stations located conveniently throughout the national forest. The current ranger districts are Blacksburg, Clinch, Glenwood, New Castle, Wythe, and the Mount Rogers National Recreation Area.

Ranger district maps can prove extremely helpful. They are contour maps that also give complete information on campsites, roads, and trails. They also show mountain peaks, streams, and even a few hollows. The map of the Glenwood Ranger District, for example, shows at least a half dozen trailside shelters, the Cave Mountain Recreation Area, the North Creek Camping Area, and the Middle Creek Picnic Area. There are comfort stations and other facilities at each of these developed areas.

The management of wildlife within the national forest is divided into wildlife management units, of which there are a dozen.

The big game hunter will find white-tailed deer throughout the Jefferson National Forest, but his chances are best on land in the high-kill counties. Grayson County, which claims big sections of the Mount Rogers National Recreation Area, is a good deer producer, but every Jefferson National Forest county in Southwest Virginia yielded deer during the last decade. The Mount Rogers National Recreation Area produces some trophy bucks. There have been no deer seasons in Dickenson County since 1980, however, because of a low population.

The vast hardwood forests of the Jefferson National Forest favor the wild turkey, and much of the recent comeback of this noble bird of the forest has been in the national forest. It provides almost unlimited hunting opportunities. The potential is good throughout the forest, and the picturesque Mount Rogers National Recreation Area promises quality hunting. Hunting in this highest land in Virginia is a unique experience. Its alpine meadows and rich coniferous forests offer a kind of hunting more typical of the far north or the western Rockies.

While bears, deer, and turkeys attract thousands of big game hunters to the Jefferson National Forest and Southwest Virginia every fall, the elusive ruffed grouse is the favorite of the bird hunters. It is the popular forest grouse found throughout the eastern mountains. The birds are abundant in the national forest and found just about everywhere. Generally, they fare best on the brushy hillsides and in the valleys, but they are also found in the more open areas high in the mountains.

Clear-cutting, a modern forestry management practice which clears patches of forest, provides some of the best grouse hunting in the national forest. With the mature trees removed, briers and fruit-bearing shrubs take over, offering good grouse hunting for many years. Open areas are also planted in autumn olive, an excellent food-bearing shrub for grouse and turkeys.

While grouse are popular, a calculated guess would say the gray squirrel is the most hunted game species of all. These frisky little animals are found just about everywhere, but they particularly like mature hardwoods and stream bottoms. Finding a place to hunt squirrels in the national forest rarely presents a problem. Just head for the nearest stand of hardwoods. The larger fox squirrel is not as abundant, but the Clinch and Walker mountain ranges of the national forest are good, and the populations seem to be expanding.

Night hunters roam the forest, primarily in search of raccoon, but opossums are more abundant, and there are a few bobcats. The raccoon, once low in numbers in Southwest Virginia, was reestablished with animals trapped in eastern Virginia and released on both public and private lands. The populations are increasing. Bobcats, however, are more limited, though they too could expand as the deer herds increase. The cats may prey to some extent on fawns and sickly adult deer.

The gray fox is more abundant in the national forest than the red, but both are more likely to be found in farming country.

The major western rivers, the Clinch, Holston, New, and Powell, flow through sections of the Jefferson National Forest and offer jump shooting for black ducks, mallards, teal, widgeon, and wood ducks. There are usually a few ducks on national forest lakes such as Cave Mountain and High Knob. Hunting is permitted, but it is very limited. Wildlife watering holes and beaver ponds also offer some shooting.

Grouse hunters kick up an occasional woodcock, but the forest is not noted for its woodcock hunting. Doves, quail, and rabbits may be found occasionally along the fringes of the forest, but this hunting is extremely spotty at the best.

Even though there are other productive and well-managed hunting lands in Southwest Virginia, the Jefferson National Forest alone could keep a hunter busy the rest of his life.

Blacksburg Ranger District
_____

ADDRESS: Route 5, Box 15
　　　　　Blacksburg, VA 24060
　　　　　Telephone 703-552-4641

LOCATION: Portions of Bland, Craig, Giles, Montgomery, and Roanoke counties.

ACCESS: U.S. Highway 460 between Blacksburg and Pearisburg provides the major access with Secondary Routes 269, 601, 613, 621, 624, 635, 700, and 808 leading off into the forest. Virginia Primary Highway 42 also provides access, with Secondary Routes 601, 606, 631, and 662 leading off it. Virginia Primary Highway 100 between Pearisburg and Narrows provides access to the western part of the district. Secondary Route 641 leads into the forest. Numerous forest service roads offer deeper access.

CAMPING: Developed campgrounds at Walnut Flats and White Rock and rough camping throughout district.

GAME: All Southwest Virginia game is found here, and Bland, Craig, and Giles are top bear, deer, and turkey counties.

Clinch Ranger District

ADDRESS: Route 3, Box 820
    Wise, VA 24293
    Telephone 703-328-2931

LOCATION: Portions of Dickenson, Lee, Scott, and Wise counties.

ACCESS: U.S. Highways 23 and 58 and Virginia Primary Highways 72 and 83 provide the major access. Secondary Routes 605, 608, 610, 619, 621, 622, 630, 631, 663, 664, 706, 723, 805, and 845, plus numerous forest service roads, provide deeper access.

CAMPING: In addition to rough camping, there are developed campgrounds at Bark Camp, Cave Springs, Flat Rock Recreation Area, and High Knob. There are also developed campgrounds at the John W. Flannagan and North Fork Pound reservoirs of the U.S. Army Corps of Engineers.

GAME: Small game, upland bird, and waterfowl usual to Southwest Virginia are found here. Dickenson and Lee counties are closed to fall turkey hunting, and Dickenson is closed to deer hunting. Lee, Scott, and Wise counties offer fair deer hunting, and Scott and Wise are good turkey areas.

Glenwood Ranger District

ADDRESS: Box 10
    Natural Bridge Station, VA 24579
    Telephone 703-291-2189

LOCATION: Almost entirely within Botetourt County, with a small portion on eastern slopes of Blue Ridge Mountains in Bedford County.

ACCESS: The Blue Ridge Parkway provides the best access, but roads leading off it may be gated. Secondary routes leading off Interstate 81, U.S. Highway 11, and Virginia Primary Highway 130 provide access from the north and east. The major secondary roads are 606, 614, 625, 640, 645, 652, and 759. Secondary Routes 602, 614, 617, 640, 694, 695, 697, 765, and 776 and Primary Highway 43 provide access from the south. Numerous forest service roads offer deeper access.

CAMPING: Primitive camping, plus developed campgrounds at Campbellville Park, Cave Mountain Lake, James River Recreation Area, North Creek, and Peaks of Otter Recreation Area.

GAME: Botetourt County is excellent for big game, and other game usual to the region is found here.

Mount Rogers National Recreation Area

ADDRESS: Route 1, Box 303
          Marion, VA 24354
          Telephone 703-783-5196

LOCATION: Primarily in Smyth County, but also portions in Carroll, Grayson, Washington, and Wythe counties.

ACCESS: Numerous secondary roads off Interstate 81 as well as U.S. Highways 21 and 58 and Virginia Primary Highways 16, 91, and 94 provide major access. The major secondary roads are 601, 604, 616, 619, 644, 653, 658, 670, 675, 684, 686, 688, 689, 726, 738, 739, 740, 750, 783, 805, 836, and 859. There are also numerous forest service roads.

CAMPING: In addition to primitive camping throughout the district, there are developed campgrounds at Comers Rock, Beartree Recreation Area, Grindstone, and Hurricane Creek and in Grayson Highlands State Park.

GAME: There is fair deer and turkey hunting in Smyth County, and also in Washington and Wythe counties. Carroll county offers fair deer hunting, but Grayson County is tops for both deer and turkey. Wythe County has a fair bear population. Other game common to Southwest Virginia is found here.

New Castle Ranger District

ADDRESS: Box 246, New Castle, VA 24127
          Telephone 703-864-5195

LOCATION: Portions of Botetourt, Craig, Montgomery, and Roanoke counties.

ACCESS: Virginia Primary Routes 18, 42, and 311 provide major access. Secondary Routes 600, 602, 603, 611, 615, 618, 621, 624, 625, 656, and 658 and numerous forest service roads offer access to more remote regions.

CAMPING: In addition to rough camping, there are developed campgrounds at Roaring Run Furnace and the Steel Bridge.

GAME: Botetourt and Craig are top bear, deer, and turkey counties, and there is fair hunting for big game in Montgomery and Roanoke counties. Birds and small game common to region are also found here.

Wythe Ranger District

ADDRESS: 1625 West Lee Street
         Wytheville, VA 24382
         Telephone 703-228-5551

LOCATION: Portions of Bland, Giles, Pulaski, Smyth, and Wythe counties.

ACCESS: Interstate Highway 77 and 81, U.S. Highways 11 and 21, and Virginia Primary Highways 16 and 42 provide the major access, but Secondary Routes 603, 608, 610, 612, 615, 617, 622, 625, 680, and 703 plus numerous forest service roads provide access to the more remote areas.

CAMPING: There are developed campgrounds at Big Bend and in the Hungry Mother State Park plus primitive camping throughout the district.

GAME: Bland and Giles counties are excellent bear, deer, and turkey areas, and Smyth and Pulaski offer fair deer and turkey hunting. Wythe County also provides deer and turkeys plus a few bears. Other game common to the region is also found on the national forest lands.

John W. Flannagan Reservoir

Of the approximately 50,000 acres of land adjacent to U.S. Army Corps of Engineers lands in Virginia, approximately 6,000 are located at two sites in Southwestern Virginia. The Commission of Game and Inland Fisheries manages the wildlife and hunting resources on these lands.

The John W. Flannagan Reservoir located in Dickenson

County is the larger of the two, and the lands around the lake are open to public hunting. Maps of the lake and surrounding lands are available from the U.S. Army Corps of Engineers, 502 8th Street, Huntington, VA 25701-2070.

No permit is required to hunt these lands, which back up against the Jefferson National Forest.

LOCATION: The John W. Flannagan lands are located in Dickenson County.

SIZE: 3,261 acres.

TERRAIN: Steep, mountain country covered with mixed hardwood and coniferous forests. Much lakeshore.

CAMPING: Well-developed U.S. Army Corps of Engineers campgrounds.

ACCESS: Virginia Secondary Routes 607, 611, 614, and 739 off Primary Highways 63, 80, and 83 provide access, but some of the more remote regions are best reached by boat. There are several public launching ramps on the lake.

GAME: Dickenson County is closed to bear and deer hunting, and turkeys are hunted during the spring season only. Grouse hunting is good, and there are fair populations of opossums and raccoon. There is some duck hunting on the lake, but the squirrel is the most abundant game species.

North Fork Pound Reservoir

To the southwest of John W. Flannagan Reservoir is the smaller North Fork Pound Reservoir, an impoundment on the North Fork of the Pound River. Near the Kentucky border, it also backs up against the Jefferson National Forest. No permit is required to hunt this land, managed for wildlife and hunting by the Commission of Game and Inland Fisheries.

Maps of the lake and surrounding land are available from the U.S. Army Corps of Engineers, 502 8th Street, Huntington, WV 25701-2070.

LOCATION: The North Fork Pound lands are located in Wise County.

SIZE: 2,722 acres.

TERRAIN: Steep, mountainous terrain covered with mixed hardwood and coniferous forests. Much lakeshore and numerous small streams.

CAMPING: At least four developed U.S. Army Corps of Engineers campgrounds.

ACCESS: Secondary Route 671 off U.S. Highway 23 provides access. There are several boat-launching ramps, and a boat ride is the quickest route to some of the more remote parts of this public hunting land.

GAME: Wise County is closed to bear hunting but open to deer and turkeys. The deer hunting is fair at the best, but the turkey hunting is improving. There is some grouse hunting and hunting for waterfowl on the lakes. There are also a few opossums and raccoon, but the squirrel offers the best hunting.

OTHER STATE LANDS

The Commission of Game and Inland Fisheries is responsible for wildlife management and hunting on some state lands it does not own. Included are state forests and a few state parks. Very little of this land is located in Southwest Virginia, but one block, the Grayson Highlands State Park, is open, and it offers good hunting.

Grayson Highlands State Park

State parks scattered across Virginia are not generally open to public hunting, but thanks to an agreement between the Virginia Division of Parks and the Commission of Game and Inland Fisheries, part of Grayson Highlands State Park near the North Carolina border is open. No special permit is needed to hunt this land.

This block of park hunting land borders on the Mount Rogers National Recreation Area in the Jefferson National Forest.

LOCATION: Grayson County.

SIZE: 1,200 acres.

TERRAIN: High country with rugged mountain peaks that reach above 5,000 feet. Haw Orchard Mountain peaks at 5,089 feet. Spectacular views of alpine scenery and mixed hardwood and coniferous forests.

CAMPING: The well-developed campground may be closed during hunting season because of risk of freeze damage to the plumbing

system, but it is usually open for primitive camping, which includes pit toilets.

ACCESS: The entrance to the park is on U.S. 58, with Mouth of Wilson
the nearest town. A good system of trails makes access to the
interior of the park reasonably good. Maps are available from the
Virginia Division of Parks, State Office Building, Capitol Square,
Richmond VA 23219.

GAME: The major game species are deer, grouse, rabbits, and squirrels,
and turkeys are making a comeback. Grayson is one of the best
deer-hunting counties in Southwest Virginia, but much of the kill
comes from private lands. The Grayson Highlands State Park and
the Mount Rogers National Recreation Area are noted for trophy
deer.

PRIVATE LANDS

The hunting pressure that has closed so much private land in
eastern Virginia to the public has not hit Southwest Virginia as
hard, and posted signs are much more rare in this part of the
state. This is not to say, however, that one should take off
blithely through the countryside with gun and dogs, completely ignoring the rights of the landowner. For one thing,
such hunting is illegal, as all private land in Virginia is technically posted. The absence of signs means the hunter needs only
oral permission. When signs are placed on the property, written
permission is needed.

The general absence of posted signs in Southwest Virginia
does mean that the hunter who seeks permission to hunt private lands is more likely to gain access. Some of the best hunting is found on private lands, and this possibility should not be
overlooked.

Most hunters look to the privately owned farmlands for
doves, quail, and rabbits, though this kind of hunting is generally not as good in Southwest Virginia as it is in other parts of
the state. There is good dove hunting, for example, in Lee,
Montgomery, Pulaski, Roanoke, Wythe, and Washington counties and the western part of Tazewell County. This kind of
hunting is available to a lesser extent in other parts of Southwest Virginia.

Big landowners from time to time make their lands available to public hunting, and in Southwest Virginia they are often coal or timber companies. For years the lands of the Penn-Virginia Corporation in Lee and Wise counties were open under a cooperative agreement with the Commission of Game and Inland Fisheries. Officially, this area was known as the Hagy Wildlife Management Area, but the agreement was terminated during the 1970s when the company began aggressively mining coal. Sometime in the future this land could very well be open to public hunting.

At present, the only corporate lands open to public hunting in Southwest Virginia are the lands of the Appalachian Power Company and the Owens-Illinois Company.

Appalachian Power Company

The Appalachian Power Company, P.O. Box 2021, Roanoke, VA 24022, owns 13,000 acres of land in Southwest Virginia that are open for public hunting. Much of this land is along the New River and in the counties of Giles, Grayson, Montgomery, Pulaski, and Russell. Some of it is adjacent to Claytor Lake. A few acres may be posted for safety or other reasons, but most of it is open to hunting, and no permit is required.

Unfortunately, no maps are available, but good contacts for information are the regional offices in the counties or the Roanoke office.

Giles is an excellent bear, deer, and turkey county, and Grayson offers top deer hunting. Montgomery County also offers bear, deer, and turkey hunting, and Pulaski and Russell are good for deer and turkeys. Ruffed grouse, squirrels, and other small game may be found on most Appalachian Power Company lands.

Owens-Illinois Company

The Owens-Illinois Company, P.O. Box 28, Big Island, VA 24526, owns 82,000 acres of land in Virginia, all of which are open to the hunting public. Much of this land is in Roanoke and Wythe counties.

Both Roanoke and Wythe counties offer good deer and turkey hunting, and hunters usually take a few bears in Wythe. There are also good populations of grouse and squirrels, a few bobcats, and opossums and raccoon.

Hunting permits are available from the company's Big Island offices. Annual fees are $4 for Virginia hunters and $10 for nonresident hunters.

PUBLIC LAKES

In addition to the small ponds and lakes on the lands of the Jefferson National Forest and those on wildlife management areas, there are several big flood-control or hydroelectric reservoirs in Southwest Virginia. The public hunting lands around most of them have already been discussed, but the lakes themselves are available for waterfowl hunting.

Waterfowl hunting is generally not as good in Southwest Virginia as it is in the eastern part of the state, but many local waterfowlers enjoy reasonably good, if spotty, shooting.

While Virginia is in the Atlantic Flyway, the migratory route the birds use in moving up and down the eastern part of the continent, Southwest Virginia undoubtedly gets some birds following the Mississippi Flyway also, particularly those lakes and rivers in the extreme western part of the state.

The black duck, the wary bird closely related to the usually more abundant mallard, is a major species in Southwest Virginia, but there are also good populations of teal, widgeon, and wood ducks during the waterfowl season. Mallards are less abundant here.

Canada geese released on South Holston Lake in the 1970s have now multiplied, and the populations are flourishing on the lake proper and on nearby farm ponds. In cooperation with the Tennessee Valley Authority, which has jurisdiction over South Holston Lake, the Commission of Game and Inland Fisheries has been able to establish breeding pairs of geese on many ponds.

Claytor Lake on the New River in Pulaski County, South Holston Lake on the South Fork of the Holston River in Washington County, North Fork Reservoir on the North Fork of the Pound River in Wise County, and the John W. Flannagan Lake on the Pound River in Dickenson County all offer waterfowl hunting at various times during the fall and winter seasons. Ice may be a problem at times, but these big bodies of water are not as likely to freeze over as the smaller ones.

Good boat-launching ramps on all of these big lakes make them accessible. A few hunters build blinds on the shores or in deep coves, but a boat anchored on a point or in a timbered cove and camouflaged with nets or burlap will serve the waterfowl hunter well.

PUBLIC RIVERS

Jump shooting, floating down a winding stream in a canoe or light boat and shooting ducks as they are flushed from the water, is probably the most popular kind of waterfowl hunting in Southwest Virginia. It is also a good way to hunt squirrels. A number of major rivers and many smaller ones offer this opportunity.

The major rivers are the New, which rises in North Carolina and enters Virginia in Grayson County to flow north through the state to enter West Virginia in Giles County, the three forks of the Holston River, the Clinch, the Powell, and the Pound. There are also a number of smaller ones that provide limited jump shooting.

The Clinch River gathers its waters in Tazewell County and flows through Russell and Scott counties before entering Tennessee. The North, Middle, and South Forks of the Holston River are confined generally to Smyth and Washington counties, though the North Fork flows through Scott County into Tennessee. The Powell River flows out of Wise and Lee counties into Tennessee, and the Pound River flows north out of Wise County into Dickenson County, where it forms the John W. Flannagan Reservoir before entering the Russell River in Kentucky. The North Fork Reservoir is on the North Fork of the Pound River in Wise County.

The New River is considered a public waterway its entire length in Virginia, but what is public on the other rivers is often debatable. A public waterway is one which can be floated without the permission of the adjacent landowners, but in the case of the others, the riparian landowner's claim extends to the center of the stream. Streams flowing through the Jefferson National Forest are public, however, and so are those flowing through other public lands.

A series of boat-launching ramps owned and maintained by the Commission of Game and Inland Fisheries provides a good access to the New River. Reading downstream, there are access points at Allosonia in Pulaski County, Claytor Dam in Montgomery County, White Thorne in Montgomery County, Narrows in Giles County, and Glen Lyn in Giles County. Numerous secondary roads, forest service roads, and farm roads provide less formal access. New launching ramps are also under construction in Grayson County at Baywood, Fries, Independence, Mouth of Wilson, Old Town, and Riverside.

The Clinch River is also being made more accessible with new boat-launching ramps under construction at Black's Ford Bridge, Cleveland Park, Nashes Ford, and Puckett's Hole—all in Russell County. At least five more are planned for this river.

Southwest Virginia has a kind of hunting found nowhere else in the state. Daniel Boone, America's most famous hunter, lived off the land here during the middle decades of the eighteenth century, and Southwest Virginians have been hunting the rugged mountains and fertile valleys ever since.

Big Game

Few states east of the Mississippi River offer better big game hunting than Virginia. Some may question this, but while Alabama is rich in deer and turkeys, it has almost no bears. The bear kill in North Carolina is often higher than that in Virginia, but the deer and turkey harvests do not approach those enjoyed by Old Dominion hunters. Continue this comparison, and in most instances Virginia will come out on top.

Bear, deer, and turkey are the major big game species in the state, and there is limited hunting for sika deer on the Chincoteague National Wildlife Refuge off the Eastern Shore. Technically, the turkey is a game bird, but it is treated as big game in Virginia. There are no wild boar in Virginia, but animals stocked in West Virginia near the Virginia border are expanding and may eventually move into the state.

The black bear is Virginia's largest big game animal, and the white-tailed deer the most abundant. Wild turkeys far outnumber the bears but do not approach the deer population.

BEAR

The black bear, Virginia's largest big game animal, is the only bear found in the state, and though widespread, it is not really abundant. Wildlife managers place the populations at 1,500 to 2,000 animals, and there is some indication that the bear's numbers may be increasing slightly.

In spite of all the horror stories that have taught Americans to fear bears, the black bear is a shy and timid animal that will avoid humans if at all possible. For this reason prime bear habitat is rather limited in the state. Bears are scattered thinly from the Blue Ridge Mountains west, with probably the heaviest concentration in the Shenandoah National Park. Authorities believe there are more bears per square mile there than in Yellowstone, a national park noted for its black bears. Bears are fully protected in parks, where hunting is prohibited, so that it serves as a sanctuary. Animals spreading beyond the park boundaries provide good hunting in neighboring counties.

There is also an isolated concentration of bears in the Great Dismal Swamp, where hunters enjoyed bear hunting for generations. The inclusion of much of the swamp in the Great Dismal Swamp National Wildlife Refuge has eliminated much of the best hunting, but the area around the refuge still produces a few bears every season.

Bear sightings are becoming more common east of the mountains, but these are usually lone animals that wander outside their normal range during breeding season or lean food periods. It is possible that a few may follow the James River in traveling between the mountains and the Dismal Swamp area.

DESCRIPTION: Outsized animals may weigh 500 to 600 pounds, but

The black bear is the largest big game animal in Virginia, but it is not as abundant as the deer and turkey.

the average adult will tip the scales at from 200 to 300 pounds. Killing a bear weighing less than 100 pounds (75 pounds dressed) or a female with cubs is illegal in Virginia. The average animal's shoulder height is not over 3 feet, and its length 4 to 6 feet. During the fall and winter hunting season most bears are glossy black, though some tend toward a dark shade of brown. Many have a white blaze on their chest. The black bear has a Roman nose and face, a feature that sets it apart from the brown or grizzly with its concave face. It also lacks the shoulder hump of other bears. The animal tends to roll when it walks, swinging its head from side to side. It is a good climber, often going up trees to escape dogs or to search for food such as acorns and apples.

HABITAT: Though some bears are noted for ranging far from their home territory, females live out their lives within a 10-square-mile range, if food and living conditions are favorable. Males range more widely, up to 100 square miles. They prefer relatively open forests with thickets that provide cover and some areas that provide fruits and grass. Water in the form of lakes, ponds, or streams should be nearby. Though omnivorous, the bear is mostly a vegetarian. It loves apples, and apple orchards make good hunting grounds. During the hunting season it feeds on acorns, pine and fir cones, and other seeds. Black bears are nocturnal only when hunting pressure makes them so; otherwise they feed during the daylight hours. Beech trees are favorite feeding spots.

SEASONS: Much of Virginia is closed to bear hunting, but there are open seasons in most of the mountain counties and in the Dismal Swamp region. Late November and December are bear-hunting weeks in western Virginia; the eastern swamp season is earlier, in October and November.

GOOD COUNTIES: Albemarle, Greene, Madison, and Nelson along the eastern slopes of the Blue Ridge Mountains; Augusta, Rappahannock, and Rockingham in the George Washington National Forest; and Bland and Giles in the Jefferson National Forest.

HUNTING METHODS: Of the 200 to 300 bears taken annually in Virginia, the great majority are taken ahead of trail hounds. This is almost completely a party hunt in which hunters and hounds are combined to form a hunting party. The dogs are used to chase bears out of the remote hollows or off inaccessible ridges to hunters waiting on stands. About the only way to enjoy this kind of hunting is to join a bear-hunting club.

A few bears are taken every year more by accident than design. Bowhunters take a few that wander beneath their tree stands during the October and November archery season, and deer or turkey hunters take a few when seasons overlap in late November and December.

Still-hunting for bears can be successful, but it requires a good knowledge of the animal and its feeding habits. Preseason scouting for bear sign is very helpful. The bear's senses of hearing and smell are excellent, and the wind carries the hunter's presence to the animal. The successful hunter works into the wind so that his deadly human scent will be carried away from the quarry instead of to it. The still-hunter walks slowly and carefully through good bear country, stopping frequently to study the country.

Bears also can be taken from tree stands overlooking an old apple orchard or other areas they are known to be feeding in. The stand should be placed so that the prevailing winds will carry the hunter's scent away from the area in which the bear is expected to appear.

Both still and stand hunters should be able to recognize bear sign—broken fruit tree branches, logs or stones flipped over, decaying stumps or logs torn apart, torn-up berry patches, trees with claw or tooth marks, footprints in soft earth, and scat (or feces). Scat is roughly cylindrical, an inch or two in diameter, and often filled with hair, insects, nutshells, seeds, or grass fibers.

ARMS AND AMMUNITION: Hunters who follow bears through thick mountain cover like to carry stubby 30/30 carbines, which are entirely adequate for taking bears bayed or treed by hounds and at short ranges. Some hound hunters even use shotguns and buckshot or .357, .41, or .44 Magnum handguns. The still or stand hunter is better off with something in the .270 or .30/06 range, however, and 150- to 180-grain bullets. A bear is tough to bring down, and the rifle and ammunition should pack plenty of shocking power. Most hunters aim for the chest cavity, the area just behind the shoulder, but a shoulder shot might be safer. It will cripple the animal, giving the hunter a chance to get closer for a killing shot to the head or neck. A bear that has been shot in the lung or heart is often capable of running off for 100 yards or more, and in thick cover this can mean losing the animal. "Always shoot a bear twice." That is the advice of most experienced hunters. The bowhunter needs sharp broadhead arrows and the strongest bow he can draw comfortably.

CARE OF THE MEAT: Once the bear is down and dead, by Virginia law it must be tagged on the spot and taken to a big game checking station. Hunters are allowed only one bear a year in the state, and the bear tag should be removed from the big game stamp and fastened securely to the animal. Many hunters cut a slit in the ear for this purpose.

The bear should then be field dressed as quickly as possible. With the animal on its back or side, make a cut through the skin at the apex of the V formed by the rib cavity and open the animal all the way to its anus, remove the sex organs, cut around the ribs to free the diaphragm, sever the windpipe and esophagus as far forward as possible, and remove the innards. The animal is now field dressed and ready to be packed out. If it is to be left for any length of time, the body cavity should be propped open to allow air to circulate; a short stick will do the job. The heart and liver should be placed in plastic bags, for both are delicious.

Skinning should be left for camp or home. Begin by slitting

the skin from the chest toward a corner of the mouth. Next skin from the rectal area out along the inner side of each back leg to the pads, and from the chest along the inside of the front legs. Skin around the pads and turn the pelt inside out to unjoint the claws, which should be left on the pelt. Skinning the head is best left to a taxidermist. Just cut through the neck and leave the head attached to the rest of the skin. After these slits have been made, the skin is simply pared away from the carcass.

Once the animal has been gutted and skinned, it is ready for butchering according to the personal tastes of the hunter and his family. Bear steaks, chops, roasts, and stew meat are delicious, and scraps can be ground and made into sausage. Some hunters like to age the animal in a cool place for several days before butchering. All fat should be removed before freezing or cooking.

COOKING: Virginia black bears killed during the fall and winter seasons have been feeding mostly on nuts and fruits, and the flesh is excellent. The meat is dark and much like beef in taste and smell. Trichinosis is commonly associated with bear meat, so it should be cooked thoroughly. Freezing at 5° for 20 days or −10° for 10 days will also take care of the problem.

BEAR RECIPES: *Barbecue Ribs* are excellent. Use your own barbecue sauce and cover the ribs generously in a baking pan. Cut and add 2 large onions, and bake uncovered in a 350° oven for an hour. Then sprinkle with brown sugar and cook another 30 minutes.

Bear Chops are tasty. Trim all the fat from the chops, and season with salt and pepper or your favorite seasoning. Place a small pat of butter on each piece of meat and grill. Five to seven minutes is about right for a 1-inch-thick chop. Do not overcook, but make sure they are done.

DEER

There are more white-tailed deer in Virginia today than there were when Captain John Smith landed on Jamestown Island. That is the opinion of those who have followed the history of hunting in Virginia. Current estimates place the state population at approximately half a million animals, and there is some feeling that this figure is near the carrying capacity of the available habitat.

Unlike the black bear, the white-tailed deer has demonstrated an ability to live on the very heels of civilization. In fact, the breaking up of the vast forests to create clearings and edges has been beneficial to the deer and is one reason why the deer population is greater today than it was nearly 400 years ago.

There is probably not a county in Virginia that does not hold at least a few deer. Deer hunting is prohibited in Arlington and parts of Fairfax County for obvious reasons of safety, and also in far western Buchanan and Dickenson counties, where they have not become firmly established. There is deer hunting in every other county in the state and in a few rural cities such as Chesapeake, Suffolk and Virginia Beach.

While deer are found statewide, the heaviest concentrations are in the southeastern counties, the Northern Neck, the Piedmont north of the James River, and the mountains from Craig, Bedford, and Botetourt counties north. Lagging a bit behind are the southwestern Piedmont, the Eastern Shore, and the mountains of Southwest Virginia. While these parts of the state offer fair to good hunting, it is not on par with the rest of the state.

DESCRIPTION: The white-tailed deer is a marvelous game animal and venison is among the tastiest wild meats in America. The hunter who can score consistently on white-tailed deer will experience no trouble hunting any other game animal. The national average weight for mature bucks is probably 130 to 150 pounds, and does average ten to fifty pounds less. The deer's color changes to a degree with the seasons, ranging from a russet or tawny coat in the summer to almost gray in the November woods. An 8-point buck is a good trophy if its antlers are evenly and widely spaced, but some real trophies run to 20 points or more. A button buck is commonly a yearling with little more than knobs on its head, while a spike buck has one or two small antlers devoid of tines. The underside of the whitetail's tail is snow white, and when alarmed it bounds away, flashing the tail in the air; hence the name whitetail. The white undercoat extends to the belly and inside of the legs, and there is a white patch under the upper throat and chin. The Virginia whitetail, *Odocoileus virginianus,* is the subspecies found in Virginia.

HABITAT: The whitetail's home range covers only about a square mile, though it may be expanded to two or three. The deer is a creature of habit, following terrain contours such as creek banks, draws, dry brook beds, and saddles between bedding and feeding areas. Within its home range the deer seems to use just about all of the cover—the oak ridges where it noses for acorns, the edges between forests and meadows, the honeysuckle patches, cutover forests, and even the open meadows. A favorite bedding area is a patch of cover in a large field. It apparently feels the open country around the cover offers good protection—room to detect approaching danger. It also likes to bed down in laps left by logging crews. Generally, it is an animal of the edges rather than the deep woods. Deer are not often far from a good source of water such as a brook, lake, pond, or river. The deer is a browser, and the list of possible foods is almost endless—twigs, ferns, grapes, apples, honeysuckle, grass, farm crops such as corn and soybeans, acorns, rhododendron, persimmons, and so on. Deer are nocturnal feeders, particularly during the hunting season, though they also feed to a lesser degree during the day. Full moons favor night feeding.

SEASON: Broadly speaking, there are three deer seasons in Virginia, or four if the October and November archery season is included. The western season is a brief two-week one that opens near the middle of November and closes near the end of the month or early in December. The eastern season is much longer, also opening near the middle of November but continuing through the first week of January. The third firearms season is a more limited one in the Great Dismal Swamp region which opens the first of October to run through November.

GOOD COUNTIES: Southampton is by far the leading deer-hunting county. Hunters there consistently take over 3,000 deer, and no other county comes close. Contributing to the high kill, however, are liberal regulations that include the long eastern season and either-sex hunting the entire season. Buckingham County is usually second in the state, but other good eastern counties include Sussex, Amelia, and Caroline. Top western counties include Rockingham, Shenandoah, Bath, Augusta, and Grayson.

HUNTING METHODS: Regulations to a degree dictate deer-hunting methods in Virginia. The use of dogs is prohibited west of the Blue Ridge Mountains, where the season runs for only two weeks, but their use is legal in the vast country east of the mountains. Local firearms ordinances also play a role in the choice of hunting methods. Rifles are generally legal in the west, but country ordinances have ruled them illegal in a number of eastern counties. In these counties deer hunters are limited to shotguns and buckshot, and their hunting ability is restricted to short-range shooting.

When hounds are the method chosen, hunters normally organize into some kind of club, often informal, where the hunters and their hounds join forces. Hunting parties split up into two groups: those who take stands along the route the quarry is expected to take and those who handle the hounds and make them drive. The driving is alternated frequently so that all members of the party get chances at a stand. Deer drives are often made during the late morning or early afternoon when there would otherwise be little activity because the deer are bedded down.

Western hunters, and many eastern hunters also, prefer still-hunting. Still-hunting is a misnomer in that the hunter does not actually sit or stand but instead moves slowly through good white-tail cover. He moves ahead as cautiously as possible but stops frequently to look and listen. It is an interesting, challenging way to hunt, and a cautious hunter may cover less than a mile in an entire day of hunting. Experienced still-hunters wear wool or other soft finish clothing that is not noisy when scratched against twigs or other vegetation.

Stand hunting, on the other hand, is done from a single position. The hunter does not move as he does in still-hunting. Tree stands are popular for this kind of hunting. They get the hunter well off the ground where he has a commanding view of a deer trail, crossing, or feeding area. The tree stand also gets the hunter well above the normal vision of the deer; a deer rarely looks up.

Both still and stand hunters, and still-hunters in particular, must keep the animal's three senses of defense in mind—its senses of smell, hearing, and vision. The deer's sense of smell is the strongest, its first line of defense. Its sense of hearing is second, and its vision last. Wind is the deer's ally. It carries these warnings to him, and the wise hunter always takes the wind into consideration, working into it if at all possible. Preseason scouting for deer sign will improve the hunter's chances considerably. This means looking for tracks in the soft places, droppings (clusters of black pellets), and buck rubs. Rubs are well-barked saplings where a buck has polished his antlers. Well-used deer trails are also obvious signs, and just jumping deer from their midday bedding areas will lead the hunter to the right place on opening day.

ARMS AND AMMUNITION: Rifles used for deer hunting in Virginia must be .23 caliber or larger, and shotguns cannot be larger than 10 gauge. Pistols and muzzle-loading guns are growing in popularity. Shotguns must also be plugged so that they cannot hold more than three shells. These simple regulations leave the deer hunter a lot of leeway. The .243-caliber rifle loaded with 100-grain bullets is a good choice, but its use is limited in brushy country. Actually, the age-old 30/30 caliber is still a good choice for hunting the thickets, but it has very limited range. The .270 with 150-grain bullets is a good all-around choice. Many hunters prefer the highly versatile .30/06, particularly if they want a single rifle that can be used for a wide variety of big game hunting. For deer, 150-grain bullets are entirely adequate. The shotgunner is limited to buckshot, and it is doubtful that he should drop below 10 or 12 gauge. Usually a full-choke barrel groups the buckshot well, but the only way to be sure is to set up a patterning board and try several loads until you find one that groups well. Then hunt with that load and that gun only. Most hunters aim for the heart and lungs by holding just to the rear of the shoulder. At close ranges, however, a neck shot will kill quickly and spoil a minimum of meat. When facing a deer head-on, a shot in the chest is recommended—or the neck if close enough. The bowhunter needs well-sharpened broadhead arrows and a bow he is comfortable with. In Virginia the arrowheads must be at least ⅞ inch in diameter, and the bow capable of propelling that arrow at least 125 yards.

CARE OF THE MEAT: First, the deer should be tagged. The deer tag from the big game license can be tied to an antler or a slit in the ear.

The manner in which a deer is handled immediately after it is killed has much do to with the quality of the venison. This means field dressing on the spot. With the animal on its back or side, make a cut through the skin from the apex formed by the rib cavity to the crotch. Care should be exercised not to prick the viscera. With the diaphragm free, reach as far forward as possible and cut free the esophagus and windpipe. Place the heart and liver in a plastic bag. Now turn the animal downhill and remove all of the intestines and other organs. Prop the body open with a short stick to keep it cool.

After it is checked by a big game checking station, the animal should be hung head down and the skin removed. Leave plenty of skin behind the head and neck if the head and antlers are to be mounted. If the weather is cool, the animal can be hung for several days before it is butchered. The animal can be butchered to fit personal tastes. Most of it will go into steaks, chops, and roasts, but there also are the scraps that can be ground into venison-burger, the ribs that are excellent barbecued, and the stew meat.

COOKING: The best venison is from a deer that is killed while it is undisturbed. This rules out animals taken ahead of hounds. Deer meat resembles beef in many ways. Its flavor, color, and texture are much the same, but it seldom has much fat. Many experienced hunters who have long since satisfied their desire for trophy deer hunt simply to put some venison in their freezers.

DEER RECIPES: *Charcoal Broiled Venison* can be excellent if properly handled. A bed of coals in a backyard grill will work well, but so will the kitchen range. Steaks from the rear quarters or tenderloin steaks are fine, but they should be about ½ inch thick. They should be placed on the grill while the meat is still slightly frozen so that the meat will cook well on the outside but still will be juicy on the inside. Do not overcook. When they are cooked to the desired taste, remove and add salt and pepper.

Roast Venison should be cooked in an oven preheated to 450°. Sprinkle flour in the bottom of roasting pan and place roast in the flour. The roast should be covered with bacon strips placed approximately ½ inch apart and seasoned with ground pepper. After the roast has been browned for 15 minutes, pour a cup of beef stock into the bottom of the pan and reduce heat to 325°. Continue to cook until a meat thermometer registers 140° if rare meat is desired. Do not cook beyond medium rare.

SIKA DEER

The sika deer is not native to Virginia or to America. In fact, it is a relative newcomer, having been introduced to the state during the late 1920s. Closely related to the elk, the sika is a native of Asia, but the animals are raised rather easily in capitivity. Back in 1927 a Maryland resident grew tired of caring for his five pet sikas and released them on the Maryland portion of Assateague Island, which straddles the Maryland-Virginia border. The upper island is a barren stretch of sand with little in the way of food and cover. Eventually, the animals discovered the heavily vegetated Virginia portion of the island, where they prospered and multiplied.

The Virginia portion of Assateague Island eventually became the Chincoteague National Wildlife Refuge, a resting and feeding stop for ducks and geese flying the Atlantic Flyway. The sika herd grew to several thousand animals, began to compete with the waterfowl for food, and even threatened to become overpopulated and a threat to their own existence.

To control the sika herds, the U.S. Fish and Wildlife Service in cooperation with the Commission of Game and Inland Fisheries has been holding controlled hunting seasons in October, November, and December. Archers only are permitted during the early weeks of the season, but late in the season a stags-only hunt is held when single-shot rifles or shotguns are permitted.

DESCRIPTION: The little sika deer is about half the size of the white-tail. Though some have been taken that weigh over 140 pounds, the average is more in the 40- to 60-pound range. Like the white-tail, its color varies from a medium brown to almost gray depending upon the season. Both young and old have light spots on their flanks. Its antlers are narrower and straighter than those of the white-tailed deer. The sika runs in a stiff-legged hop instead of bounding. It has almost no tail, but when it is alarmed, the white hairs on its rump spread out in fanlike fashion.

HABITAT: The sika's habitat on Assateague is a mixture of pine forests and tangled underbrush on low, sandy terrain and rounded dunes. Intermixed are marshes, ponds, and grassy meadow. Much of the vegetation is stunted.

SEASONS: Hunting is usually allowed in October, November, and December. The bowhunting season comes first, followed by the firearms season.

GOOD COUNTIES: Assateague Island is located off the oceanside of Accomack County near the Maryland border.

HUNTING METHOD: The sika is an extremely shy animal that feeds mostly at night. Early morning and late afternoons offer the best hunting when the animals leave the cover and venture into the open. Regulations limit the hunting methods, and most hunters either still-hunt or wait on stands. Still-hunting means walking slowly and stopping frequently to look and listen, working generally into the wind. Like the white-tailed deer, the sika deer has excellent senses of smell and hearing and only fair vision. Hunters who draw permits are assigned to specific areas.

ARMS AND AMMUNITION: Only single-shot rifles or shotguns are permitted. Rifles must be .23 caliber or larger, and shotguns from 20 to 10 gauge. Slugs only are permitted in shotguns. Rifles in the .243 or .270 range are entirely adequate, and bullets should be from 100 to 150 grains. Bowhunters must use bows capable of casting the selected arrows 125 yards, and the arrows must be tipped with broadheads at least ⅞ inch in diameter.

CARE OF THE MEAT: Animals taken in early October require careful handling because of the warm weather. The animal must be tagged and field dressed just as soon as it is determined that it is dead. Roll it on its back and slit the belly skin from the apex of the V formed by the rib cavity to the anus. Reach as far forward as possible to sever the windpipe and the esophagus and then turn the animal on its side and remove the intestines and all of its organs. Place the heart and liver in a plastic bag. As quickly thereafter as possible hang the sika head down, and remove the skin, and let the animal cool in a cool place—the shade at the minimum. Later it can be butchered into steaks, chops, roasts, and stew meat and the spare scraps ground into burger meat.

COOKING: A member of the large deer family that includes both the white-tailed deer and the larger American elk, the sika's meat is also tasty if given the proper care from the time of the kill to the table.

SIKA DEER RECIPES: *Sika Roast* can be a simple but delicious meal. Wrap a 2-pound roast in aluminum foil and seal it tightly. Place it in an oven set at 300° and leave it for an hour. When done there will be a good deal of juice in the foil. This should be saved to pour over the meat when it is served. Salt if desired.

Sika Meatballs are easy to make and tasty. The ingredients are 1½ pounds ground sika meat, 1 small grated onion, 1 large grated potato, 2 large grated carrots, 1 egg, 2 tablespoons flour, ¼ teaspoon salt, a dash of pepper, 1 can cream of mushroom soup, and 1 can evaporated milk. Combine all of the ingredients except milk and soup in a mixing bowl. Shape the meat into patties and fry in a heavy skillet with enough cooking oil to prevent sticking. When they are well browned and cooked, place them in a greased casserole dish. Now pour the milk and soup over the meat and bake in the covered casserole for about 40 minutes with the oven set at 350°.

TURKEY

The wild turkey was just as abundant as the white-tailed deer when our ancestors from Europe arrived in this land—or possibly even more so. Turkeys too have made a dramatic comeback in Virginia, though it is doubtful that their numbers were ever as dangerously low as was the deer population. On the other hand, the current population of slightly less than 100,000 birds probably does not approach the abundant population our ancestors knew, nor will they ever approach that level. The wild turkey in Virginia is primarily a bird of the big hardwood forests, a kind of habitat that has been drastically reduced in the state and is not likely to return. The demand for agricultural lands, subdivisions, highways, and fast-growing pines that can be turned into fiber are too great for the restoration of our once expansive forests.

Still, the turkey has demonstrated a degree of adaptability along its modern comeback trail. It approaches the white-tailed deer in its ability to live on the heels of civilization, and it has shown a willingness to accept a less than ideal habitat. The mature hardwood forests with their thick canopies and limited understory may still be the bird's preferred habitat, but today the wild turkey lives in all kinds of cover. This flexibility bodes well for the future of turkey hunting in Virginia.

Today there are turkeys just about all over Virginia. There probably are at least a few birds in every county, though their numbers are extremely low in a number of eastern counties—primarily in the Tidewater region. Ironically, this is where the early settlers first became acquainted with the big bird. Fall turkey-hunting seasons reflect this distribution. While the entire state is open to spring turkey hunting, fall hunting is not allowed in what can be described roughly as the eastern one-fourth of the state. Approximately twenty-five eastern counties and rural cities are now closed to fall hunting, and so are Buchanan, Dickenson, and Lee counties in the west.

Even though the wild turkey is found just about statewide, it is truly abundant only in the Piedmont and mountain regions. Currently, the best mountain hunting begins in Bland and Giles counties, extends eastward to include Bedford County, and then follows the mountains north to the West Virginia border. Most of the foothill counties in the upper Piedmont are reasonably good, but those counties just south of the James River are better.

This distribution picture is subject to change, however, as the turkey continues its comeback in Virginia. Some of the far Southwest Virginia counties such as Tazewell and Wise show real promise, and there is good habitat in the Jefferson National Forest, which spreads over much of this part of the state.

The combined fall and spring kill runs about 10,000 birds, but it is almost sure to increase.

DESCRIPTION: The wild turkey, particularly the male, is a handsome
    bird of the forest. The sight of one thrills hunter and nonhunter
    alike. The dominant color of the bird is bronze or dark copper,
    though gobblers are likely to appear black in the forests. The male

birds are known as gobblers or toms. The scaly legs, unfeathered and skinny from the knees down, are usually reddish gray, and the tom has black spurs about an inch in length. The tail is squared, and the wing feathers are edged in white. The gobbler has a beard that hangs from the breast, a stiff, black adornment that looks somewhat like the tail of a horse. Hen birds on rare occasions have this beard. On an adult gobbler the beard will average about 8 to 9 inches, but on some birds it is much longer—and a real trophy. Normally a hen's head and neck are covered with very fine feathers that give them a bluish effect. An adult gobbler's head, on the other hand, has all kinds of adornments, including a wattle that hangs from the chin and throat, lumpy and fatty caruncles on its lower neck and throat, and a frontal caruncle just above its bill. Its head is pale, almost white, except when it struts before a hen in the springtime. The wild turkey is slimmer and generally smaller than the common barnyard variety. Gobblers will average from 19 to 24 pounds, though some outsized ones may go to 25. The smaller hen will average 8 to 13 pounds.

HABITAT: The wild turkey is primarily a bird of the forest, and it prefers mature ones that choke out the understory. Mature oaks not only provide food in the form of acorns but also provide good visibility from the forest floor. The turkey's vision is its first line of defense. The mature trees also provide safe roosts. The bird needs a nearby source of water in the form of a pond, lake, or stream, some openings or nearby fields where it can graze and feed on insects in the spring and summer, and fall and winter food in the form of nuts, seeds, wild grapes, and other fruit.

SEASON: Virginia hunters enjoy both fall and spring hunting, and the annual harvest is usually divided fairly evenly between the two seasons. The current season limit is two birds. The fall season opens around the first of November and runs through December, while the spring season runs from the middle of April through the middle of May. Turkeys are also legal during the archery season that opens in mid-October to continue well into November, be-yond the opening of the fall turkey season. Many eastern counties are not open during the fall season, however, and some have very brief seasons. Only gobblers are legal in the spring, but a bearded hen qualifies. Fall hunters are allowed to take one hen.

GOOD COUNTIES: Bath County in the west and Buckingham County are often the top two counties in the state. Other top western counties include Alleghany, Augusta, Botetourt, Giles, Rockbridge, and Shenandoah. In addition to Buckingham, good eastern counties in-clude Albemarle, Amelia, Caroline, Cumberland, and Fluvanna.

HUNTING METHODS: In the opinion of many who have hunted most or all of America's rich variety of game species, the wild turkey is the most difficult of all. The bird is extremely wary, and nature equipped it with a set of eyes that are a challenge to modern radar. Its eyes are set well back on the sides of its head, giving it excellent vision in at least three directions of the compass. Its sense of hearing is also excellent, and it has no trouble sorting the steady trod of the hunter from the other sounds of the woods. The wild turkey is rarely an easy bird to bag. Scouting, if at all possible, should precede a hunting trip. In Virginia one of the best signs to look for is scratchings, leaves on the forest floor scattered by birds looking for food. Even a lone turkey can leave a lot of sign. Experienced hunters can tell the direction the turkey was going by studying the scratchings; it throws the leaves to the rear as it proceeds. Soft places in the earth will reveal tracks, and scat or droppings are often evident. The scat is looped or spiraled and often twisted in a knob at one end.

Spring hunting, though relatively new to Virginia, is considered the epitome of turkey hunting by many. The very heart of spring hunting is the effort by the hunter to imitate the yelp of a lovesick hen. It is breeding time, and the old gobblers are interested. Only gobblers are legal in the spring. The usual procedure is to roam the woods at daybreak until an old gobbler sounds off. He is usually still on his roost. The hunter then moves as close as he dares, builds a scanty blind or locates a natural one such as a brush pile or clump of vegetation to conceal himself, and begins to work his yelper. The aim is to get the old gobbler interested enough to wander within shotgun range. The spring hunter dresses in camouflage and masks his face. There are numerous turkey calls on the market, from cedar boxes to mouth-operated ones. The box is the easiest to master.

The turkey dog is the key to fall hunting in Virginia. The typical turkey dog is an English pointer or setter in which the pointing instinct has been suppressed insofar as turkeys go. Its sole responsibility is to find the birds and flush them. The hunter might get a chance shot at a flushed bird, but the real goal is to go to the site of the flush, build a blind, call in the dog, and then call the scattered birds to the blind. Confused and scattered, they will usually respond to the yelp of a mother hen imitated on a turkey call.

ARMS AND AMMUNITION: The shotgun is the traditional arm for turkeys in Virginia. It should be a full-choke 10 or 12 gauge, and most have long, 30-inch barrels, though barrel length is not particularly important as long as it holds a tight pattern. The shotgunner aims for the bird's head and neck, and a thin pattern might not put enough shot in the bird to bring it down. A carrying sling is handy but not essential. High brass shells loaded with sizes 4 to 6 are the usual choice. Fours are preferable if they hold a tight pattern. The best approach is to shoot the various loads at a patterning board and use the load that holds the best pattern out to about 40 yards. Rifles are also legal for turkeys in Virginia, but the heavier calibers destroy too much of the meat. The .22 Magnum with hollow-point bullets is a good turkey rifle, and it extends the hunter's range up to 100 yards. Riflemen attempt to place their bullet at the base of the neck where it will kill quickly and damage a minimum of meat. Turkeys are also legal during the archery season that runs from the middle of October into early November. Broadhead arrows with blades at least ⅞ inch wide are required and recommended for turkeys. The bow must be capable of shooting the arrows at least 125 yards.

CARE OF THE MEAT: Turkeys, particularly those killed in late April or early May, require immediate attention if the delicious meat is to taste its best, but do not overlook tagging and clearing them through a big game checking station. If the bird is not to be plucked immediately, it should be field dressed. This is no more than opening up the bird and removing the intestines and other organs. If the gizzard is to be saved, place it in a plastic bag. Ideally, the bird should be plucked first and then gutted. Some hunters insist upon dipping the bird in boiling water to facilitate the removal of the feathers, but plucking the bird dry is no problem, and there is less risk of damage to the meat. Once plucked and gutted, the bird should be kept in a cool place until it is ready to be cooked or placed in the freezer. Some hunters prefer to skin their birds.

COOKING: The meat of the wild turkey is delicious, every bit as much as the meat of the farm-fattened birds that grace most American tables at Thanksgiving—and often better. The early settlers learned this quickly when they ventured inland. The old gobbler, the quarry of the spring hunter, may require a bit more cooking, but it too is excellent.

TURKEY RECIPES: *Roast Turkey* is the favorite dish of most turkey hunters. To roast an 8-pound (dressed weight) turkey, you need 1 tablespoon flour, melted butter or margarine, salt, pepper, paprika, 1 small sliced onion, ½ cup chopped celery, and whatever stuffing you prefer. Using a conventional oven, preheat it to 350°. Shake the flour in a large-size brown-in-bag and place it in a 12 × 8 × 2–inch dish. Rinse the turkey and pat it dry. Stuff the turkey with your favorite dressing, brush the entire surface with butter, and sprinkle it with seasonings. Spread the onion and celery in the bottom of the bag, and place the turkey in the bag. Cover the breast and thighs with small pieces of foil to prevent browning too rapidly. Close the bag with a twist line, make six ½-inch slits in the top, and bake for 2 to 2½ hours.

For *Wild Turkey Soup*, Rob Keck, executive vice president of the National Wild Turkey Federation, recommends 1 turkey carcass, 4 to 5 quarts water, 4 medium carrots, 1 small head of cabbage, 3 stalks of celery, 1 teaspoon salt, ½ teaspoon pepper, ½ teaspoon poultry seasoning, turkey gravy, and stuffing left over from a roast turkey dinner, and 1 pound of small macaroni precooked. Keck removes as much meat as possible from the turkey bones, places the bones in an 8-quart pot, and covers them with water. He simmers this for 2 hours or long enough to loosen the remaining meat from the bones, but not so long that the bones will fall apart in the broth. While the bones are simmering, he grinds all of the vegetables in a meat grinder. When the bones are done, they are lifted from the broth, and then the ground vegetables, the juice from the vegetables, and the seasonings are added to the broth. Leftover stuffing and gravy are added, and this simmers for another 2 hours. The remaining meat is cleaned from the bones and added to the soup. When the vegetable bits are tender and the broth tastes just right, the cooked macaroni is added. Keck lets the soup stand for several hours before serving. This allows the flavor to develop. The soup will serve a crowd, he says.

Small Game Mammals

An abundance of gray squirrels, fox squirrels in the western part of Virginia, spotty cottontail rabbit populations, and a few marsh rabbits along the coast, a small population of snowshoe hare in the Highland County, and gray and red foxes make up Virginia's small game mammals.

While the cottontail rabbit is the number one game animal nationwide, that is not the case in Virginia. The frisky little gray squirrel rules supreme here. More people hunt gray squirrels than any other small game animal. Many a Virginia rural youth has cut his hunting teeth on rabbits and squirrels, though that first rabbit may have been taken from a box trap instead of with a gun. No other species of game has provided more hours of pure hunting joy over the generations than the rabbit and squirrel. But rabbit and squirrel hunting is by no means limited to the youngsters. Mature hunters whose interests may eventually turn to more glamorous game periodically return to the squirrel woods and the rabbit patches.

FOXES

There are two kinds of foxes in Virginia, the smaller gray fox and the larger red. The gray is the native Virginia fox, but the red was introduced from England centuries ago. Fox chases with a pack of hounds are popular in Virginia, and riding to the hounds is steeped in tradition. It is a colorful sport featuring registered hounds, fast horses, and hunters in red coats. To protect this kind of hunting, guns are prohibited for fox hunting in the counties of Albemarle, Amelia, Charlotte, Clarke, Culpeper, Fairfax, Fauquier, Halifax, Lee, Loudoun, Louisa, Rappahannock, and Warren. Fox hunting is strictly the joy of the chase in those counties. Many foxes escape the hounds to run again.

Fox hunting with hounds is popular in other parts of Virginia also, but not on the same grand scale. These hunts feature dog crates in the back of pickup trucks and hunters on foot or in four-wheel drive vehicles. They too enjoy listening to the hounds, and they often hunt at night when the scent is stronger and the dogs run better.

In the rest of the state, foxes can be hunted with guns, but this kind of hunting has never become particularly popular, possibly because hound hunters frown on it.

DESCRIPTION: Both the gray and the red foxes are fairly small, weighing between 7 and 12 pounds, not much bigger than a large house cat. The shoulder height is 14 to 16 inches, and the bushy tail 14 or 15 inches long. The legs of the red are slightly longer then those of the gray, but it is the color of the two animals that sets them apart. Their names are highly descriptive. The red is more coppery in color than red, and the gray is a salt-and-pepper color bordered with enough brown to confuse the inexperienced hunter,

The gray squirrel is the most popular small game animal in Virginia.

who might mistake it for a red. The gray will hole up in a den or use dense cover to elude the dogs, or climb a tree occasionally. The red does not hole up or climb and prefers to run in more open country. It is much faster than the gray. Both animals are elusive.

HABITAT: A fox may roam over a 10-square-mile area, or even farther during the breeding season or when food is scarce. The gray is an animal of the deep woods, the forests, and the thickets, whereas the red prefers the more open farming country.

SEASONS: The chase seasons when no guns are allowed are long in Virginia, either continuous or running from early fall through March. The guns season generally runs from early November through January.

GOOD COUNTIES: Both the gray and red foxes may be found in suitable habitat throughout the state, but the red is most abundant in the piedmont and tidal areas, and the gray just about statewide in forested country. It is more abundant than the red in the western part of Virginia.

HUNTING METHODS: While foxes are hunted primarily with hounds in Virginia and seldom shot, the possibilities of gun hunting are almost unlimited. Hunters placed on stands can take them in front of hounds and are not limited to the usual hunting hours of a half hour before sunrise to a half hour after sunset. They can also be lured within gun range by predator calls; the ones that imitate the wails of a dying rabbit are good. They can be tracked in the snow or simply stalked in areas where they are known to be abundant. The fox can be a challenging quarry for the gun hunter.

ARMS AND AMMUNITION: Hunters waiting for the hounds to run a fox by them usually carry 20- to 12-gauge shotguns bored full or modified and loaded with express or Magnum size 2 or 4 shot. Hunters operating predator calls also can use shotguns, but a rifle might be better. Calibers range from the 5mm and .22 rimfire Magnum through the various .22 center-fires. The stalking or tracking hunter should by all means arm himself with a rifle.

CARE OF THE FUR: The fox has no food value, but its fur is usually valuable. To remove the fur, use a sharp knife and make slits from the anus along the back sides of both hind legs and cut through the tailbone near its base. With the animal hung by its back feet, work the skin down over the body and off the head. The feet and tail should be left on the fur and the bone removed from the tail. Once the skin is removed, it should be placed on a stretcher, fur side out, and allowed to dry in a cool place.

HARE

Of the several varying hares found in America, only the snowshoe lives in Virginia, and its population is small and largely limited to Augusta and Highland counties. It is called a varying hare because its fur changes from a brownish gray in the summer to snow-white in the winter.

DESCRIPTION: Besides its changing color, another unique feature of the snowshoe hare is its hind feet. They are almost 6 inches long, and they broaden from the heel to the splay toes. They serve as snowshoes in the deep snow, permitting the animal to move freely without bogging down. These surprising hare can leap long distances, often covering as much as 15 feet in a single bound. Its senses are strong: 3- to 4-inch ears that are as sensitive as radio antennas when held erect, a seemingly always twitching nose, and sharp, black eyes that sometimes give it away against a background of snow and white fur. The snowshoe is capable of running for hours without tiring.

HABITAT: The snowshoe hare seldom seeks the impenetrable thickets the cottontail prefers. It is more a creature of the open woodlands. The little animals love conifers, and that is a good place to put down the hounds used to hunt them. They browse during the hunting season on the bark, twigs, and tips of pine, spruce, fir, cedar, aspen, willow, and other plants and trees. Their forms (bedding places) are often on slight elevations, and they are conspicuous in the snow.

SEASONS: The season is the same as that for the cottontail rabbits west of the Blue Ridge Mountains, usually November, December, and January.

GOOD COUNTIES: Highland County is the only one with an appreciable snowshoe hare population.

HUNTING METHODS: The traditional way to hunt snowshoe hare is with beagle hounds, much the way cottontail rabbits are hunted. Hunters look for tracks and well-used trails and release the dogs. Once up and going, a hare may run for a mile or more, but eventually it will return to the area from which it was jumped. Hunters take stands along the expected return route, and if there are enough hunters, they cover all possible routes. The stand should give the hunter a commanding view and a clear field of fire, but if at all possible some concealment will improve his chances. Favorite hounds include the larger 15-inch beagles, foxhounds, and beagle-foxhound crosses. Unlike the cottontail, the hare seldom if ever holes up. Hunters without hounds can still-hunt, walking slowly through an area where there is plenty of sign in the form of tracks, trails, and gnawed twigs and branches.

ARMS AND AMMUNITION: The beagle owner will want a 20- to 12-gauge shotgun bored modified or improved cylinder, and size 6 shot. High brass shells are advisable, but many hare have toppled to field loads. The still-hunter will want a .22 rimfire rifle with hollow-point bullets.

CARE OF THE MEAT: If at all possible, hare should be field dressed immediately upon being bagged. This is easy to do. Just slit the belly skin from the apex of the V formed by the rib cavity to the anus and snap out the intestines and other organs. To prevent getting blood on clothing, place the hare in a plastic bag.

COOKING: The meat of the snowshoe hare is dark and tasty on the table, a favorite game dish of many hunters.

HARE RECIPES: *Barbecued Hare* is prepared by soaking the animal overnight in cold water to remove traces of blood. Cut it into 6 pieces and marinate it 1 to 3 hours in 2 ounces of barbecue sauce, 1 tablespoon of Worchestershire sauce, and 1 cup dry white wine. Place it in a cooking pan, pour in the marinade, add ½ cup wine, and salt and pepper. Seal the pan tightly with aluminum foil and place in a 300° oven. Cook for 2 to 3 hours.

Fried Hare is fine if the animal is young. First quarter the animal and wash and dry it. Season the pieces with salt and pepper, dip in 1 beaten egg, dredge in flour, and fry slowly in oil for an hour. Turn the pieces often so they will brown evenly.

RABBITS

The cottontail, the number one game animal in America, is the most widely distributed rabbit in Virginia, though there are some small marsh rabbits in the coastal regions.

The cottontail's fortunes bounce around in Virginia like a rubber ball. The rabbit populations has always tended to be somewhat cyclic, but not enough so to disturb bunny-hunting enthusiasts. During the 1970s, however, the cottontail population seemed to hit a new low, and it stayed there. Always abundant during the summer and early fall, the rabbit seemed simply to disappear by the time the November opening rolled around. The Commission of Game and Inland Fisheries suspected tularemia, a common rabbit disease, but the rabbit is subject to a wide range of parasites, and it is the favorite prey of just about every predator imaginable, including stray cats and wild dogs.

The cottontail's salvation has been its ability to bounce quickly back from a low population. It is extremely prolific. During the early 1980s the cottontail picture began to brighten considerably, and the hunting forecast for the future appears reasonably bright.

Cottontails are distributed throughout Virginia, and there is probably not a city or county that does not have some bunnies. They occur within the limits of most cities. Within that wide range, however, the rabbit populations tend to be spotty, and their abundance varies from year to year.

While cottontails are found on a number of public hunting areas, they are most abundant in the farmlands of eastern Virginia and the valleys of the western mountains. Crop farming favors the cottontail because of the edges it creates. The hunter who can get permission to hunt some productive farms is lucky indeed.

The marsh rabbit is found primarily in the Dismal Swamp region.

DESCRIPTION: The cottontail rabbit varies in weight from 2 to 3 pounds live weight, and its body is mostly a grayish-brown, but this varies somewhat with the kind of cover it lives in. The rabbit's camouflage is almost perfect. It has a good deal of white on its belly and the underside of its short tail. It flashes that tail when jumped, and that is the basis for its name. The average rabbit is between a foot and a foot and a half long, and it has long 2- to 3-inch ears. The cottontail is not a fighter, relying instead upon its excellent camouflage for concealment and its speed for escape. Its hearing and sight are excellent. The marsh rabbit is darker brown, and its tail is gray underneath. Its feet are also brown. It is approximately the size of the cottontail.

HABITAT: The cottontail is an animal of the edges—the edges of pastures, hayfields, parks, yards, roads, highways, and just about anywhere heavy vegetation gives away to more open cover. They like patches of rough cover close to grass or other food. That cover can be piles of brush, brier patches, honeysuckle—any dense vegetation that gives the animal reasonable protection from its many enemies. Rabbits live out their lives in a relatively small area, seldom leaving it unless forced to do so. The marsh rabbit lives in marshes and feeds on marsh grasses.

SEASONS: November, December, and January are the traditional rabbit-hunting months in Virginia, though the month of February has now been added east of the Blue Ridge Mountains. This change may not endure for long.

GOOD COUNTIES: Rabbits are found throughout the state except at the highest elevations, but they are most abundant in the Shenandoah Valley farmlands. The marsh rabbit is most abundantly in the coastal area.

HUNTING METHODS: The pint-sized little beagle hound is the very heart of cottontail hunting. Without the little hounds, rabbit hunting becomes a somewhat solitary kind of hunting. Sizable packs of hounds, usually five to ten dogs, are often put down in rabbit country, though a hunter can do fine with a pair of dogs or even a lone one. Hunters are guided to rabbit country by scouting and sighting a number of animals near dusk, by finding rabbit droppings, and late in winter by observing their tracks in fresh snow. The droppings are small piles of pea-sized dark, round pellets that are fairly easy to spot. The animal's back feet leave oblong, solid imprints in the snow that tend to widen from the back to front. The front feet make much smaller but like-shaped imprints.

Once the dogs are down in the selected hunting terrain, the hunter can contribute by stomping on brush piles, kicking clumps of grass, and wading through honeysuckle in an effort to get a rabbit up and going. The usual mistake is to move too rapidly. The modern cottontail seems to feel its best defense is to take full advantage of its excellent camouflage and remain concealed. The hunter can walk within a couple of feet of a rabbit, and it will hug its form—unless the hunter stops. That is when the animal becomes suspicious, apparently feeling it has been detected. It is then likely to flush from its form.

Most beagle owners refuse to shoot a rabbit on the jump, preferring to let the dogs have their fun and enjoy the music of the chase. The cottontail will almost always return to the area from which it is jumped. That is home. It may run a tight circle and return quickly, but many older rabbits cover an amazing amount of country before returning. Hunters like to remain in the area, take up stands along likely return routes, and await the rabbit's return. Stands should offer good views of old roads, clearings, or other such spots the rabbit must cross. These give good fields of fire. A cottontail is seldom running flat out on the return trip. It has no reason to do so. The short-legged little hounds are no threat, and the cottontail has no trouble maintaining a safe distance. It hops along, stops frequently, and turns on the speed only when it has to cross a clearing or the hounds press too closely.

The hunter who does not own hounds has a number of choices. He and a partner, or even the lone hunter, can walk crisscross patterns through likely rabbit cover, moving slowly, stopping frequently, and kicking or stomping on likely cover. This calls for fast shooting at a target moving rapidly away. The inexperienced hunter will often shoot behind the fleeing bunny. An interesting time to hunt cottontails is after a fresh snow when rabbit tracks lace good habitat. Tracking is easy once you unravel a trail from the maze of tracks. One trail will lead out of the confusion and off to a nearby brush pile or other cover. If there are no tracks leaving that cover, then the hunter has his quarry located. The hunter armed with bow and arrow or a little .22-caliber rimfire rifle will want to search the cover bit by bit, hoping to locate the rabbit and try for a head shot. The shotgunner, on the other hand, can simply kick the animal out and hope to take it going away.

There are several other options available to the hunter who prefers the little .22-caliber rimfire. One is to simply take a stand late in the day near an edge which rabbits are known to inhabit. They will venture into the open just before dusk, offering shots for the waiting hunter. Another possibility is stalking, a form of hunting that requires good eyes and a lot of patience. Experienced hunters can spot rabbits in their beds and take them with head shots. The animals' black eyes often give them away. Cottontails like to sit on the sunny side of hills in extremely cold weather.

ARMS AND AMMUNITION: All kinds of guns get put to use for hunting rabbits, but the best is a light, fast-swinging shotgun with a short barrel and bored improved cylinder or modified choke. Light field loads in size 6 are fine. The cottontail is not nearly as hard to bring to the bag as the squirrel. The rifle fan will want to use a .22-caliber rimfire with hollow-point bullets.

CARE OF THE MEAT: Rabbits should be field dressed on the spot. It can be done quickly and easily. Because of the risk of tularemia, rubber gloves should be used when field dressing and cleaning rabbits. Slit the belly skin from the apex of the V formed by the rib cavity to the anus and snap the innards out. Before putting the rabbit in the game pocket, it should be placed in a plastic bag to prevent staining the clothing. As quickly as possible, however, it should be placed in a cool place until it can be completely dressed. Completing the cleaning job back home is simple. Just remove the fur, which comes off easily, by simply ripping it off in patches; cut off the head and feet; and the rabbit is ready for the pan.

COOKING: The meat of the rabbit is dark and delicious. Young cottontails are particularly good, and some place the meat at the top of the wild game possibilities.

RABBIT RECIPES: *Fried Rabbit* is simple and tasty. Cut one rabbit into serving pieces and wipe off the excess moisture. Shake the pieces in a paper or plastic bag containing ¾ cup flour, 1 teaspoon salt, and ½ teaspoon pepper. Place in a 9-inch heavy skillet or electric skillet containing a cup of hot cooking oil, and set at medium high heat. Brown on both sides. Sprinkle with 1 cup chopped onion. When rabbit is almost done, in about 20 minutes, turn the heat to medium low and pour off the oil. Add water and let simmer for another ½ hour, or until tender. If a thickened gravy is desired, remove the rabbit from the pan and mix 2 heaping tablespoons flour and ½ cup water. Stir into contents of the pan until it comes to a boil and thickens.

Rabbit Casserole can be made by first cutting the rabbit into serving pieces and soaking in salt water. Young rabbits should be soaked 1 to 2 hours, but older ones 12 to 18 hours. Use 1 teaspoon salt per 1 quart of water. After the meat has been soaked, wrap it in a damp cloth and store overnight in a cool place. Butter a casserole dish and add a layer of rabbit pieces. Sprinkle with ½ teaspoon salt, fresh ground pepper to taste, ½ teaspoon ground thyme, and 3 large bay leaves. Add 5 slices of bacon and repeat layering until the ingredients are used up. Pour one cup of water over casserole, cover, and bake at 350° until tender. This is usually 1 to 2 hours, depending upon the age of the rabbit. Finally, remove the cover and sprinkle 1 cup of seasoned bread crumbs over the casserole, bake 30 minutes, and the dish is ready.

SQUIRRELS

There are two game squirrels in Virginia, the abundant gray and the larger but more sparsely distributed fox squirrel. The Delmarva fox squirrel, an extremely handsome animal, has been introduced to the Eastern Shore, but its numbers are limited and it will not likely be available to hunters in the near future. It is classified as an endangered species.

The little gray squirrel, the true bushytail, is a frisky, always busy animal found throughout the state. Its status as a game animal is undoubtedly highest in the mountain counties, however, where hunters of all ages and both sexes pursue the animal with zeal.

While the gray squirrel is found statewide, the big fox squirrel is found only in the western part of Virginia, generally from the Blue Ridge Mountains west. In fact, they are legal game only west of the Blue Ridge Mountains and in the northern counties of Fairfax and Loudoun.

Except for some of the coastal marsh areas, there is probably not a public hunting area in Virginia that does not offer good squirrel hunting. Attempting to pinpoint the best locations would be futile. Probably the best place to hunt squirrels is the most convenient one.

Knowledgeable hunters seek out the hardwood ridges, a spot dear to squirrel hunters everywhere. Timber cutters usually spare the hardwoods on the cliffs. They are too difficult to log, and once bared they erode badly. Consequently, the old oaks rich in mast and hollows for dens are havens for squirrels. There is no better place to hunt, and ridges are found from the eastern Piedmont region, where the terrain levels off into the coastal plains, to the high western mountains.

Another favorite location for the squirrel hunter is the hickory grove, or even a lone hickory laden with nuts. Hardwoods adjacent to cornfields are also good in the fall before the corn is harvested.

DESCRIPTION: Salt-and-pepper gray is the best way to describe the color of the gray squirrel, but it is tinged with a little buff or brown that gives it a different cast at times. Its underparts are white. Its average weight is a pound to a pound and a half, and its length is about 18 inches from the tip of its nose to the tip of its long bushy tail. The little animal is agile and seemingly always on the move except when it is crunching on a nut or dozing high in an old oak. The larger fox squirrel is almost twice the size of the gray, and its average length is over two feet. Most Virginia fox squirrels tend to be a bit more buff or brown than the gray and more grizzled in appearance. They seldom possess as much white, and they are much slower, less agile animals.

HABITAT: The gray squirrel is primarily an animal of the big woods, preferring large stands of hardwood timber, but it will settle for much less than that. The animal is fairly adaptable and is often found in pine forests, though such cover is far from ideal. It tends to live near the edges, but rich hickory groves and mast-laden oaks may keep it deep in the woods. The fox squirrel prefers a different type of habitat, the more open, park-like lands with rows of oaks, the river valleys, and the farmlands. It is seldom found deep in the forests, and the big woods are not to its liking.

SEASONS: Squirrel seasons are long in Virginia, beginning as early as the first of September in a few southern counties, and from then until the end of January there is squirrel hunting somewhere in the state. The general season, however, runs from early November through January. Squirrels are also legal during the mid-October to early November bowhunting season.

GOOD COUNTIES: Gray squirrels are found throughout the state, and good concentrations are likely to occur just about anywhere. Fox squirrels are found in Fairfax and Loudoun counties and west of the Blue Ridge Mountains.

HUNTING METHODS: Countless numbers of squirrels are killed by hunters out after other game such as turkeys, rabbits, grouse, and so on, but most serious hunters take them either by still-hunting or waiting on a stand. Still-hunting can be an exciting, challenging way to hunt. The hunter moves slowly and as quietly as possible through hardwoods known to have squirrels or having the appearance of good squirrel country and stops frequently to look and listen. The bark of a squirrel often gives its location away, or the hunter might sight one in the distance and attempt to stalk within range. Stalking is challenging and a good training for hunting in general. The hunter uses the trunks of large trees, hills, and ravines to conceal his approach.

The stand hunter must scout the woods before his hunt, locate an area where the animals are feeding, and then get on the stand before dawn or an hour or so before dusk. The best stand is within gun range of a nut-laden hickory or other nut tree the animals are obviously feeding in. The litter beneath the tree will reveal the feeding activity. Later in the fall or winter when the nuts are gone, about the only place to take a stand is near a den tree. Often a whole colony of squirrels may use a single den tree. Well-used holes in the tree will help locate the best one. If dens are scarce, they build leafy nests in the crotches of trees. The stand hunter takes his game as it leaves the den in the morning or returns to it at dusk. The hunting time is more limited than it is at the early fall nut tree. Since nut or den trees may attract a number of squirrels, experienced stand hunters often refrain from retrieving their game when it falls, particularly if they are hunting with a light .22-caliber rifle. Getting up from a stand to pick up a downed squirrel can be much more disturbing than the mild report of the rifle or shotgun. It is better to make sure the animal is dead, mark down its location, and let it lie until the end of the hunt. Soon the game will be moving again, and there will be another opportunity to shoot. If the hunter has selected a good location, he may bag his limit of bushytails without ever moving from his stand.

Many hunters also combine squirrel and duck hunting by drifting down a wooded stream in a canoe or light boat. Squirrels coming to the water's edge to drink offer good shooting, and so do those in the trees near the stream. Even if he is hunting squirrels only, however, the canoe or boat hunter is limited to the shotgun in Virginia; shooting a rifle from a boat is illegal.

A few hunters also use squirrel dogs when in pursuit of bushytails. Good squirrel dogs come from a variety of breeds, but most of them seem to hunt by sight instead of with their noses. The dog's job is to locate the squirrels and tree them until the hunter can arrive with his firearm.

ARMS AND AMMUNITION: Squirrel hunting attracts both shotgun and rifle fans, and also a few archers. The shotgun should be bored full or modified, but gauge or barrel length is of little consequence. Some hunters even do well with the little .410 gauge. The squirrel is reasonably tough, however, and high brass shells are recommended. Size 6 shot is a good choice. The .22-caliber rifle is the choice of many squirrel hunters; any caliber larger than that is too powerful. Riflemen who are good enough to make head shots will do fine with solid-point bullets, but most are better off with hollow-points. A squirrel shot through the midsection with a solid-point bullet may make it to the den to die a slow death, but a hollow-point will drop it instantly. Broadhead arrows are legal for squirrel hunters, but many prefer the blunt small game tips. Squirrels are legal game during the special bowhunting season that runs from mid-October into November.

CARE OF THE MEAT: If practical, the squirrel should be field dressed at once, though this is not often done. Usually the time between the bagging of a squirrel and cleaning it is fairly brief. Field dressing the animal is simply a matter of slitting the belly from the edge of the rib cavity to the anus and removing the intestines and other organs. If it is to be carried in a game pocket, it should be placed in a plastic bag to prevent staining the clothing.

COOKING: Usually those squirrels taken in October and early November are the tastiest because many of them are still young and tender. Regardless of its age, however, the squirrel, whether it is a nut-fattened gray or a jumbo fox, is excellent eating. Just ask any mountain family.

SQUIRREL RECIPES: *Brunswick Stew* made with squirrels is a favorite throughout Virginia. The ingredients are 2 quartered squirrels, 2 teaspoons salt, 1 can condensed tomato soup or 1 cup canned tomatoes, 1 onion sliced thin, 2 potatoes also sliced thin, 1 cup green lima beans, 1 tablespoon sugar, salt and pepper, 1 can whole-kernel corn, and ¼ pound of butter. Place the pieces of squirrel in a deep kettle with 2 teaspoons of salt and cover with water. Simmer for about an hour and a half or until tender. Remove the squirrels and debone them. Cut into 1-inch chunks, return the meat to the broth in the kettle, and add the tomato soup or stewed tomatoes, onion, potatoes, lima beans, sugar, and salt and pepper to taste. Cook until the potatoes and beans are tender, add the corn and butter, and cook another 5 minutes.

For *Baked Squirrel* roll pieces of 2 or more squirrels in seasoned flour and brown in vegetable fat heated in a frying pan on top of stove. Place the squirrels in a casserole dish and cover with 1 can mushroom soup mixed with 1 can chicken broth. Cook in a slow oven at 325° until tender. Add one 4-ounce can of mushrooms and cook for an additional 10 minutes.

Upland Birds

For generations the lovable and popular bobwhite quail was the very heart of bird hunting in Virginia. In fact, when someone mentioned bird hunting, it was automatically assumed that the bird under consideration was the bobwhite. Bird hunters were quail hunters, bird dogs were pointers or setters trained to hunt quail, and bird guns were light, open-bored shotguns used to hunt quail. That was the picture in Virginia from long before the Civil War right up to World War II. It was the day of family farms and patch farming that left plenty of edges and cover for the quail. The quail and quail hunting flourished. There was

For generations the bobwhite quail was the number one game bird in Virginia, but today the dove may have taken over that spot. (Photograph by Wallace Hughes)

never any doubt that the bobwhite quail was the very heart of bird hunting in Virginia. There were, of course, ruffed grouse in the mountains, a few woodcocks, some interest in snipes, and doves, but doves seldom drew a second glance.

The picture is quite different today. The dove that no one took seriously is now by far the most abundant game bird in Virginia, and possibly the number one game bird in the state, and grouse hunting is at an all-time high. A few hunters have discovered the joy of woodcock hunting, but the snipe is still a neglected bird. The biggest change in bird hunting, however, has come with respect to the once popular bobwhite. There are still many avid quail hunters in Virginia, but the hunting has dropped off sharply, reflecting a trend that began near the end of World War II when family farms began to disappear, and in their place came commercial farms that left little in the way of cover and food for the quail. There has also been a gradual shift from crop farming to cattle and grass. Pheasant have been introduced, and there is currently a brief season in November, but wildlife managers hold little hope for the future of pheasant hunting in Virginia.

Still, with a half dozen birds to chose from, interest in bird hunting in Virginia is high.

DOVE

Abundant and more accessible to most hunters, the dove may have replaced the long popular bobwhite quail as the number one game bird in Virginia. Virginia dove hunters take over a million birds annually.

The mourning dove, the only dove found in the state, nests here, and many of the birds taken every season are resident doves. There are good flights of migrants also, but these birds are more likely to arrive late in the year when the harsh weather to the north sends them south.

The commercial farming operations that feature large fields of grain may have eliminated quail cover, but they have proved attractive to the mourning dove. Doves appear to be increasing slightly in the state in spite of the heavy hunting pressure they are subjected to every fall.

Doves are found all over Virginia except for the deep woods and higher mountains, but they are most abundant in the Piedmont region. They are found primarily in the agricultural areas from the Eastern Shore to far Lee County and from the grainfields along the Potomac River to the dove-rich country near the North Carolina line.

The majority of the birds bagged annually in Virginia come from private farms. Some farmers grant hunting permission, and others charge a fee—usually modest. There are also a number of public hunting areas managed for doves. Fort Pickett near Blackstone is in the heart of the very best dove-hunting country in the state, and the managed dove fields often provide good shooting. There are also a number of wildlife management areas where fields are managed for doves; among them are Amelia, Briery Creek, Chickahominy, Elm Hill, Hardware River, James River, Powhatan, and White Oak Mountain.

Hunting is limited to Wednesdays and Saturdays on most public hunting lands managed for doves.

DESCRIPTION: Mostly gray with a pinkish-beige breast and belly, the mourning dove is an attractive, graceful bird with a small head, streamlined body, and a long pointed tail. The average adult bird will weigh from 4 to 5 ounces, but birds taken early in the season are often the young of the year and smaller. The birds are extremely prolific, breeding a half dozen times during the late spring and summer. Their numbers would be greater if the birds were better nest builders. Their flimsy nests are often destroyed by storms.

HABITAT: The dove drinks at least once a day and so is never far from water. It feeds on small seeds, corn, peanuts, and various grains. It prefers open spaces for both drinking and feeding, and it will avoid tall grass, weeds, and other vegetation. For feeding it prefers freshly harvested fields where there is limited vegetation and also freshly cultivated fields where it picks up the sown seeds. When watering, it prefers sandbars and the bare banks of lakes, ponds, and streams.

SEASONS: September and October are the major dove-hunting months in Virginia, but there is also a late season the last week or so in December and early January.

GOOD COUNTIES: Doves are found throughout Virginia, but the best hunting usually occurs in the agricultural region of the southeastern part of the state.

HUNTING METHODS: The most popular way to hunt doves is to station hunters all around a grainfield or a freshly sown field in which the birds are feeding. The hunters attempt to intercept the birds as they fly to and from the field. The constant shooting keeps the birds flying; otherwise, they settle down in the middle of the field beyond the range of the hunters. The fast birds, swerving and dipping as they fly, are tough to hit, and the hunter who can bag his limit of twelve doves with a couple of boxes of shells is above average. Lone hunters, or small parties, can use decoys placed in trees, or they can station themselves along flyways the birds are known to use as they fly to and from a field. Some hunters also take stands near watering holes or roosting areas. Camouflage clothing helps, and most hunters build scant blinds or use natural ones.

ARMS AND AMMUNITION: The dove hunter needs an open-bored shotgun, light and easy to swing. Gauges 12 to 20 are fine, and most prefer an improved cylinder choke. Field loads in size 8 are the usual choice in ammunition.

CARE OF THE MEAT: Doves taken on a hot September afternoon should be kept in a cool place if at all possible. Usually there is some shade nearby. On most afternoons there are long stretches between shooting, and one way to pass the time is to pluck the birds already bagged. This way, a hunter might end the hunt with most of his birds already plucked. All that remains to be done is to gut the birds and wash them in cold water. Some hunters prefer to pop out the breasts of doves and discard the rest—of which there is very little in the way of meat. A dove's wings and legs are hardly worth the effort. To pop out the breasts, first clip off the wings and break the skin at the base of the neck on the breast side. Insert a finger or thumb in the V formed by the breasts and pull sharply. The breast will pop out. Wash it in cold water, and it is ready for the pan or the freezer.

COOKING: The meat of the mourning dove is dark but excellent, particularly the breasts. Some insist the meat is better when the feathers are plucked from the bird instead of popping out the breasts as described above, but either way the dove is excellent on the table.

DOVE RECIPES: *Broiled or Grilled Doves* are easy to do and very tasty. Dip the birds in butter and cook them on a charcoal grill or under the oven broiler. Cook 5 to 10 minutes, remove, and salt and pepper lightly. This is an ideal way to cook dove breasts.

Charlie Elliott of Georgia lives near some of the best dove hunting in America, and *Dove Pie* is one of his favorites. He recommends 6 to 8 doves, 4 boiled eggs, Crisco, flour, celery, an onion, butter, nutmeg, salt, black pepper, and water. Season the doves with salt and black pepper and boil until they are tender. This usually takes about an hour. Add a small piece of celery and half an onion and continue to cook until they are done. With Crisco, cold water, and flour, make enough pastry for 2 thin crusts, Place first crust in the bottom of a 3-inch-deep square pan. Place boiled doves in the pan on the crust and pour stock from doves for gravy. Chop eggs over the doves, and sprinkle with a little nutmeg and black pepper. Chop plenty of butter in the pan with the doves, and sift a dusting of flour over the doves and gravy. Place a very thin crust over the top and bake until a golden brown.

GROUSE

Few kinds of hunting are more demanding physically than grouse hunting. In Virginia the best hunting is in the mountains, where the terrain is often steep and the cover thick. If the hunter owns good dogs, however, he can let them do much of the rough work. Today the grouse and quail probably run neck-in-neck in popularity, with the grouse favored in the western part of the state and the quail in the east. It has not always been so, but the dropping off of the quail population has caused many bird hunters to show more interest in the ruffed grouse.

Generally, grouse are found from the Blue Ridge Mountains west, but the eastern slopes of the mountains are good, and so are some of the western Piedmont foothills. The Piedmont hunting is spotty at best, though there is usually some good shooting along the James River and at the Marine Corps base at Quantico. For years the best grouse hunting has been found in Southwest Virginia.

There is almost unlimited public hunting land for the grouse hunter. In fact, few hunters in Virginia enjoy a wider choice of public hunting land. The George Washington and Jefferson national forests provide over a million acres of public hunting land for the grouse man. Some of it is rarely ever hunted. Most of the western wildlife management areas also hold grouse.

DESCRIPTION: The ruffed grouse is one of three forest grouse found in America, and the only grouse that lives in Virginia. The birds are about the size of a bantam chicken, or an average of a pound to a pound and a half in weight. Like all members of the big grouse family, its legs are feathered almost to the feet. Color phases vary from a reddish brown to almost gray, but most birds found in Virginia lean toward the lighter brown phase. Their fan-shaped tails make the birds easy to identify, but many hunters rely upon the bird's explosive flush to tell them a bird has left the ground.

HABITAT: Though the ruffed grouse is a bird of the forest and can survive in the deep woods, it prefers more open, scrub timber, where the sun finds its way to the earth and briers and vines spring up. While it likes conifers for protection from the winter weather, it uses the more open areas for sunning and dusting and for the seeds, berries, and grapes they offer for food. The modern forestry practice of clear-cutting patches of woodlands favors the ruffed grouse. Abandoned farms and old orchards are particularly good, though they offer a transition kind of hunting that falls off as the land grows back into forest.

SEASONS: November, December, and January are grouse-hunting months in Virginia both east and west of the Blue Ridge Mountains.

HUNTING METHODS: The serious grouse hunter employs well-trained dogs, usually one of the pointing breeds, though some hunters also use flushing dogs. The pointing dogs locate the birds and hold them on a point until the hunter arrives, but the flushing breeds work back and forth before the hunter, always staying within gun range, and rout the birds out. The pointing breeds, usually an English pointer or setter, are the preference of most Virginia grouse hunters. The wide-ranging dogs so popular for quail hunting do not make good grouse dogs. The plodding dog that ranges close to the hunter, takes its time, and moves cautiously once it scents birds is the choice of the grouse hunter. Because grouse are extremely jumpy and often flush wild even ahead of the most cautious dog, many grouse hunters like to approach a grouse point from the front instead of moving in behind the dogs as is customary. Caught between the dog and the hunter, the bird may hold a little longer on the ground, or if it does flush wild, its flight may carry it within shotgun range.

Many hunt grouse successfully without dogs. They know their hunting country well, know where the birds are likely to be found, and simply walk them up. The best approach is to walk a zigzag pattern through good cover and pause frequently. The birds often flush when the hunter pauses, apparently feeling they have been spotted.

ARMS AND AMMUNITION: A light, fast-swinging, open-bored shotgun is the arm of the grouse hunter. The shooting is usually fast, sometimes little more than a snap shot. The boring should be improved cylinder and the gauge 20 to 12. High brass, size 6 shot are the usual choice, but the grouse is not a tough bird. Some hunters prefer the lighter field loads in size 8.

CARE OF THE MEAT: In extremely cold weather it may not be necessary, but field dressing the birds on the spot is bound to improve the taste. Doing so is simple. Just slit the belly to open the bird and remove the intestines and other organs. Place the bird in a plastic bag before putting it in the game pocket. The birds should be placed in an ice chest and kept cool as soon as possible. Back home, the heads are removed, the birds are plucked dry and washed clean, and they are ready for the pan or freezer.

COOKING: Grouse hunters insist the grouse is the tastiest bird that flies, though others might prefer the dove, quail, or some other favorite. In any event, the grouse is a delight on the platter, and being sizable, a couple of birds make a good meal. Its meat is a bit dry but very tasty.

GROUSE RECIPES: *Fried Grouse* can be prepared in the same manner as fried chicken. Cut the birds into frying-size pieces, salt and pepper, and fry until pieces are golden brown. Use bacon fat to cover the bottom of the pan. The pieces should be turned so they are browned evenly on all sides. When they are well browned, cover the skillet and cook slowly over moderate heat for approximately 30 minutes.

A simple *Grouse Casserole* can be made by cutting the bird into serving pieces and removing all of the shot. Mix 1 can of cream of chicken soup with 2 or 3 finely chopped carrots and 1 or 2 finely chopped onions. Pour the soup mixture into the bottom of a casserole and place pieces of the bird in the mixture. Sprinkle lightly with garlic salt and cover with several strips of hickory-smoked bacon. Cover and bake for 2 to 3 hours at low heat. Baste with soup mixture several times during the cooking process.

PHEASANTS

The pheasant is not native to Virginia, or to America, for that matter. The birds were introduced from Asia over 100 years ago, and in parts of the United States they offer excellent hunting. Various species of pheasants have been released in Virginia by the Commission of Game and Inland Fisheries, but none show much promise. There are a few pheasant scattered about Virginia, some from former releases made by the commission and others that stray from private shooting preserves or privately owned flocks; and there is a brief season on pheasant, but the harvest is extremely low.

Many shooting preserves stock ring-necked pheasant, and this is about the only satisfactory hunting in Virginia. Pheasant never seem to lose their wild instincts even when reared in capitivity, and birds released in the wild quickly assume their native instincts.

DESCRIPTION: The male ring-necked pheasant, often called the cockbird, is a gaudy, handsome bird with a green head, a red mask arount its eyes, and a long tail. The general color of its body is brown, but it is mixed with edgings of black and a bit of green and red near the base of its tail. The female lacks the bright colors and is a more subdued brown. The cock is noted for cackling as it takes to the wing. The birds average from 2 to 4 pounds.

HABITAT: Pheasant flourish best where there are good croplands, but they also need a mixture of grass and brush nearby.

SEASONS: Pheasant hunting generally parallels the quail season in Virginia—early November through January, but not into February as is true of the eastern quail season.

GOOD COUNTIES: None, though the most birds are probably on the Eastern Shore and in the northern Shenandoah Valley.

HUNTING METHODS: Pheasant can be hunted in a variety of ways. Some hunters use pointing dogs, but the birds tend to run on the ground and do not hold well for dogs. Other hunters like flushing dogs, which fan back and forth before the hunter but always stay within shotgun range. Many hunters simply walk the birds up, forming a line if there are several hunters and combing good pheasant cover. Pheasant drives are also popular. Hunters split up with part waiting at the end of rows of corn while the rest walk the rows and drive the birds to them.

ARMS AND AMMUNITION: Most pheasant hunters like heavy loads and reasonably tight chokes. The birds are tough, and shots do not often come at close range. High brass size 4 to 6 loads and a 12-gauge shotgun with a modified choke are a popular combination, though some hunters prefer a full-choke barrel.

CARE OF THE MEAT: As is true of all game birds, the pheasant should be field dressed on the spot. Just open the bird and remove the intestines. It can be plucked or skinned later. Keep it cool, in an ice chest if possible.

COOKING: The delicious white meat of the pheasant rates near the top, or possibly at the top, among the game birds of America. The pheasant is an excellent eating bird, though the old cocks can be tough. Hunters are about evenly divided between plucking and skinning the birds. Skinning is faster, but many insist the plucked birds are tastier.

PHEASANT RECIPES: *Fried Pheasant* is much like southern-fried chicken. The ingredients, in addition to 1 pheasant per person, cut into frying pieces, include butter or cooking oil, salt, pepper, flour, and milk. Salt and pepper each piece to taste and dredge in the flour. Place in a heavy skillet holding ¼ inch of oil, cover, and cook over medium heat until brown. Brown both sides. During the last few minutes of cooking, remove the cover but continue to cook until pieces are golden brown. Remove the meat, pour off the excess oil, and add flour to the residue. Stir until the flour is light brown. Add the milk slowly, stirring constantly, until it begins to boil, and the preferred thickness is attained. Salt and pepper.

The ingredients for *Broiled Pheasant* are 1 or 2 birds, butter or margarine, salt, and pepper. Cut the birds in halves lengthwise, brush on melted butter or margarine inside as well as out, and rub with salt and pepper. Place under the broiler and brown on both sides. Remove from the broiler, turn the heat down to 325°, and brush the birds again with butter or margarine. Wrap each half separately in aluminum foil, completely sealing the edges. Place on a cookie sheet or in a large pan and bake in the oven for about an hour. Large birds may require a bit more time.

QUAIL

Numerous books have been written about hunting the bob-white quail, and some of them have become classics. Over the generations no bird has been more popular, not only in Virginia but all over the South. It so nearly fits the mold of the ideal game bird—handsome, excellent on the table, reasonably abundant, explosive when it flushes, and, best of all, it holds well for a pointing dog. That trait alone has endeared "old Bob" to generations of hunters who place nothing above moving in behind a brace of staunchly pointing bird dogs.

The quail is extremely popular among many hunters, particularly the older ones who remember the hunting as it was in the old days. While not as good as it once was, there is still good quail hunting in Virginia, and those who own good dogs and spend the hours in the field will find birds.

The bobwhite is primarily a bird of the agricultural lands, and where such exists it is found throughout the state from the flat coastal plains of the Eastern Shore to the remote valleys of the west. It loves abandoned farms, especially old croplands rich in seeds and weeds. It also frequents freshly cutover woodlands and young pine plantations.

The most successful quail hunters own excellent dogs, usually more than one, and they own dogs good at locating single birds as well as coveys. Coveys often flush wild, not allowing the treasured covey shot, but if the hunter can follow their flight and mark down where they alight, he can enjoy some excellent shooting for the scattered birds. While the coveys are often found in the open, they invariably take to the rough cover when flushed. This may be a nearby hardwood lot, pine forests, swamps, thickets, or other cover. The shooting is tricky but exciting. For this type of hunting the hunter needs a strong-nosed, patient dog that will take the time to locate the single birds. English setters or pointers are still the choice of most bird hunters, but other breeds such as the Brittany and German short-haired pointers are seen more and more in the quail fields. Wide-ranging pointers or setters can be difficult to keep up with in much of the thick cover that the modern quail hunter must work.

The best quail hunting is found on private lands, usually crop farms, and many hunters seek this kind of hunting territory. Many even lease farms for hunting. Both Fort A. P. Hill near Bowling Green and Fort Pickett near Blackstone offer good quail hunting. One of these military reservations could well be the best bet for the quail hunter who must rely upon public hunting land. There are also quail on a number of the wildlife management areas in the Piedmont region and in Southside Virginia, but the hunting is not as likely to be as good as that found on private lands.

One good possibility for the hunter who is limited to public hunting lands is the thousands of acres of corporate timberlands open to public hunting. Most of these lands are managed for fast-growing pine, and young pine plantations can provide good hunting for the first four or five years after they are planted with seedlings. Westvaco and some of the other companies will direct the quail hunter to such land.

Watching the dogs work, come on point, and then hold staunchly is one of the joys of quail hunting. Few other forms of hunting can approach this kind of thrill. Add fast wing shooting at a handsome bird, and you have all of the ingredients of a fine day afield.

DESCRIPTION: A small, chunky bird noted for its cheery call, the average bobwhite quail weighs about 6 ounces, but some will go to 9 ounces. Its basic color is brown, but it is flecked heavily with white and buff. The throat of the male is milky white, and a white band runs from the base of its beak past the eyes and along its outer neck. In the female the throat and line are buff, and this is the most accurate way to tell the two apart. Many experienced hunters say they can pick the cockbirds out in flight.

HABITAT: Quail fare best in agricultural lands that feature grain such as wheat, and where some edges and food are left for the birds.

Farms where a lot of lespedeza is grown for hay are also popular places for the birds. Open pinewoods, brushy fields, and abandoned farms are also good. The birds also like some rough cover nearby. It offers then escape from the weather as well as predators.

SEASONS: November, December, and January are hunting months in Virginia, and the season runs well into February east of the Blue Ridge Mountains.

GOOD COUNTIES: The best hunting is found in the southeastern part of Virginia, generally south of the James River.

HUNTING METHODS: Pointing dogs are the very heart of quail hunting, and hunting without them can be frustrating and a hit-and-miss affair at the best. The hunter puts his dogs down in good cover and generally gives them just about complete freedom in locating the birds. He may direct them to a degree by whistles and hand signals. Once the dogs point the birds, the hunter moves rapidly in and attempts to take some game from the covey rise. He also has to keep an eye on the escaping birds so that he can lead the dogs to the scattered single ones. These often offer the best shooting as the scattered birds are more likely to sit tightly for the pointing dogs than will a complete covey. Dogs are also all but essential in locating dead birds that often fall in rough cover where the naked eye of the hunter is far from good at separating the dead quail from the surrounding cover.

The dogless hunter might find a few birds by concentrating his efforts in what appears to be the best cover. He may walk up a few, but the explosive flush of the birds may be so noisy and unexpected that he will have trouble getting himself together for a fast shot.

ARMS AND AMMUNITION: A light, 20-gauge shotgun with a 26-inch barrel bored improved cylinder is best for hunting quail. Load it with size 8 field loads. Some may prefer the 16 or 12 gauge, and some real experts even hunt with the little .410 gauge, but it is not generally recommended. Fine quail-hunting guns are treasured possessions, often passed on from generation to generation, but there are plenty of good ones on the market for the modern hunter.

CARE OF THE MEAT: Quail, particularly if the weather is warm as it is early in the season, should be field dressed and kept in an ice chest if possible. Just open up the birds and remove the intestines and other organs. Many hunters spot hunt today, moving by jeep or pickup truck from one good area to another. When this is the case, it is easy to carry an ice chest in the vehicle and deposit the birds there before moving on to another field. For generations the only accepted way to dress a quail was to pluck it, and this can be done dry, but today there is a move toward skinning the birds because it is faster. To skin a quail, clip the wings off, break the skin at the throat, insert a finger or thumb, and pull sharply, separating the breast from the neck, back, and skin. With the breast clear, skin out the legs, and the bird is ready to be washed for the pan or freezer.

QUAIL RECIPES: *Fried Quail* is much like fried chicken. The meat is white and delicious. Some like to add a couple of small pieces of chicken when frying quail. The ingredients are 6 or 8 quail (plus several pieces of chicken, if desired), oregano, flour, cooking oil, salt, and pepper. Salt and pepper the birds and dust lightly with oregano. Roll in flour and place in a preheated heavy skillet containing 4 tablespoons of vegetable oil. Brown at not more than 325°. When they are brown on all sides, add a small amount of water to the skillet, cover tightly, and simmer until the birds are tender. Add a little water if needed to keep them from getting too brown.

For *Roast Quail* it is best to pluck the birds instead of skinning them. Stuff the body cavities with buttered bread crumbs mixed with chopped pecans. Roll the birds in flour. Place then in a casserole and pour over them some browned butter that has been mixed with hot water—not too much. Add ⅛ cup sherry per bird, cover, and bake in a slow 300° oven until tender, approximately 1½ hours.

SNIPE

The Wilson's or common snipe is found in swamps and wetlands throughout Virginia, but it is more prevalent in the eastern part of the state, particularly in the Tidewater region. Hunters tend to confuse the snipe and woodcock, generally referring to woodcocks as snipes. Both are migratory birds, but they are seldom found together. Snipes frequently fly over waterfowl blinds, and duck hunters probably bag more of them than most other hunters. Slipping along over the marshes, the snipe can present a challenging target. The snipe favors more open areas than does the woodcock, and it uses seasonal wetlands that may dry up during the summer months.

Very few hunters go out specifically for snipes, but in addition to duck hunters, quail, rabbit, and even a few grouse hunters bag them. It is an underharvested bird in Virginia, one that can support a lot more hunting than it does.

The birds migrate mostly at night, but they seldom appear in flocks. Sometimes they appear scattered rather thickly through good cover, but not together. The hunter will usually jump them one at a time, however, and seldom in pairs or flocks.

DESCRIPTION: Its coloration somewhere between brown and gray, the snipe has a boldly striped head and a long bill. The long bill is used for digging in the mud and soft earth for insects, crustaceans, worms, and snails. The birds average 4 to 5 ounces.

HABITAT: Bogs, wet meadows, swamps, and marshes are the home of the snipe.

SEASONS: Mid-October through January is snipe-hunting time in Virginia.

GOOD COUNTIES: Snipes are most abundant in the eastern Piedmont and the coastal regions of the state.

HUNTING METHODS: Snipes are hunted so infrequently in Virginia that serious hunting methods have not been developed, but walking them up is the usual way. Of course, a knowledge of the country and the areas the birds are using is helpful. If there is a breeze, move with it. The birds flush with the wind and then either swing across it or back into it. They may swing back over the hunter's head, giving him an excellent shot.

ARMS AND AMMUNITION: The snipe hunter needs a light gun, and something in the 20 to 16 gauge will serve well. It should have a short, open-bored barrel, and field loads of size 9 shot are the usual recommendation.

CARE OF THE MEAT: The fact that snipes were once slaughtered by market hunters speaks for the little bird's value on the table. Many are taken during warm weather, and like all game birds they should be field dressed. Open them up and remove the intestines and other organs, and keep as cool as possible.

SNIPE RECIPES: Try *Baked Snipe* by placing the breasts on sheets of aluminum foil. Cover each breast with dry onion soup and 3 butter patties. Close foil and bake at 350° for about 1 hour. This recipe can be strengthened by adding ¼ cup of wine.

For *Grilled Snipes*, split the birds in half. Make a paste of butter, grated lemon rind, and parsley and rub on cleaned birds. Grill over medium heat for 1 hour, basting frequently with lemon-butter.

WOODCOCK

The woodcock, often confused with the snipe, is found throughout the state where there is suitable habitat, but it is rarely abundant in Virginia, though good concentrations occur occasionally. It is a migratory bird, and good flights pass through the state, but they are highly unpredictable. Few forms of hunting are marked by more uncertainty. There are also scattered populations of resident birds that probably never leave the state.

One comforting thing about woodcock hunting, however, is that once a good location is found, it is likely the birds will return to it year after year. Then the problem becomes one of catching them when they are there. Woodcocks often migrate at night, and they can move in overnight, stay awhile, and move on again.

Attempting to pinpoint the best woodcock hunting in Virginia is all but impossible. There are always a few migratory birds that follow the mountains south, but they are scarce in the Southwest Virginia. Some hunters enjoy good success along the Shenandoah River, and to the east bird hunters at Fort Pickett pick up good bags occasionally. They are also found at Fort A. P. Hill and on the Quantico Marine Corps base.

The tendency of the birds to sit tightly for a pointing dog is one of the joys of woodcock hunting. Many hunters like to start their young dogs on woodcocks.

DESCRIPTION: Brown on their backs, the breasts of woodcocks are almost orange, and there are black bands across the top of the head. The bird's long bill, chunky body, short neck, and short, rounded tail make it easy to identify. Once he has seen a woodcock, the hunter has no further trouble knowing the bird. The wing is also rounded but noticeable only in flight. Its eyes, set far back on its head, allow it to see in all directions without moving its head and neck. The woodcock is slightly larger than the bobwhite quail, averaging 6 to 10 ounces.

HABITAT: The woodcocks' preferred habitat includes alder thickets, moist, leafy bottoms, and wooded swamps, but they are often flushed on the sides of hills where they appear to be enjoying the winter sun. Its livelihood depends upon there being available soft ground it can probe with its long bill, primarily for worms. Frozen ground sends it scurrying south.

SEASONS: November and December are woodcock-hunting months in Virginia.

GOOD COUNTIES: Not really good anywhere but best from the Shenandoah River east in the state.

HUNTING METHODS: A close-working pointing dog is the road to woodcock-hunting success. English setters are popular, but so are pointers and Brittany spaniels. If the hunter is successful in locating some boggy areas where the birds are stopping temporarily, the dogs will do the rest. The woodcock puts out plenty of scent, and it will hold well for the dog. In fact, they will sometimes sit until almost stepped upon by the hunter.

The dogless hunter has no recourse except to walk slowly through known woodcock cover, stopping frequently, with the hope that he will flush some birds. Experienced hunters do this successfully, but they know areas where the birds are likely to be found. Often the same area furnishes them good shooting year after year.

ARMS AND AMMUNITION: The woodcock hunter wants a light shotgun, one that swings easily and is bored improved cylinder. The little 20 gauge loaded with sizes 8 or 9 field loads will serve well.

CARE OF THE MEAT: Many hunters do not like woodcock, insisting they have a livery taste, but others rank the timberdoodle right up there with the bobwhite quail. It depends upon one's taste, probably, but the woodcock can be tasty on the platter. Most recipes seem to dwell on the breasts of the birds, but the legs, which are white meat, are also good. Woodcocks are usually taken in cool weather, and few hunters bother to field dress them, but opening the birds to remove the intestines and other organs would improve the taste in most cases. The birds can be plucked dry, though many hunters prefer to skin them.

WOODCOCK RECIPES: For *Broiled Woodcock*, most hunters like to parboil the birds first to make them tender. Then open the bird down the back, roll it in flour, and lay it to broil with the breast down. Make gravy of 2 tablespoons flour in cold water with butter, pepper, and salt. Stir in the liquid in which the birds were parboiled. Use the gravy to serve with the birds after they have been broiled. They can also be served with bacon and toast, or slash the broiled breasts three times when done, put a little butter, pepper, and salt in each slash, and place on toast. Pour liquid from pan over them.

Parmesan Woodcock Steaks are the choice of many bird hunters. Usually the breasts only are used, but the legs can be prepared in the same manner. Parboil if the birds are old. Skin and bone 4 woodcock breasts, pound each with a meat mallet to ¼ inch thick. Salt and pepper to taste and dredge in a mixture of ½ cup each flour and Parmesan cheese. Fry in ¼ pound hot butter until golden brown, 3 to 5 minutes for each side.

Waterfowl

Ducks, a great variety of them, are the very heart of waterfowl hunting in Virginia, but there are also both Canada and snow geese and Atlantic brant along the coast. Then there are the coots and rails, not waterfowl in the true sense, but included here because they occupy much the same kind of water or marsh habitat. Like ducks, they are migratory and subject to federal regulation, though a migratory bird stamp is not required of the hunter who limits himself to rails.

Just about any kind of waterfowl hunting imaginable is available in Virginia's rich system of bays, sounds, ocean waters, tidal rivers, fast inland rivers, lakes and reservoirs, and beaver and farm ponds.

Virginia is in the Atlantic Flyway, and most of the ducks and geese that use that flyway stop off in Virginia sometime during the fall and winter seasons. The lakes and rivers in the extreme western part of the state attract a few strays from the Mississippi Flyway.

The big Chesapeake Bay attracts the diving species such as canvasbacks, redheads, scaup, and sea ducks, and the coastal marshes are favored by the black ducks. Back Bay, probably Virginia's most popular waterfowling area, draws a great variety of both diving and dabbling ducks, and the inland marshes hold black ducks, mallard, pintail, widgeon, and wood ducks. Black ducks, mallard, and woodies also frequent the inland rivers. The big lakes also draw a few diving ducks as well as dabblers.

Canada geese are reasonably abundant in the Tidewater region, and there are numerous resident populations in the Piedmont area. The American brant migrates through Virginia, offering good shooting along the Eastern Shore. Greater snow geese are also abundant in the Tidewater area, and there are big flocks of swans in the Back Bay area.

Currently swans are protected year-round in Virginia.

DUCKS

There are probably no fewer than two dozen ducks that at one time or another during the course of the year use Virginia waters. A few such as the black duck, mallard, and wood duck breed here and rarely leave the state. The rest are mostly migrants that breed to the north and pass through Virginia on their migratory routes. Seen commonly in the state, in addition to the blacks, mallard, and woodies, are gadwalls, baldpates, pintail, teal, shovelers, redheads, ring-necked ducks, canvasbacks, scaup, goldeneyes, buffleheads, old-squaws, ruddy ducks, and to a lesser extent eiders.

DESCRIPTION: The average duck bagged in Virginia will probably weigh a little less than 2 pounds. Teal are the smallest, considera-

While waterfowl hunting is best along the coast, it is fair to good throughout Virginia.

bly less than a pound, but some big mallard may tilt the scales at 4 to 5 pounds. A 2½-pound mallard is nearer average. The better eating ducks, such as the mallard, teal, and gadwall, feed mostly on vegetable matter. They are grouped generally as dabbling or puddle ducks. Diving ducks, on the other hand—such as the red-head, scaup, goldeneye, and old-squaw—also include fish, insects, and crustaceans in their diet. Their food value drops accordingly. Though they spend most of the time on the water, ducks are excellent flyers and seem equally at home in the air. The duck's legs are short, its feet webbed, and its bill more or less spatulate. Heavily feathered, some ducks lose a third of their weight when they are plucked and dressed.

HABITAT: The dabbling ducks prefer the marshes and shallow water, but many of them also frequent the rivers and inland ponds. Many such mallard also visit agricultural areas where they feed in open fields. Divers such as the scaup raft up and spend a lot of time on

open water. Most ducks spend at least part of the day in shallow water, however, where feeding conditions are favorable. Depending upon the species, ducks will be found in all kinds of water from the open ocean to tiny beaver ponds and small headwater streams.

SEASONS: Virginia hunters normally enjoy a long season split into three segments, one in early October, one in late November and early December, and one that runs from mid-December well into January.

GOOD COUNTIES: While the Tidewater counties offer the greatest concentrations of ducks, there is probably not a county in Virginia that does not offer some duck hunting.

HUNTING METHODS: Shooting over decoys from a blind is the traditional way to hunt ducks in Virginia. The setup includes a well-camouflaged blind at the edge of a marsh or over open but shallow water, a set of decoys, and either a boat or a good retrieving dog for retrieving the game. Most experienced duck hunters are also good with various duck calls. Hunters using marsh blinds can often get by without a boat or dog if the water is shallow enough to wade in hip boots or chest waders. The placing of decoys is important to the success of this kind of hunting, but regardless of how they are located before the blind, it is important that some open water be left among them for the decoying ducks. If there is a skim of ice on the water, an area should be cleared to provide some open water. When ducks approach the blind, the hunters should crouch low and remain absolutely motionless until the birds are within shooting range. Blinds can be less sophisticated than the elaborate ones seen along most coastal waters. A well-camouflaged hunter can get by with a skimpy one set up quickly just for a single hunt or even a natural one such as offered by scrubby vegetation. While coastal hunters are accustomed to putting out a lot of decoys, sometimes as many as fifty to sixty or more, the inland hunter on a river or pond can get by with less than a half dozen. Inland ducks are not accustomed to seeing large concentrations of birds on the water. Beaver ponds, farm ponds, quiet stretches of streams, and quiet coves in big lakes all offer possibilities for hunting from blinds, and points in lakes offer chances for pass shooting at ducks. Particularly popular among inland hunters is jump shooting, drifting slowly down a stream in a canoe or light boat and shooting ducks as they flush from the water. Getting within range of the wary birds is a problem. The boat or canoe should be painted a camouflage pattern or at least a subdued tone. Anything shiny should be concealed, and the hunters should be dressed in camouflage clothing. Hugging the banks of the stream helps, as ducks are often resting in cover near the shore. Most inland rivers meander, and the curves in the stream offer good cover. Hunters hug the inside banks and often surprise ducks feeding just around the bend. Jump shooters take most of their ducks as they flush before the boat, but they also frequently get chances at birds trading up and down the river. Flushed birds may also circle back over the hunters if they decide to head upstream. Some hunters like to walk the banks of streams and jump shoot, but they need a good retriever for those birds that fall in the water—and many do.

ARMS AND AMMUNITION: Ducks decoyed to a blind are usually taken at close ranges, and an open-bored shotgun is fine. Most duck hunters like 12-gauge guns, but anything from 20 to 10 gauge will work. It should be bored modified or improved cylinder. The same gun will take ducks on a jump-shooting trip. For ammunition, high brass size 6s are the usual choice. Lead shot have been outlawed in most coastal areas, however, and the only choice is the lighter steel shot. When this is the case, size 4 might be a better choice. Much depends upon the gun, and shooting both 4s and 6s is the only sure way to learn which is best.

CARE OF THE MEAT: Since ducks are usually killed during cold weather, field dressing them is unnecessary. They should be dressed as soon as possible after the hunt, however, to keep them in the best condition. Ducks can be plucked dry, but many hunters prefer to dip them in boiling water first. Others dip them in melted paraffin, let the paraffin turn hard, and then peel it off. The paraffin takes the feathers with it. Once picked, the birds should be opened and the intestines and other organs removed. Many hunters clip off the wings before plucking, because they provide very little meat.

DUCK RECIPES: For *Chesapeake Barbecued Duck*, the ingredients are ½ pound butter, ½ cup catsup, 1 tablespoon sugar, 1½ tablespoons lemon juice, 1 tablespoon Worchestershire sauce, fresh ground pepper, 1 tablespoon salt, 1 clove garlic pressed, 1 small chopped onion, and ½ teaspoon Tabasco sauce. Split whole ducks in half and flatten with a cleaver. Allow half a duck per person or one breast. Combine barbecue sauce ingredients in a saucepan, cover, and simmer for 5 minutes. Bake the duck in a flat pan at 375° for 1 hour, basting with the sauce every 10 minutes. Turn duck on the other side and cook and baste for another hour.

The ingredients for *Roast Duck*, preferably a mallard, are 1 duck, 1 tablespoon Burgundy or claret wine, 1 cup water, 1 teaspoon salt, ½ teaspoon pepper, 1 teaspoon celery salt, ½ cup chopped celery, and ½ cup chopped onion. Place the duck in a coverable pan and add wine and water. Sprinkle with salt, pepper, celery salt, chopped celery, and chopped onion. Place uncovered in oven set at 500° and leave for about 20 minutes, or until brown. Cover the pan, reduce the heat to 350°, and cook for approximately 2 hours.

GEESE

The majestic Canada goose with its white chin strap and familiar call is the first to come to mind when geese are mentioned in Virginia, but the greater snow geese, the American brant, actually a maritime goose, and the whistling swan are also found in Virginia. Swan are protected, but the other three are fair game, the brant just recently.

Canada and snow geese populations seem to be growing in Virginia, and the recent opening of a season on brant indicates that these birds are making a comeback. There is much support for an open season on swans, but it is unlikely that one will be declared anytime soon.

DESCRIPTION: The Canada goose is a gray-brown bird with a long black neck, a black head, and white patches beneath the chin and over the eyes. The average weight is 5 to 8 pounds, with some outsized males going to 11 or 12 pounds. The snow goose is smaller, averaging 6 to 7 pounds, and is all white except for its black wing tips. Its neck tends to be shorter than that of the Canada goose. The brant is much smaller than the geese, averaging 2½ to 3 pounds, and in build it more nearly resembles a duck with its somewhat stubby neck. Its head and neck are black with a white ring around the neck, and it has a white body behind a black chest. Its wings are a brownish gray. The swan, all white and much larger at 16 or 17 pounds, has a long gooselike neck.

HABITAT: The Canada goose is primarily a bird of the open water and large fields, but it is found just about all over Virginia. On the Eastern Shore huge flocks feed on agricultural lands late in January. Snow geese also feed on agricultural lands, but in Virginia they seem to spend most of the time in the marshes and open water of Back Bay. The brant is a salt-water goose, rarely found far from the ocean front, and swans are most abundant on the shallow waters of Back Bay.

SEASONS: November, December, and January are goose-hunting months in Virginia.

GOOD COUNTIES: Brant and snow geese are found only in the Tidewater region, and Canada geese are most abundant there. Canadas, however, occur just about statewide.

HUNTING METHODS: Most geese, both Canadas and snow, are taken from blinds, either over water or in grainfields. Life-size decoys are used before the water blinds, but in the fields stake blinds cut from plywood and painted gray are the usual choice. Both kinds are effective when used in combination with a good call. Young birds or lone birds looking for company are usually the easiest to decoy. Some hunters dig pit blinds in the fields, but well-concealed blinds above the ground are just as effective and easier to build. Some farmers object to pits being dug in their fields. These two types of blinds produce the bulk of the goose kill just about every year. Most other birds are taken in the course of duck hunting or occasionally by other hunters who get chance shots at the birds.

ARMS AND AMMUNITION: The goose hunter needs a full-choke shotgun in gauges 10 or 12 and size 2 to 4 shot in heavy loads. The goose is not tough to bring down, but it is a big bird and a strong one. Some hunters even use size 1 shot, particularly where steel shot are required.

CARE OF THE MEAT: Taken during the cold winter months, the goose is rarely field dressed, but it should be kept out of the sun. Geese can be plucked dry but dipping them in boiling water will make the job easier. Hunters who bag a lot of geese often invest in mechanical pluckers. They make the job much faster. Once the feathers are removed, the bird is opened up and its intestines and other organs are removed, as is the case with any game bird.

GOOSE RECIPES: *Roast Canada Goose* is a recipe supplied by Remington Farms in the heart of Maryland's best goose hunting on the Eastern Shore. The ingredients are 1 Canada goose, 2 tablespoons Burgundy or claret wine, 2 cups water, 1 tablespoon salt, 1 teaspoon pepper, 1 tablespoon celery salt, 1 cup chopped celery, and 1 cup chopped onion. Place the dressed goose in a pan with a cover. Pour wine over the goose and add water. Sprinkle with salt, pepper, celery salt, chopped celery, and chopped onion. Set oven at 500° and place uncovered goose in oven for about 20 minutes, or until brown. Cover the pan, reduce the heat to 350° and cook for 2½ to 3 hours.

Here is another approach to *Roast Wild Goose*. Stuff the dressed goose with nontart apples, close the body cavity, salt and pepper, and roast in a hot oven for 20 minutes. Then reduce the heat to a moderate level and roast until the meat is tender. Baste the bird frequently with the drippings.

COOT

The American coot is included in the waterfowl hunting regulations, though it is actually a gallinule that is not often sought by hunters. It is a marginal game bird at the best. The birds are usually abundant on Back Bay and also on some of the inland lakes such as Lake Anna and Lake Chickahominy. Coastal hunters often refer to it as blue pete.

DESCRIPTION: A relatively small bird that may average close to 1 pound, the American coot is mostly slate gray with a black head and neck and a white bill. It is often seen walking in the marshes.

HABITAT: It prefers the open water most of the day but will seek the coves and marshes for food and for protection from the weather.

SEASONS: Coots are fair game during the November, December, and January waterfowl season.

GOOD COUNTIES: Hunting is best on the waters of the tidal area.

HUNTING METHODS: Coots do not decoy, and that is one of the reasons they are not popular among hunters. Working a reed-choked shoreline, hoping to get within range before they flush, is one way to hunt them. One effective way to hunt them is to work from the open water in a boat and drive the birds slowly into a cove. If not approached too quickly or closely, they will simply swim away without flushing. Once they are in the cove, they are likely to fly back over the hunters in the boat when flushed. They prefer to fly over open water instead of going inland.

ARMS AND AMMUNITION: Any shotgun used for waterfowl will serve fine on coots. It should be bored improved cylinder or modified. Any gauge of 20 or up is fine. High brass size 6 shot are about right.

CARE OF THE MEAT: Killed during the cold months of late November, December, and January, coots are seldom field dressed, but at the end of a trip they are skinned in the manner of small game instead of plucked. They should also be trimmed of any fat that has accumulated. Some hunters prize the gizzard of the coot because it is quite large.

COOT RECIPES: *Fried Coot Breasts* are a favorite of those who like to eat coots. Fillet the breasts of 2 coots from the bone and cut off the legs. Marinate the meat for about 24 hours in a mixture of 2 quarts of water, 1 cup salt, and 1 tablespoon vinegar or cooking wine. The other ingredients include 1 cup seasoned flour, ¼ cup bacon fat or cooking oil, 2 cups milk, ¼ teaspoon garlic salt, ½ medium-sized grated onion, and a can of cream of mushroom soup. Roll the meat in the seasoned flour and fry it in the bacon fat or cooking oil until golden brown. Make a smooth paste with ½ cup of the remaining flour and some milk. Pour remaining fat out of the pan and stir in the flour paste. Then stir in the remaining milk and add the garlic salt, onion, and mushroom soup. Cover the pan and allow the meat to simmer in the sauce over low heat for 2 hours.

RAILS

Rails are really not considered waterfowl, but they live in the salt and freshwater marshes along the bay and ocean and the big tidal rivers. Their habitat is much the same as many of the more popular ducks in Virginia, and they are subject to federal regulations as are ducks and geese. Rail hunting begins early, however, and it is generally over by the time the major duck and goose seasons open. The rail hunter is not required to purchase a migratory bird hunting stamp.

There are two major rails in Virginia, the big clapper of the saltwater marshes and the little sora of the freshwater marshes. The clapper gets most of the attention, though there is plenty of good sora hunting for those willing to look for it. Much less common are the king and Virginia rails.

Clapper rail are found on both the ocean and bay sides of the Eastern Shore, and to a less extent along the western shore of the Chesapeake Bay. Several public hunting areas on the Eastern Shore offer good clapper rail hunting, and the inshore marshes of the barrier islands should be good. A hunting permit can be obtained from the Nature Conservancy. One of the most popular rail-hunting areas, however, is the broad expanse of public marshes that stretches out from Wachapreague.

The less-sought-after sora rail is found in the tidal marshes of the major rivers flowing into the Chesapeake Bay, but they are most abundant where the water ranges from fresh to brackish. Tidal marshes along rivers such as the James, Mattaponi, Pamunkey, and Rappahannock offer sora hunting, but most of it is on private land, and the permission of the owner is needed.

DESCRIPTION: The rail is a chunky, chickenlike bird with a short tail and long legs. Generally, they are weak fliers, not capable of sustained flight. The larger clapper rail is more gray than brown, and it weighs from about 10 ounces to a pound. The little sora weighs only a couple of ounces, rarely more than 3. It has a brownish back, gray underparts, and a black face patch.

HABITAT: Clappers live in the salt marshes where they skulk through the grass or walk along the mud banks. The habitat of the sora is much the same except that it is found in the freshwater marshes.

SEASONS: Mid-September to mid-November is rail-hunting time in Virginia.

GOOD COUNTIES: The counties of the Eastern Shore and those along the James, Mattaponi, Pamunkey, and Rappahannock rivers are the rail-hunting counties.

HUNTING METHODS: The traditional way to hunt both sora and clapper rails in Virginia is to hire a guide with a boat. The hunter stands in the bow of the boat while the guide poles the boat slowly through the marshes. This can be done only at high tide, however, when there is enough water in the marshes to float the boat. Unfortunately, there are few if any guides who offer this service today, but a pair of hunters can team up, one doing the poling while the other shoots from the bow of the boat. They can alternate at the poling and shooting. There is also a trend today toward wading through the marshes if the ground is firm enough, and many marshes in Virginia are firm. Hip boots or chest waders are recommended. The rail is not a fast flier, but skittering off over the marshes with its long legs dangling, it offers a challenging target.

ARMS AND AMMUNITION: Salt marshes can be tough on a shotgun, and many hunters do not like to carry their prize guns into the marshes. Any open-bored shotgun will serve the rail hunter well, and gauge is not important. If he wades, however, he will appreciate a light gun. Light field loads in size 9 are the recommended rail-hunting load, but sizes 7½ to 8 will be satisfactory.

CARE OF THE MEAT: Rail are seldom field dressed, but they should be cleaned immediately at the end of the hunt. Most rail hunts do not last over a couple of hours. Rail are usually skinned, particularly the larger clappers. The sora may be plucked. Opening the birds and removing the insides will take only a couple of minutes.

RAIL RECIPES: *Fried Rail* are easy to prepare. Dust the birds with seasoned flour and fry them in butter. When they are well browned, lower the heat, cover the pan, and let them simmer for about 20 minutes. For gravy, remove the rail to a hot plate and stir enough flour in the drippings to absorb them; then gradually add milk until the gravy is of the right consistency.

For *Roast Rail* the birds should be plucked instead of skinned, and this recipe should be particularly good for the little sora. Stuff the body cavities with buttered bread crumbs mixed with chopped pecans. Roll the birds in flour, place them in a casserole, and pour over them some brown butter that has been mixed with a little hot water. Add ⅛ cup of sherry per bird. Cover and bake in a 350° oven until tender. This normally takes about 45 minutes.

Night Hunting ——————————

The comeback of the raccoon has seen the flourishing of night hunting in Virginia. The lowly opossum has always attracted some attention from those who like to listen to trail hounds on a bright winter night, but it was not until the coon had made its way back to abundance that the modern level of interest was reached.

While the raccoon is by far the most popular quarry of the night hunters, there is some interest in bobcats, and it is just about impossible to keep some hounds from treeing a scaly-tailed possum. Fox hunters often run their hounds at

The raccoon is the favorite quarry of night hunters in Virginia. The animal can move surprisingly fast on the ground.

night also, but this popular hunting is a daytime pursuit as well.

The bobcat, though fairly common in Virginia, is seldom seen. They are scattered statewide, but they are most abundant in the mountains in the west and the Dismal Swamp area in the east.

The opossum, versatile and highly adaptable, is found just about all over the state, even in the major cities. It seems equally at home in the remote woods or the busy farming country.

The raccoon, which night hunting is mostly all about, is also found statewide. It is most abundant, however, in the swamp country in the eastern part of the state.

BOBCAT

Estimates of the relative abundance of bobcats in Virginia range from scarce to fairly common. Few game animals are harder for biologists to get a handle on.

Trappers take a few cats, and bear and deer hunters take

them occasionally, but hunting bobcats in Virginia can be a frustrating experience. Bagging one, however, will make it all seem worthwhile. The little cats make handsome trophies.

The use of highly trained cat hounds is the most productive approach to hunting bobcats, but there are few such dogs in Virginia. Most cats are treed by coonhounds, and coon hunting probably accounts for the bulk of the small annual kill.

DESCRIPTION: A bobcat looks larger than it actually is because of its fur, which is long and thick. The average weight is only 15 to 20 pounds, though some exceptional ones go much larger. Color ranges from a grayish brown in summer to gray in the winter. Dark bars and flecks and spots of black give it a spotted appearance, but the cat is a handsome animal, and its fur is valuable. In many ways it resembles a big house cat. Sly and secretive, it is seldom seen by man. It moves mostly at night.

HABITAT: The bobcat is an animal of the deep woods, be it swamp or mountain country.

SEASONS: November, December, and January are bobcat-hunting months in Virginia.

GOOD COUNTIES: The mountain counties and the rural cities adjacent to the Dismal Swamp.

HUNTING METHODS: The most effective way to take bobcats is to hunt them with well-trained cat hounds, dogs that may be hard to develop on Virginia's limited bobcat population. Some hunters lure them within rifle range with dying rabbit calls, but this kind of hunting is illegal at night. It can be done during daylight hours but is not as effective then.

ARMS AND AMMUNITION: Night-hunting parties normally carry a single firearm, a little .22-caliber rifle for shooting treed opossums and raccoons. At close range this is entirely satisfactory for treed bobcats, but a .22-caliber Magnum would be a better choice if bobcats are the primary quarry.

CARE OF THE MEAT: The bobcat has no value as a food animal, but its fur is extremely valuable and should be handled with care.

OPOSSUM

There was a time in Virginia when night hunting meant possum hunting. Before World War II raccoon were scarce in Virginia for the most part, and the opossum was the only choice for those who liked to spend evenings under the starlit skies with their trail hounds. It was fun then, and it still is, but the raccoon offers a greater challenge today, and it is a more highly prized animal. Opossums and raccoon are treated together under the game laws of Virginia, but most hunters discourage their hounds from chasing possums. It is mostly an unwanted animal today.

The opossum is abundant throughout the state, and no animal is more underharvested. Its fur has some commercial value, but a couple of dollars is top price for a prime pelt.

DESCRIPTION: The opossum is unique on this continent in that it is the only animal that carries its young in a pouch—a marsupial, in other words. Averaging 5 to 6 pounds, the opossum with its white, narrow face, pointed nose, black eyes, and scaly, hairless tail is easy to recognize. The body is mostly gray but white underneath. It is noted for feigning death, or "playing possum," when cornered. This is its last line of defense.

HABITAT: Though primarily an animal of the forests, the opossum will den up just about anywhere. It prefers hollow trees, but logs, drainpipes, old buildings, woodchuck holes, openings in rock piles, and the like provide it protection from the weather and its enemies. Persimmons are a favorite fruit.

SEASONS: Opossum seasons are long, from early September or October through January, but the early months are usually chasing months during which the animals can be run with hounds but not killed.

GOOD COUNTIES: Opossums are abundant throughout the state.

HUNTING METHODS: Just about any dog will tree an opossum, but the hounds are best. Put down in good hunting territory, they are likely to pick up a trail very quickly. Since the opossum does not move as fast as the raccoon, the chase is likely to be shorter. A productive persimmon tree is a likely place to start a chase. When treed in small saplings, the opossum often can be shaken from its perch; otherwise, it is shot out of the tree.

ARMS AND AMMUNITION: A single firearm to a party is the usual approach to firearms. A light .22-caliber rimfire rifle will do the job on opossums.

CARE OF THE MEAT: The opossum is a notorious scavenger, and for this reason the meat may have a strong taste. In the old days it was customary for night hunters to take the animals live if possible, lug them home in a gunny sack, and pen them up. After they were fed sweet potatoes and other vegetables for several weeks, the meat was cleared of its strong taste and became a delicacy. The opossum can be skinned quickly by slitting along the inside of the back legs and pulling the skin up the body and over the head. The skin should be stretched on a pelting board for the fur market, but the animal should be gutted and washed for table use.

OPOSSUM RECIPES: *Yams and Possum* have long been a popular southern dish. First parboil the dressed and washed animal in water containing red pepper and salt. When the meat is tender, remove it from the water and place it in baking pan that has been greased lightly. Surround the meat with yams, quartered if very large, and bake until a golden brown. The oven should be set at 300° for the best results.

Fried Possum is also tasty if the meat is first parboiled in salty water until tender. The animal should be cut into small pieces first. After the meat has been parboiled, it should be seasoned with red pepper and salt, rolled in flour, and fried in hot fat.

RACCOON

Like the deer and the wild turkey, the raccoon has made a dramatic comeback in Virginia, and coons are now found just about statewide. They roam mostly at night, however, and many people do not realize they may have raccoon almost in their backyards.

Raccoon have always been reasonably abundant in the eastern swamps, but even today they are far from abundant in Southwest Virginia.

Locating raccoon in Virginia is rarely difficult. Some of the very best hunting is found in the eastern farmlands and on the lands of the big timber corporations. There is also good hunting in many of the wildlife management areas and the two national forests. Raccoon are generally more abundant in the George Washington National Forest than in the Jefferson, where the animals are still on the comeback trail.

While both trappers and hunters dip into the raccoon population, the night hunters take a good share of the harvest. They are a dedicated group who invest large sums of money in such prize trail hounds as the black and tan, bluetick, English coonhound, redbone, and treeing walker. Coon-hunting clubs are popular, and there is a lot of good-natured rivalry between hunters and hunting clubs.

DESCRIPTION: The raccoon's black face mask and ringed tail make it easy to identify. The rest of the body is a mixture of gray and brown with black peppering. The average weight for an adult coon is 12 to 15 pounds, though some grow much larger. Heavily furred and fat, the raccoon is a rotund animal but capable of moving rapidly on the ground, and it is also an excellent climber as well as a swimmer.

HABITAT: The raccoon is an extremely adaptable animal, and given a chance it will quickly expand its numbers. Basically, it needs a bit of forest, some nearby water, and an adequate food supply. A list of possible food is almost endless, but it includes a wide variety of plants and grass, berries and fruit, fish, small rodents, and the eggs and young of various forms of wildlife.

SEASONS: Early September and October through February are the months that coons are hunted in Virginia. Only chasing is permitted early in the season, but by November hunters are allowed to bag some animals.

GOOD COUNTIES: While the raccoon is now found just about statewide, the counties in the eastern part of the state offer the best hunting.

HUNTING METHODS: There is only one way to hunt raccoon effectively, and that is with well-trained trail hounds. Hounds work best on warm, moist nights when the animal's scent is strong on the ground, but night hunters do not wait for perfect conditions. A good knowledge of the country he hunts is invaluable to the coon hunter as he can put his dogs down where they are most likely to pick up a trail. Many hunters prefer streams, ponds, or other wet areas to start a hunt. Wet ground is a good place to pick up a trail. The dogs locate the game, trail it, and eventually tree it. The hunters' work is following the hounds and going to the tree where they either shoot the quarry or pull the hounds away and look for another chase.

ARMS AND AMMUNITION: One .22-caliber rimfire rifle to a hunting party is the usual approach to arms. All it is used for is to shoot the treed quarry out of the tree.

CARE OF THE MEAT: Taken during the cool, or chill, of the night and usually shot in the head with no damage to the edible portions and no shot-up intestines to taint it, the raccoon is excellent eating if properly field dressed. This means removing the skin cleanly and gutting the animal for cooling throughout. The skin is removed by slitting along the insides of the back legs and working it up over the body and head. The fur of the raccoon is valuable in the fur market, and it should be placed on a stretcher and stored in a cool place to cure.

RACCOON RECIPES: *Baked Raccoon* is prepared by removing the excess fat and then parboiling the animal in water containing spicewood twigs or a large onion. As it parboils, add 1 teaspoon salt, 1 pod red pepper, and 1 tablespoon black pepper. When it is tender, remove the meat and pat it dry. Place in a baking pan oiled lightly with vegetable oil and bake at 325° until brown.

For *Fried Raccoon*, remove the excess fat and parboil in water containing several spicewood twigs, a large onion, two peeled potatoes, 1 teaspoon salt, 1 pod red pepper, and 1 tablespoon black pepper. When it is tender, remove the meat and wipe off excess moisture. Cut into pieces, roll in cornmeal, and deep fry in very hot fat.

Varmints _____

In the eyes of the law there are three kinds of animals in Virginia: songbirds and endangered species, which are protected year-round; game animals, which enjoy the protection of closed and open seasons; and those that receive little or no protection. The latter group includes crows, English sparrows, frogs, skunks, starlings, turtles, and woodchucks, and they are loosely referred to as varmints. Hunting them has become very popular in Virginia, but the primary emphasis is on crows and woodchucks. Frogs and turtles are sometimes taken for their food value.

Crows and woodchucks are the most popular targets of Virginia varmint hunters. The crow is a real wing-shooting challenge.

Actually crows enjoy a closed season, but there is no bag limit on them—or any other varmint. Varmints are available only to the properly licensed hunter, however, and since most are on private land, the permission of the owner is needed.

The crow is the quarry of the wing-shooting enthusiasts, and the dedicated rifleman enjoys hunting woodchucks. Both become better hunters from the experience and the shooting practice.

CROW

Finding crows is rarely a problem, but they are most abundant in the farming areas where food is easier for them to come by. Hunting on wildlife management areas, national forests, state forests, and other lands managed by the Commission of Game and Inland Fisheries is prohibited except during the regular seasons on game species. This eliminates some of the best crow-hunting weeks, but finding private land to hunt on is rarely a problem, for the birds can become pests at times.

Crows offer an excellent opportunity to practice wing-shooting on live targets, and they present a wide array of targets from birds decoyed by fake crows and owls to tough pass shooting.

DESCRIPTION: The average crow weighs only a pound, but its heavy feathers and wingspread of 2 to 3 feet make it look much larger. Its color is jet black and its raspy voice unmistakable. The crow is an extremely wary bird.

HABITAT: Crows build their nests in tall trees, and trees are also their favorite roosting place. In Virginia they like to roost in thick pine forests but will also use hardwoods and even low shrubs such as willow clumps. Their preference is such cover surrounded by big open areas. They feed primarily in agricultural fields, particularly grainfields.

SEASONS: Crow hunting is limited to Wednesday, Thursday, Friday, and Saturday in Virginia, and the season is split, running from August 1 to December 31 and from the first Wednesday in February through the last Saturday in March.

GOOD COUNTIES: Crows are found throughout the state.

HUNTING METHODS: A lot of crows are killed by hunters after other game, but the serious crow hunter locates an area which the birds are using, sets up a blind or selects a natural one, puts out his crow and owl decoys, and calls the birds in with either a mouth-operated call or a mechanical one. The mechanical call is more foolproof. Dedicated crow hunters dress in camouflage, and some even mask their faces. The crow has extremely sharp eyes and will flare off from the careless hunter before he gets a shot.

ARMS AND AMMUNITION: The ideal crow arm is an improved-cylinder shotgun in gauge 20 to 12, and it should be loaded with high brass size 8 shot. From a more practical standpoint, however, just about any shotgun and load will take crows. The goose hunter might want practice for his favorite hunting and so will use his 10- or 12-gauge shotgun with a long barrel bored full choke. The duck hunter, on the other hand, might like a shotgun bored improved cylinder or modified if he is accustomed to shooting over decoys. The crow is not a tough bird to bring out of the air if solidly hit, and many hunters use crow hunting to clean up odds and ends of ammunition left from the regular hunting seasons.

CARE OF THE MEAT: Rarely is the crow used on the table, though its dark flesh is edible. Most crow hunters simply leave the birds in the field. This goes against the code of many hunters, but it is well to keep in mind that the birds will not go to waste. Many forms of wildlife live by scavenging, and every scrap of meat will soon disappear. Crows not taken by hunters often die from poisoning if farmers need to control them to protect their crops.

WOODCHUCK

Woodchucks are found all over Virginia, though they are rare in the high mountain forests and the coastal marshes. Finding good woodchuck hunting is seldom difficult, but the animals are most abundant in farming country, particularly where there is a good deal of grass farming. The best woodchuck hunting comes during the summer months, and since public lands managed by the Commission of Game and Inland Fisheries cannot be hunted except during the regular seasons on game species, the wildlife management areas, the national and state forests, and other public lands are generally not available to the woodchuck hunter. Woodchucks become pests as they often riddle fields with their intricate system of burrows, however, and many farmers welcome responsible varmint hunters.

A popular time to hunt woodchucks is late June or early July after the first hay crop has been mowed and the animals are easier to spot in the short grass. Hunting in pastures is good all summer, and usually there are additional hay harvests later in the summer that expose the animals in the hayfields. The woodchuck offers the rifleman an excellent opportunity to keep his shooting sharp for the fall and winter big game hunting. Many guides say their best hunters are those who hunt woodchucks through the summer months.

DESCRIPTION: Rotund and squatty, the woodchuck waddles when it walks, but it can duck into its den with amazing speed. Big woodchucks are sizable animals, but the average adult weights about 5 to 10 pounds. The animals are generally a grizzled brown, and the tail is fully haired. When spotted, the woodchuck usually is standing upright on its back legs, but it drops on all four feet to feed.The woodchuck is the only true hibernator in Virginia.

HABITAT: Woodchucks love pasture and hayfields, and they usually take up residence nearby, building their systems of dens and burrows near the edge of the field. They often use honeysuckle or other cover to conceal the entrance to their dens.

SEASONS: Although there are no closed seasons on woodchucks, the serious hunter waits until the middle of June to shoot them. By then the young have been weaned, and there is no risk of robbing the young of a mother. Hunting can be good well into the fall when the animals begin to hibernate.

GOOD COUNTIES: Woodchucks are found throughout Virginia.

HUNTING METHODS: A combination of stalking and stand hunting is the usual approach to woodchuck hunting. Most hunters dress in camouflage to help conceal their approach or presence. If the hunter has a good colony of chucks located, simply taking a stand late in the day and waiting is a good approach. The hunter who has to stalk within range needs all of the concealment available to do so successfully, and even then he may have to crawl on his belly. Some hunters drive around the farming country to locate the chucks and then seek permission to hunt them. Binoculars are handy in studying the fields in search of game. Many shots are at long ranges. In fact, many expert riflemen like it that way, and bipods and beanbags to steady the rifle are helpful. Most long-range shots are taken from the prone position.

ARMS AND AMMUNITION: The woodchuck hunter needs a flat-shooting rifle, something like the .243, .22/250, or the old .22 Hornet. The .222 Magnum is popular, and so is the .22 Magnum rimfire up to 100 yards. A good telescopic scope is almost a necessity. Many chuck hunters load their own ammunition.

CARE OF THE MEAT: The woodchuck feeds almost entirely upon vegetable matter, and the young ones, particularly, are good to eat. Unfortunately, however, many hunters do not take advantage of this. Since it is usually shot in warm or even hot weather, the woodchuck should be dressed as quickly as possible. The animal is easy to skin. Simply slit the skin along the inside of the back legs and peel up over the body. It is unnecessary to save the head, so that skinning step can be omitted; just cut off the head and discard it with the skin. The skin has no value in the fur market. Open up the animal, remove its innards, and cut it into pieces as desired. Normally, the limbs are removed and the carcass is either halved or quartered. Wash it thoroughly in cold water, and the meat is ready for freezing or cooking.

WOODCHUCK RECIPES: *Chuckburgers* are one possibility. Strip the meat from the bones and grind it in a meat grinder. Mix the meat with ½ cup bread crumbs, ¼ cup ground onion, 1 teaspoon pepper, 1 beaten egg, and 1 tablespoon melted fat and shape into patties. Make a batter of 1 beaten egg and ½ cup cracker meal. Dip the patties in the batter and fry in hot fat. When they are brown, place them in a casserole, cover lightly with currant jelly, and bake in a 300° oven for approximately an hour.

For *Fried Woodchuck*, boil the pieces of meat in salt water until they are tender. Some add a tablespoon of vinegar to the boiling water. Remove the meat and wipe off the excess water before rolling it in flour and frying in hot fat until brown. Salt as preferred.

Trapping

In their quest for fur, adventuresome trappers have probed the most remote parts of America and staked a strong claim to a share of the history of this country. The names of creeks, rivers, and mountains bear witness to their early travels; trapper creeks, otter lakes, and beaver runs are all over the North American continent. Trapping is a rich part of our outdoor heritage.

In Virginia, trapping valuable furbearers, like hunting, is regulated by the Commission of Game and Inland Fisheries, and the two have much in common. Unfortunately, there is

The muskrat is the most abundant of Virginia's long list of furbearers. (Courtesy of Virginia Commission of Game and Inland Fisheries)

some conflict where there is common interest in a game or furbearing species. The best example is the raccoon, popular among hound men but also valued by trappers because its fur commands a good price on the market. To a less extent the same is true of the gray and red foxes. This fur is even more valuable than that of the raccoon. But the conflict is unwarranted. Both hunting and trapping are closely regulated, and this assures a surplus of game, so that all can enjoy the harvest.

Like the hunter, the trapper needs a state license, and he also needs the permission of the landowner or a permit if he plans to trap on lands managed by the Commission of Game and Inland Fisheries. Each trap the trapper sets must have a tag bearing his name and address, and he is required to visit his traps at least once every 24 hours.

The recognized furbearers in Virginia are the beaver, bobcat, fox, mink, muskrat, nutria, opossum, otter, raccoon, skunk, and weasel. The skunk and weasel do not enjoy the protection of a closed season, but their fur is valuable, and many trappers take them.

The beaver, one of the most prized furbearers in America, is abundant in the state, and in some areas it reaches nuisance numbers. It prefers small brooks where there are plenty of trees for its dams, but it is also found in larger ponds, lakes, and reservoirs. It may also use rivers and larger streams, but not to the extent that it does the smaller streams.

Never abundant, the bobcat is secretive and rarely seen. It lives throughout Virginia from the western mountains to the eastern swamps, but primarily in well-forested country.

There are both gray and red foxes in Virginia, but the gray is our native fox, the red having been introduced from England. Both are found statewide, but the red prefers the more open agricultural areas, and the gray the dense cover of the forest.

The mink is another highly prized furbearer that is found statewide, seldom far from water. It roams the banks of streams and the shores of lakes and ponds.

For sheer numbers no furbearer comes close to the muskrat. "Rats" live mostly in the water, and they are particularly abundant in the brackish coastal marshes. They are also found inland along streams and in lakes and ponds. Because it likes to burrow into banks, the muskrat is a threat to earthen dams.

The nutria, much larger than the muskrat but somewhat similar in appearance, was introduced to America from Brazil around the turn of the century. It is a creature of the marshes and is found only in the Back Bay area in Virginia.

The opossum may occur just about anywhere from the mountains to the coast, but the otter, closely related to the mink, is most abundant east of the Blue Ridge Mountains. It is now fully protected west of the mountains. The otter is a large animal that may grow to 25 pounds and is rarely found far from water. It feeds mostly on fish.

A creature of the edges, the skunk is found just about throughout the state, and so is the little weasel, though weasels are not nearly as abundant.

December, January, and February are trapping months in

Virginia, a time when the fur is prime and likely to bring the best prices in the fur market.

Of the four kinds of traps used to catch Virginia fur-bearers, the leghold is by far the most popular and most used. The other three are the body-gripping trap, the box trap, and the snare.

Depending upon what kind of spring is used, the leghold may be a long spring, jump, coil spring, or guarded trap. The long spring is the least costly, but the jump and coil springs are easier to conceal and are good for confined spaces where there might not be enough room for the long spring. The guarded trap has an additional spring that presses against the animal's body to immobilize it.

The body-gripping trap is a killer trap that is generally used in water only. The Virginia law restricts its use on land because of the threat to small domestic animals.

Snares are used both in water and on land. Generally made of wire, the snare loop cannot be more than 8 inches in diameter, and it should not be more than 10 inches above the ground. Snares are set along runways both on land and under the water and at the entrances to dens. The animal enters the loop, and as it presses against the wire, the loop tightens around its neck.

Box traps are big and cumbersome, and they have limited use. Animals are usually taken alive with them.

While furbearers are taken for their valuable furs, some species also have considerable food value, particularly the beaver. Its meat is highly prized. Properly cleaned and prepared, the meat of the raccoon is also good. Muskrat are popular as food animals in some parts of the country, and so is the opossum. Food is a by-product of trapping, and some trappers sell the meat regularly. Others use it on their own tables.

Hunting and trapping are important parts of the rich outdoor heritage enjoyed by Virginians from the coast to the mountains. Food for the table, trophies for the wall, and furs that put a little cash in the pockets are the end results, but these tangible prizes are definitely secondary. The real values are lungs filled with clean air, well-toned muscles, and minds temporarily relieved of day-to-day problems. No human being is better fitted to tackle the problems of this complex world than the hunter or trapper fresh from a stint in Virginia's fields, woods, or marshes.

APPENDIXES

INDEX

APPENDIX A

Governmental Agencies

Virginia Commission of Game and Inland Fisheries
4010 West Broad Street
P.O. Box 11104
Richmond, VA 23230-1104
Telephone 804-367-1000

Regional Offices

Box 1001
Tappahannock, VA 22560
Telephone 804-443-2810

Route 6, Box 484-A
Staunton, VA 24401
Telephone 703-332-9210

Route 1, Box 157
Marion, VA 24354
Telephone 703-783-4860

HCO2
Box 238
Buckingham, VA 23921
Telephone 804-969-4696

U.S. Fish and Wildlife Service
8301 Willis Church Road, Route 156
Richmond, VA 23231
Telephone 804-771-2481

Wildlife Refuges

Back Bay National Wildlife Refuge
4005 Sandpiper Road
P.O. Box 6286
Virginia Beach, VA 23456
Telephone 804-721-2412

Chincoteague National Wildlife Refuge
Box 62
Chincoteague, VA 23336
Telephone 804-336-6122

Great Dismal Swamp National Wildlife Refuge
Suffolk Post Office
Box 349
Suffolk, VA 23434
Telephone 804-539-7479

Presquile National Wildlife Refuge
P.O. Box 620
Hopewell, VA 23860
Telephone 804-458-7541

George Washington National Forest
Harrison Plaza, P.O. Box 233
Harrisonburg, VA 22801
Telephone 703-433-2491

Ranger District Offices

Deerfield Ranger District
2304 West Beverley Street
Staunton, VA 24401
Telephone 703-885-8028

Dry River Ranger District
112 North River Road
Bridgewater, VA 22812
Telephone 703-828-2591

James River Ranger District
313 South Monroe Avenue
Covington, VA 22426
Telephone 703-962-2214

Lee Ranger District
Route 1, Box 31A
Edinburg, VA 22824
Telephone 703-984-4101

Pedlar Ranger District
2424 Magnolia Avenue
Buena Vista, VA 24416
Telephone 703-261-6105

Warm Springs Ranger District
Route 2, Box 30
Hot Springs, VA 24445
Telephone 703-839-2521

Jefferson National Forest
Room 957
210 Franklin Road S.W.
Roanoke, VA 24001
Telephone 703-982-6270

Ranger District Offices

Blacksburg Ranger District
Route 5, Box 15
Blacksburg, VA 24060
Telephone 703-552-4641

Clinch Ranger District
Route 3, Box 820
Wise, VA 24293
Telephone 703-328-2931

Glenwood Ranger District
Box 10
Natural Bridge Station, VA 24579
Telephone 703-291-2189

Mount Rogers National Recreational Area
Route 1, Box 303
Marion, VA 24354
Telephone 703-783-5196

New Castle Ranger District
Box 246
New Castle, VA 24127
Telephone 703-864-5196

Wythe Ranger District
1625 West Lee Street
Wytheville, VA 24382
Telephone 703-228-5551

U.S. Army Corps of Engineers, Huntington District Office
502 8th Street
Huntington, WV 25720-2070
Telephone 304-529-5395

John W. Flannagan Reservoir
Route 1, Box 268
Haysi, VA 24256
Telephone 703-835-9544

North Fork Pound Reservoir
Route 1, Box 369
Pound, VA 24279
Telephone 703-796-5775

U.S. Army Corps of Engineers, Norfolk District Office
803 Front Street
Norfolk, VA 23510-1096
Telephone 804-441-7606

Gathright Dam and Lake Moomaw
P.O. Box 432
Covington, VA 24426
Telephone 703-962-1138

U.S. Army Corps of Engineers, Wilmington District Office
P.O. Box 1890
Wilmington, NC 28402-1890
Telephone 919-251-4827

> John H. Kerr Reservoir and Dam
> Route 1, Box 76
> Boydton, VA 23917
> Telephone 804-738-6662
>
> Philpott Reservoir
> Route 6, Box 140
> Bassett, VA 24055
> Telephone 703-629-2703

Virginia Division of Forestry
P.O. Box 3758, University Station
Charlottesville, VA 22903
Telephone 804-977-6555
and
2229 East Nine Mile Road, P.O. Box 635
Sandston, VA 23150
Telephone 804-737-4791

> *Field Offices*
> _____
>
> Pocahontas State Forest
> 9200 Beach Road
> Chester, VA 23832
> Telephone 804-796-4250
>
> Cumberland State Forest
> Route 1, Box 250
> Cumberland, VA 23040
> Telephone 804-492-4121
>
> Appomattox-Buckingham State Forest
> Route 3, Box 133
> Dillwyn, VA 23936
> Telephone 804-983-2175

Virginia Division of State Parks
203 Governor Street
Suite 306
Richmond, VA 23219
Telephone 804-786-2132

Virginia State Travel Service
101 North 9th Street Office Building
Richmond, VA 23219
Telephone 804-786-4484

Shenandoah National Park
Luray, VA 22835
Telephone 703-999-2243

Blue Ridge Parkway
2657 Mountain View Road
Vinton, VA 24179
Telephone 703-982-6213

APPENDIX B

Conservation Organizations

Virginia Bear Hunters Association
Route 3, Box 81
Waynesboro, VA 22980

Virginia Deer Hunters Association
P.O. Box 34746
Richmond, VA 23234-0746

The National Wild Turkey Federation
770 Augusta Road
Edgefield, SC 29824

Quail Unlimited
P.O. Box 10041
Augusta, GA 30903-2641

Ruffed Grouse Society
1400 Lee Drive
Coraopolis, PA 15108

Ducks Unlimited
1 Waterfowl Way
Lone Grove, IL 60047

North American Hunting Club
P.O. Box 3402
Minnetonka, MN 55343

Safari Club International
4800 West Gates Pass Road
Tucson, AZ 85745

Virginia Wildlife Federation
4602 D West Grove Court
Virginia Beach, VA 23455

Izaak Walton League of America
1401 North Kent Street
Level B
Arlington, VA 22209

The National Rifle Association
1600 Rhode Island Avenue, N.W.
Washington, DC 20036

Virginia Trappers Association
2132 Shipyard Road
Chesapeake, VA 23323

APPENDIX C

Public Shooting Preserves

Kenny F. Barnard
Route 1, Box 139
Amelia, VA 23002
Telephone 804-561-2670

Hoot Owl Hollow Farm
Amelia County
Pheasant, quail

John Cowden
Star Route A, Box 21A
Milboro, VA 24460
Telephone 703-925-2314

Fort Lewis Lodge
Bath County
Pheasant

Russell O. Peoples
Route 2, Box 326-D
New Castle, VA 24127
Telephone 703-864-6179

Hermit Valley Preserve and Kennels
Craig County
Quail

Juanita R. Christensen
P.O. Box 563
Rixeyville, VA 22373
Telephone 703-937-4310

King Kennels Shooting Preserve
Culpeper County
Pheasant, quail

Andrew W. Dykes, Jr.
3831 River Road West
Goochland, VA 23063
Telephone 804-556-6585

Orapax Plantation
Goochland County
Pheasant, quail

Ronald O. Edwards
Route 2, Box 72
Center Cross, VA 22437
Telephone 804-443-4592

Plain Dealing Shooting Preserve
King & Queen County
Pheasant, quail

D. T. Glascock
Box 160
Fairfax, VA 22030
Telephone 703-273-1515

D. T. Glascock Shooting Preserve
Loudoun County
Ducks, pheasant, quail

Ed Allen
Route 2, Box 66-A
Providence Forge, VA 23140
Telephone 804-966-2582

Ed Allen's Hunting Preserve
New Kent County
Chukar, pheasant, quail

David Pomfret
P.O. Box 1265
Orange, VA 22960
Telephone 703-854-4540

Oakland Farm Shooting Preserve
Orange County
Chukar, pheasant, quail

Johnny H. Lambert
c/o Primlumber, Inc.
Route 1, Box 265-C
Claudeville, VA 24076
Telephone 703-251-8012

Primland Shooting Preserve #1
and #2
Patrick County
Pheasant, quail

Harry E. Lowry
Route 3, Box 282
Farmville, VA 23901
Telephone 804-223-8233/8222

Loraine Farm Shooting Preserve
Prince Edward County
Pheasant, quail

Dean M. McDowell
14710 Deepwood Lane
Nokesville, VA 22123
Telephone 703-594-2276

Merrimac Farm Shooting Preserve
Prince William County
Pheasant, quail

Lon S. Marks
Route 1, Box 156
Capron, VA 23829
Telephone 804-658-4150

Indiantown Shooting Preserve
Southampton County
Quail

M. Dewey Howell, Jr.
101 Philhowere Drive
Suffolk, VA 23434
Telephone 804-539-6296

Magnolia Shooting Preserve
City of Suffolk
Chukar, pheasant, quail

APPENDIX D

Mean Temperatures

Northwest Mountains and Valley

Location: Berryville					Range: −13.0 to 103.0			
Sept.	Oct.	Nov.	Dec.	Jan.	Feb.	Mar.	April	May
66.0	54.9	44.1	34.1	30.9	33.8	41.6	53.9	62.0

Location: Buchanan					Range: −4.0 to 107.0			
Sept.	Oct.	Nov.	Dec.	Jan.	Feb.	Mar.	April	May
68.3	58.0	47.1	38.0	37.5	39.1	46.5	57.0	65.4

Location: Big Meadows					Range: −14.0 to 90.0			
Sept.	Oct.	Nov.	Dec.	Jan.	Feb.	Mar.	April	May
59.5	50.4	39.5	29.8	28.6	29.3	36.0	47.8	56.8

Upper Piedmont and Coastal Plains

Location: Ashland					Range: −7.0 to 105.0			
Sept.	Oct.	Nov.	Dec.	Jan.	Feb.	Mar.	April	May
68.4	57.6	47.3	37.5	36.0	38.3	45.5	56.3	65.1

Location: Charlottesville					Range: 1.0 to 107.0			
Sept.	Oct.	Nov.	Dec.	Jan.	Feb.	Mar.	April	May
69.4	59.4	48.6	37.9	36.0	37.7	45.6	57.1	66.0

Location: Falls Church					Range: −13.0 to 102.0			
Sept.	Oct.	Nov.	Dec.	Jan.	Feb.	Mar.	April	May
67.8	57.0	46.0	35.3	33.9	35.8	43.5	54.7	64.2

The Northern Neck

Location: Fredericksberg   Range: −7.0 to 106.0
Sept.	Oct.	Nov.	Dec.	Jan.	Feb.	Mar.	April	May
68.9	57.8	47.1	36.9	34.7	36.8	44.6	55.7	65.3

Location: Warsaw   Range: −4.0 to 106
Sept.	Oct.	Nov.	Dec.	Jan.	Feb.	Mar.	April	May
70.1	59.7	49.4	39.3	37.1	39.0	46.5	57.3	66.3

Lower Tidewater Virginia

Location: Back Bay   Range: 8.0 to 103.0
Sept.	Oct.	Nov.	Dec.	Jan.	Feb.	Mar.	April	May
72.6	63.8	53.5	35.9	40.4	42.0	48.3	57.7	65.6

Location: Cape Henry   Range: 12.0 to 104.0
Sept.	Oct.	Nov.	Dec.	Jan.	Feb.	Mar.	April	May
72.6	63.1	53.2	43.5	41.4	41.7	48.0	57.3	66.0

Location: Painter   Range: −5.0 to 103.0
Sept.	Oct.	Nov.	Dec.	Jan.	Feb.	Mar.	April	May
70.2	60.4	50.4	40.7	38.9	40.1	46.6	56.2	65.3

Southside Virginia

Location: Bedford   Range: −3.0 to 104.0
Sept.	Oct.	Nov.	Dec.	Jan.	Feb.	Mar.	April	May
68.2	58.4	47.9	38.9	37.9	39.5	47.1	57.4	65.7

Location: Boykins   Range: 0.0 to 104.0
Sept.	Oct.	Nov.	Dec.	Jan.	Feb.	Mar.	April	May
71.2	60.5	50.9	41.5	39.4	42.0	49.2	60.0	67.1

Location: Charlotte Court House Range: −1.0 to 106.0
Sept.	Oct.	Nov.	Dec.	Jan.	Feb.	Mar.	April	May
68.7	58.3	47.7	38.5	36.4	38.0	45.4	56.8	65.3

Southwest Virginia

Location: Catawba   Range: −8.0 to 101.0
Sept.	Oct.	Nov.	Dec.	Jan.	Feb.	Mar.	April	May
65.6	56.1	45.5	36.6	35.0	36.4	43.6	54.6	62.9

Location: Blacksburg   Range: −12.0 to 100.0

Sept.	Oct.	Nov.	Dec.	Jan.	Feb.	Mar.	April	May
64.1	54.1	43.1	34.1	33.1	34.5	41.8	52.5	61.2

Location: Wytheville   Range: −10.0 to 96.0

Sept.	Oct.	Nov.	Dec.	Jan.	Feb.	Mar.	April	May
64.4	54.7	43.9	35.4	34.3	36.0	43.	53.4	61.6

Books on Hunting

Big Game

American Bears, by Paul Schullery. Outdoor Life Book Club, P.O. Box 2000, Latham, NY 12111.

The Whitetail Deer Hunter's Handbook, by John Weiss. Winchester Press, 220 Old New Brunswick Road, Piscataway, NJ 08854.

Advanced Wild Turkey Hunting and World Records, by Dave Harbour. Winchester Press, 220 Old New Brunswick Road, Piscataway, NJ 08854.

Small Game

All about Small-Game Hunting in America, by Russell Tinsley. Winchester Press, 220 Old New Brunswick Road, Piscataway, NJ 08854.

Squirrels and Squirrel Hunting, by Bob Gooch. Tidewater Publishers, P.O. Box 456, Centreville, MD 21617.

Upland Birds

The Dove Shooters' Handbook, by Dan M. Russell. Winchester Press, 220 Old New Brunswick Road, Piscataway, NJ 08854.

Grouse and Woodcock, by Nick Sisley. Stackpole Books, Cameron and Kelker Streets, P.O. Box 1831, Harrisburg, PA 17105.

Modern Pheasant Hunting, by Steve Grooms. Stackpole Books, Cameron and Kelker Streets, P.O. Box 1831, Harrisburg, PA 17105.

Coveys and Singles, by Bob Gooch. A. S. Barnes and Co., Inc., P.O. Box 3051, San Diego, CA 92038.

The Complete Hunter's Almanac, by Jerome J. Knap. Pagurian Press Limited, Suite 1106, 335 Bay Street, Toronto, Canada.

Waterfowl

Hunting North American Waterfowl, by John O. Cartier. E. P. Dutton & Co., Inc., 2 Park Avenue, New York, NY 10016.

Goose Hunting, by Charles L. Cadieux. The Stephen Greene Press, Brattleboro, VT 05301.

Night Hunting

All about Small-Game Hunting in America, by Russell Tinsley. Winchester Press, 220 Old New Brunswick Road, Piscataway, NJ 08854.

Varmints

All about Varmint Hunting, by Nick Sisley. Stackpole Books, Cameron and Kelker Streets, P.O. Box 1831, Harrisburg, PA 17105.

Trapping

Trapping, by Harold McCracken and Harry Van Cleve. A. S. Barnes and Co., Inc., P.O. Box 3051, San Diego, CA 92038.

Miscellaneous

Fish and Game Cooking, by Joan Cone. EPM Publications, Inc., Box 490, McLean, VA 22101.

Index _____